INTERNATIONAL POLITICAL ECONOMY SERIES

General Editor: Timothy M. Shaw, Professor of Political Science and International Development Studies and Director of the Centre for Foreign Policy Studies, Dalhousie University, Nova Scotia, Canada

The global political economy is in a profound crisis at the levels of both production and policy. This series provides overviews and case-studies of states and sectors, classes and companies, in the new international division of labour. These embrace political economy as both focus and mode of analysis; they advance radical scholarship and scenarios.

The series treats polity–economy dialectics at global, regional and national levels and examines novel contradictions and coalitions between and within each. There is a special emphasis on national bourgeoisies and capitalisms, on newly industrial or influential countries, and on uneven patterns of power and production, authority and distribution, hegemony and reaction. Attention will be paid to redefinitions of class and security, basic needs and self-reliance and the range of critical analysis will include gender, population, resources, environment, militarization, food and finance. This series constitutes a timely and distinctive response to the continuing intellectual and existential world crisis.

Recent titles include:

Towards a Socio-Liberal Theory of World Development

Arno Tausch
Federal Ministry of Labour
Division of European Integration, Vienna
Austrian Embassy, Warsaw
and Associate Professor of Political Science
Innsbruck University

in collaboration with

Fred Prager
Vienna Institute for Comparative Economic Studies

St. Martin's Press   New York

First published in the United States of America in 1993

Printed in Great Britain

ISBN 0–312–06210–9

Library of Congress Cataloging-in-Publication Data
Tausch, Arno, 1951–
Towards a socio-liberal theory of world development / Arno Tausch
[with Fred Prager].
p.   cm. — (International political economy series)
Includes bibliographical references and index.
ISBN 0–312–06210–9
1. Economic development.   2. Capitialism.   I. Title.   II. Series.
HD82.T33   1993
338.9—dc20   91–27475
                                                                      CIP

Opinions expressed in this book are those of the author
and not necessarily those of the Austrian Government.

'Third World discourse that intends to promote Third World interests may eventually serve to legitimize a growth-impeding social structure by omitting to criticise the structural foundations of the behavior of the Third World's privileged classes.'

Hartmut Elsenhans, 1983: 26

'Thus, it is not necessary to change the entire world, to have a New International Economic Order, in order to abolish poverty. Rather, if each country would embark on a programme to abolish the poverty within its borders, the world would soon be changed in the process.'

Keith Griffin, 1981: 226

Contents

List of Figures

List of Tables

List of Abbreviations

BHN	Basic Human Needs
CIA	Central Intelligence Agency
CIS	Community of Independent States (formerly USSR)
CH	Switzerland
CEPAL	United Nations Economic Commission for Latin America (Comision Economica para América Latina)
CSFR	Former Czechoslovakia
CMEA	Council for Mutual Economic Assistance
CND	Canada
DYN	Growth
EC	European Community
GINI	Index of Inequality, designed by C. Gini, ranging from 0 (absolute equality) to 1 (perfect inequality)
GDP	Gross Domestic Product
GNP	Gross National Product
GDR	(Former) German Democratic Republic
GATT	General Agreement on Tariffs and Trade
ILO	International Labour Office
IMF	International Monetary Fund
LDC	Less Developed Countries
LFPR	Labour Force Participation Ratio
MNC	Multinational Corporation
NIDL	New International Division of Labour
NIC	Newly Industrializing Countries
NATO	North Atlantic Treaty Organization
SIPRI	Stockholm International Peace Research Institute
SPSS	Standard Statistical Package for the Social Sciences
TNC	Transnational Corporation
UK	United Kingdom
UN	United Nations
US	United States
UK	United Kingdom
USSR	(Former) Union of Socialist Soviet Republics
WHO	World Health Organization
WTO	(Former) Warsaw Treaty Organization
CSSR	(Former) Czechoslovak Socialist Republic
MRDF	Machine Readable Data File

CSPS   Central School of Planning and Statistics (Warsaw)
RIDC   Research Institute for Developing Countries
GUS   Polish Central Statistical Office (Warsaw)
IBRD   International Bank for Reconstruction and Development
        (Washington)
CSIC   Spanish Council for Advanced Studies (Madrid)
ICPSR   International Consortium for Political and Social Research
        (Ann Arbor, Michigan)

Preface

This book, which tries to reformulate development theory in the light of the traumatic changes that have taken place in the world since 1989, was greatly influenced by the working group on development theory in the European Association of Development Research and Training Institutes, headed by Zbigniew Bablewski and Bjoern Hettne.

I hope I have developed convincing evidence about the necessity of a socio-liberal reformulation of development theory that combines social justice as a precondition for a successful capitalist development with the possibility of pluralism and democracy. A great number of scholars commented on earlier drafts of this work. I mention here especially my teachers, the late Eduard Maerz (Vienna), the great disciple of Austromarxism, and the late Karl Wolfgang Deutsch. It was their desire to acquaint Third World thought with the work of Otto Bauer, but their deaths prevented them from realizing this project. John-Ren Chen, of the Department of Econometrics at Innsbruck University, provided useful comments and criticisms and in many ways supported my work. Kunibert Raffer, of the Department of Economics at Vienna University, was very helpful in communicating his disagreement to me, formulated within the framework of the world systems approach.

I very much enjoyed the opportunity to write part of this book during an appointment at the University of Hawaii at Manoa. The Department of Political Science supported my work in a very valuable way and debated the results of my research. Mark Nakamura, with dedication to his work, drew the figures; Dick Chadwick and Edna Lee supported my computer work; Dunbar Campbell offered many comments.

I was able to finish the final version of this book at the Federal Ministry of Labour in Vienna, where I had the opportunity of observing the political realities of a changing Europe 'from within'.

My thanks go to Macmillan, the originating publishers: to the series editor Tim Shaw for his advice on my earlier drafts, to Tim Farmiloe, Clare Wace, Tony Grahame and Keith Povey for their patience with my work at different stages in the production process. Melanie Sully and Father Richard Lennan commented on earlier drafts. My wife Krystyna and our children greatly encouraged me to write this book.

Vienna   Arno Tausch

Fred Prager: An Appreciation

Born Vienna, 2 September 1911
Died Vienna, 24 April 1993

Exile is a heavy burden on anyone who has to suffer it. Fred Prager, born and raised in the very Red Vienna which this book is so much about, was a political activist all his lifetime; when the Nazis came to power and there was a clerical dictatorship in Austria it became clear, that, for him, a Jew and a socialist, he had to leave Europe. He was able to go to a far-away country, away from the 'Shoah', in which so many of his friends, relatives and like-minded were murdered, and he went to South Africa. Exile is a heavy burden, but Fred belonged to the group of very few people here on Earth who had to suffer it twice. In flamboyant opposition against everything inhumane, he soon got into trouble with the Nationalist Party and the South Africa it represented. His tales about his years in South Africa, solitary confinement, the years of opposition, have already been told but not yet published. His moving photographs about the suffering African majority in South Africa in the 1940s and 1950s more than anything else stand for the very essence of his life, which was in the spirit of Isaiah, 58.

Shortly before this book appeared in print, Fred, who had done so much to aid its appearance, died: one week after the celebrations of the ghetto uprising in Warsaw, and in the midst of the events in South Africa, which he followed so closely from his second exile, in his native Austria, to which he had returned in the years of Bruno Kreisky.

It is to the people of South Africa, then, the oppressed majorities and those people who went to that country because they had nowhere else to go, that I now – in memory of Fred – dedicate this book.

'Then shall thy light break forth as the morning, and thine health shall spring forth speedily; and thy righteousness shall go before thee.'

ARNO TAUSCH

1 Introduction

At first sight it might appear provocative to write a book which is at least partially optimistic about international development. The well-known Filipino social scientist W. Bello (1989) has been quite correct in summarizing recent trends in the social development of regions of the world economy in the following way:

Africa faces serious collapse on a continental scale. In 1990, per capita incomes will drop to their independence levels and drought, desertification, deforestation, civil war and hunger affect the lives of millions of human beings.

Latin America faces a lost decade in terms of development. In 1990, regional per capita incomes will barely reach 1980 levels, the debt burden amounts to US$ 400 billion, and in the past four years there has been a capital transfer from the region to the developed centres to the tune of US$ 100 billion each year.

In just two years, infant mortality rose in Brazil, a former 'miracle' country, from 66 to 74 per 1000 live births. In Bolivia, poor families offer their children to the well-to-do, and tuberculosis is back in Peru. In the Philippines, poverty has risen as a consequence of restructuring and the fall of the international price of sugar and coconuts, and now affects 60 per cent of the population.

In the (former) socialist countries leading political forces now believe that growth can only be assured by a further re-integration into the capitalist world economy, and that many egalitarian principles and policies must be dismantled under the discipline of the world market.

In their heroic attempt to estimate the world-wide distribution of incomes after allowing for inter- and intra-country inequalities, Berry et al. (1981) came to the conclusion that the top 5 per cent of the world income recipients (including former socialist countries) control over 30 per cent of the world's consumption expenditures. The GINI index of our globe is 0.609, which is in the vicinity of the most inegalitarian developing countries, such as Brazil. The poorest 20 per cent of the global population have a share in world consumption of only 2.52 per cent, while the mean consumption of the top 5 per cent is 61 times higher than the mean consumption of the poorest billion inhabitants of our globe. In terms of basic human needs satisfaction, however, there certainly has been a narrowing of the gap between rich and poor. Although we do not as yet have basic human needs (BHN) data from many countries adjusted for intra-country economic inequality, the GINI indices for average calorie intakes, primary and secondary school enrolment ratios and life expectancies, as distributed among the nation states, refute the pessimistic conclusions to be drawn from the commodity-distribution-oriented analysis inherent in Berry *et al.* (1981).

Table 1.1   GINI indices of global basic human needs satisfaction

Calorie intake per capita	0.12
1 + 2 School enrolment	0.21
Life expectancies	0.13

Source: M. D. Ward, 1981.

What is even more important, inequalities in BHN (adjusted for population) among countries did not increase over time (Ward, 1981), while commodity production oriented inequality measures did (Berry *et al.*, 1981). Looking systematically into the patterns which determined social, political and economic development from the middle of the 1960s onwards leads to the very core of development theory. It is my assumption that such patterns determine why some nations had a more rapid increase in life expectancy, a more rapid fall in infant mortality, faster economic growth, better income distribution and more political stability than other nations. These assumptions, I believe, were already inherent in the debates among the social democratic parties of the European continent shortly before and during the presently ending long economic cycle. Such assumptions regarding the viability of a socio-liberal development strategy are confirmed, using advanced statistical methods with data from all nations of the capitalist world economy for the period from 1960 onwards. These theories become all the more important since the breakdown of the Leninist regimes in East Germany, the CSSR, Hungary, Russia and Romania and the continuing legitimation crisis of Leninist socialism the world over.

The processes of stagnation in semi-periphery and periphery countries such as in Africa notwithstanding, there has been overall progress in the living conditions of millions of people on earth during the 1960s, 1970s and 1980s, progress which can best be measured by the very pronounced increases in life expectancy and decreases in infant mortality in all subgroups of the developing world. Even in the low-income countries, whose per capita income in 1988 was under $500 per annum, there was such increase over a quarter of a century. This group of countries, with 2884 million inhabitants, is the real yardstick for any development theory. Their average life expectancy is now 60 years (China and India 63 years, other low-income countries 54 years), while in the industrialized countries before the Second World War it was only 56 years (World Bank, *World Development Report*, 1990). In China and India there was a reduction in the infant mortality rate from 114 per 1000 live births to 59, better than in some regions of the former USSR, the motherland of socialism (see Chapter 8). For the 980 million people living in the other 42 poorest countries of the world which form the group of low-income countries together with China and India, there was a reduction in the average infant mortality rate from 149 to 98, thus overtaking some middle-income countries with a far superior level of industrialization such as Brazil, Nigeria, Peru, Turkey or apartheid South Africa some years ago. Development over the last quarter of a century meant, above all, dramatic shifts in the global distribution of BHN satisfaction (see also World Bank, *World Development Report*, 1988: 324–25; Ward, 1981; World Bank, *World Development Report*, 1990).

The two largest countries of the world in terms of population, India and China, which between them share almost 40 per cent of the world's population, experienced very creditable economic growth rates during the era of 'structural adjustment' to a changing world economy in the 1980s. 'Structural adjustment' is understood here to measure the ability of a given country to maintain its growth rate in the second half of the present Kondratieff cycle, especially during the 1980s, after the two oil price shocks. My concept thus differs from that of the World Bank, and is a purely empirical concept. Average life expectancies – the best single yardstick for a country's social development – have advanced in some nations, most notably in the Asian NICs (newly industrializing countries Hong Kong, Singapore, Taiwan and South Korea) throughout the last three decades. Economic growth even under very adverse conditions has continued at very respectable rates in Scandinavia, Japan and the 'little dragons' (see also Chapter 3). From a cross-national perspective, my work will not exclude developments in the former socialist countries. Within what has remained of former world socialism, pretty much the same causally interpreted patterns have emerged as in the larger world economy. Egalitarian patterns of income and wealth distribution at the onset favoured subsequent growth and stability. Growth needs social reform, but the older a political system becomes, the more necessary are pluralism and the market. There is, indeed, a problem of state classes (Elsenhans, 1983) most violently emerging in ethnically heterogeneous societies.

In the history of political thinking, the Austromarxists drew up perhaps the clearest formulation of what a socio-liberal transformation of society could mean. This statement does not, of course, disregard the parallel between the Austromarxist consensus on reform and development, formulated by Otto Bauer in the Linz Party Programme of 1926, with the reform strategy of Swedish Social Democracy, to which Ernst Wigforss made a lasting contribution. Research on the relationship between these two socio-liberal reform perspectives is also important because Polanyi, who was in many ways formed by the experience of Red Vienna before the Austrian civil war in 1934, foresaw such a socio-liberal perspective in his 'Great Transformation' of 1944. More than Polanyi himself, O. Bauer, the main author of the Linz Programme, was emphatic in his belief that capitalism, in order to survive, needs mass consumption, social reform and mass demand. For Polanyi, the experience of Red Vienna, described in full detail in appendix IX to the 'Great Transformation', was an unprecedented rise in the living conditions of the working class on the European continent, and yet incompatible with the logic of capitalist development. Wigforss and his followers realized that capitalism needs just that, and thus was responsible for the long-run development miracle of Sweden from the time of the Great Depression onwards while other countries were plunged into civil war and fascism (Tilton, 1979). Workers' protection, social insurance, social welfare, the struggle of the unions for improved and healthier working conditions and the development of workers' co-operatives were all part of the theory of Austromarxism, but it was Swedish Social Democracy that realized this theory under more favourable political conditions than in Austria. Polanyi's comrades took it for granted that first and foremost there must be a commitment to pluralist democracy, in sharp contrast to both the fascist movements on the right and the Bolshevik theory on the left (Kadan and Pelinka, 1979).

The Party Programme of 1926, which must be regarded as the essence of Austromarxism, rejects the idea of armed struggle to achieve socialism, but underlines the protective right of the working class to fight back against the imminent danger of fascism, should a fascist dictatorship arise. It is noteworthy that the content of the reform package, proposed by O. Bauer in part IV of the Programme, has many parallels with what contemporary macro-quantitative development research regards as basic conditions for a successful national development. The very precondition which brings about a lasting change in the class character of the state is the organization of national defence: a professional army will be prepared to massacre workers, while Social Democracy envisaged a citizen force based on conscription under democratic control.

To be sure, the Programme – as one of the most important documents of Marxist thought in the twentieth century – contains a very pronounced dose of liberal prescriptions. O. Bauer himself was very apprehensive about the mere substitution of private capitalism by state capitalism (see also Tausch, 1991a). Almost prophetically, Bauer foresaw the severe conflict of nationalities in systems dominated by state bureaucracies. His theory on nationalism – the most coherent Marxist work ever written on that issue so vital for an understanding of present-day conflicts in the former socialist world – was written in 1907, before the outbreak of the First World War. State classes aggravate the nationality conflict. All obstacles to the development of an international division of labour have to be eradicated: cartels and monopolies must be abolished; import duties and restrictions against factor mobility only serve to support local monopolies and power structures (Party Programme, 1926, doc. Kadan and Pelinka, 1979: 82–88). Another feature of the socio-liberal transformation of society is a far-reaching agrarian reform, which is necessary to overcome patterns of extensive land use. It is surprising, in view of contemporary quantitative results, how precisely Austromarxism pinpoints the negative development effects of extensive land-use (Tausch, 1991a). The agrarian project aims not to establish a Soviet-type of collective agriculture, but to protect and develop family-based agriculture, leading towards the free and voluntary association of peasants within co-operatives. Bureaucracies stand in the way of a successful capitalist development. Human capital formation is recognized to be of fundamental importance; measures to enhance the educational chances of children from working-class and peasant households have absolute priority. There must be immediate measures to alleviate the lot of those living under slum and bad housing conditions. Their entitlements and rights must be drastically increased *vis-à-vis* the property owners.

Taxation is another factor in the proposed scheme of development. Indirect taxes should, as far as possible, be abolished and there must be a progressive system of taxation on incomes, wealth and inheritance. Minimal incomes from both wage labour and property should be tax-exempted. Within a framework of what political scientists later called 'national integration' (Deutsch, 1979b), the state, especially the judicial system, must not reflect the class interests of the wealthy and the property owners, but of the entire population. The proposed social reforms are based on worker participation in the decisions of industry, protection against unemployment and work accidents, a general scheme of an eight-hour working day, protective measures for apprentices, old age pensions, sickness benefits, financial insurance for the disabled and those households that have lost an income earner. The courts must be entitled to enact measures provided under a code of labour and industrial legislation even when the interests of the capital owners are opposed to such measures. Female emancipation receives short but far-reaching treatment in the 1926 reform package: all sexist forms of inequality must be abolished, contraceptives must be legalized and should be available to all sectors of the population. Abortion must be made legal upon medical and social indication. Mortality reduction, especially the reduction of infant mortality, is of overriding importance for the whole development concept contained in the 1926 reform programme. Educational policy, including pre-school and kindergarten education, comprehensive schools from age 6 to 14 and free access to institutions of higher education are further points in the package. In view of the contemporary resurgence of religious fundamentalism in the world it is necessary to point out that, for the sake of development, all state religions must be abolished; the state as such cannot be tied to any religion, and there must be free competition between all forms of ideologies and religions in a framework of liberalism and plurality.

My recognition of the empirical validity of liberal arguments in the tradition of Olson and Weede makes it necessary to rethink anew the liberal aspects inherent in the socialism of the great reformers in this century, like Bauer, Mariategui, Polanyi, and Wigforss. It would be wrong to interpret their 'liberalism' as 'supply-side socialism' just as it would be wrong to interpret my findings as 'supply-side development theory'. Under different sets of circumstances, though, state capitalism or state expenditures under a capitalist system produce negative results; and under certain circumstances, state socialism contributes to certain results, and these results might be connected with inefficiency, social stagnation, or, as the case of the capitalist 'rim-countries' will show in Chapter 8, there might be an upsurge of 'military Keynesianism' in the present phase of the Kondratieff cycle.

It is this theoretical framework which guides my empirical research. Social justice in a framework of pluralism and the market (de Kadt) is the basic principle which explains success and failure in the world system. The contenders are modernization theories and '*teorias de la dependencia*' (usually translated as 'dependency theory')/world systems theories. While *dependencia*/world system approaches have traditionally explained differences in development performance in terms of the changing, but hierarchically reproduced, world-wide division of labour, in which there is a certain stability in the centre–periphery structure, neo-*dependencia* approaches no longer exclude the successful capitalist development of the newly industrializing countries. Neo-*dependencia* approaches (especially theories of the 'new international division of labour' and feminist world system analyses) have a feature in common: they predict a rise in marginality in the former core countries, accompanying semi-peripheral capitalist development. But while such neo-*dependencia* authors stress the functionality of 'non-capitalist' relations of exploitation and rediscover marginality – defined as the exclusion of population groups from the innovation process (Apter, 1987) – an important controversy has arisen. This is about the relationship between the world capitalist system and non-capitalist relationships of domination in both historical and contemporary dimensions and involves such authors as R. Brenner, H. Elsenhans and D. Senghaas. The exploitation of 'non-capitalist' spheres, such as the Polish serf-economy in the 'long sixteenth century', is located within the more general disability of the 'state classes' in the Third World to innovate, to base accumulation precisely on the appropriation of relative surplus value, and to create mass demand and social structures without blatant forms of discrimination in facilitating capitalist development. The emerging critique of state classes by authors originally writing within the framework of 'critical' development theory has another interesting aspect: development economists of the 'pioneering' generation, like Lewis, Myrdal and Prebisch, have drawn attention to the responsibility that states in the Third World have for the way things are.

Is the search for a synthesis between socialism and liberalism (Prebisch, 1984) an alternative to established world systems approaches to explain development and underdevelopment? Such a synthesis, first, corresponds to the mentioned traditions of reform inherent in European social democracy in the inter-war period. And secondly, it corresponds very well with the empirically observable determinants of world development between 1960 and the mid-1980s. Liberal economic theories in the tradition of M. Olson would maintain that, on the other hand (i) with increasing political systems age, state sector influence and 'distributional coalitions' tend to thwart growth; and (ii) inequality proves to be a major stumbling block for long-term capitalist development.

While some of the last formulations by the very founder of (bourgeois) dependency theory, R. Prebisch, would agree at least with the first of these propositions, it can be shown that institutional inflexibility and lack of mass demand – the two most important hypotheses derived from Olson – have also played a major role in the reformulation of the world systems approach by Elsenhans and Senghaas. To test such perspectives, which lay emphasis on a greater chance of periphery countries for long-term political and social reforms, a methodological innovation is introduced here, developing further life expectancy research in the tradition of a Plateau curve of basic human needs satisfaction. Otherwise I use well-established research instruments, as applied in macro-quantitative development theory testing. I confirm a 'redistribution with development' perspective of world-wide per capita real income growth from 1960 to the mid-1980s. Basic human needs satisfaction and the redistribution of incomes and of land are not only compatible but are a precondition of stable growth patterns (Table 7.1). This serves to contradict the essence of pessimistic modernization theories, which were the historical starting point of the *dependencia* critique. Demographic patterns and human capital formation by the state via secondary schooling play an important role in the determination of inequality (Equation 7.3), while 48 per cent of economic growth 1965–83 is explained for the 68 countries with complete data by: (i) changes in the organization of national defence (conscription); (ii) public efforts at human capital formation; (iii) a changing state tax structure with greater reliance on direct taxes; (iv) increasing institutional age, combined with high government expenditure, which indeed blocks growth, as Olson predicts yet – contrary to his expectations about free factor mobility as an agent of growth – transnational capital first dynamizes host economies, but then forms part of the power structure, dominated by the state classes, thus blocking long-term growth.

Expectations by various authors about a Plateau-effect of basic needs attainment with increasing levels of industrialization are confirmed by my statistical investigations. Olson's theory is confirmed for life expectancy and its increases over time since 1960. State class control over the economy in an ethnically heterogeneous environment is the best predictor for long-term social stagnation measured in terms of how much energy input of a society (and thus environmental degradation) is used to guarantee a certain level of basic human needs attainment (Table 7.4).

I confirm the original critique by some *dependencia* authors, like Cardoso and Palma, against stagnationist and 'narodnik' analyses. The stagnationist school, however, *is* relevant in terms of economic growth, *which is blocked in a long-term perspective by TNC penetration.* But critics like Cardoso are right, when we consider TNC investment for export production in so called 'free zones'. Precisely those countries which already let a larger share of their labour force work in such zones had the most dynamic growth of *employment* in the period in question. I am cautious about attempts in international journals to explain political instability and political violence by such phenomena as US military aid and deprivation (Muller). Rather, the room for manoeuvre of the government, measured by the government savings (debt) ratio per total savings and military expenditures, plays a major role in the determination of violence. Instability of the executive is connected with income concentration, limited party competition, limited financial room for manoeuvre of the government and low levels of past investment expansion (Tables 7.7–7.9). This finding, of course, bodes ill for the post-1989 attempts at IMF-type stabilization policies in Eastern Europe. Income concentration rises, the party system does not work properly, state debts are high, government savings are extremely negative and there is a severe contraction in investment leading, most probably, to military interventions, at least in some countries. Government consumption plays a major role in today's staggering Third World debt of more than $1400 billion whenever we consider government sector influence and institutional stability jointly in the regression equation (Table 7.10). Again, traditional indicators of 'dependence' do not explain how this rapid rise in the rate of debt came about. Furthermore, my approach could lead to the development of some thought about the socio-psychological consequences of state class control in an institutionally rigid environment (Tables 7.11–7.12). Conflicts are more and more located at the individual level, while state classes keep their power in institutionally rigid set-ups. Furthermore it is shown that – quite in line with Olson's expectation – blatant social discrimination, especially against women, is connected with long-term economic stagnation, irrespective of the industrialization level reached by a society at the start of the measurement period.

Up to this point, my analyses were derived at the level of the world economy. In Chapter 8 I look at the implications of former state socialism. I start out from a very pessimistic analysis of development trends in the socialist world during the 1980s. Stagnating human development, lack of redistribution and a strong hard core of the state class in the heavy industrial sector characterized the leading European former socialist countries in the interior, while there was a compelling economic need – within the system – to alleviate external imbalances with the capitalist world economy by arms exports. My macro-quantitative model does not spell out how far the present reconstruction movement can go. But it does tell us something about the consequences of its possible failures and the continuation of the command type of economy: stagnating productivity and a renewed arms sales drive to the Third World. Stagnating Third World societies, not very heavily penetrated by transnational capital, have been the main clients of Soviet-bloc arms sales to the South. By their lower price and maintenance costs, these weapons systems somewhat alleviated the explosive debt situation of militarized Third World state classes at given or pretended security needs of Third World countries. Long-term instability in such regimes increases, while claims about their 'development' in combination with 'trickle down' cannot be maintained.

I also present a politometric analysis of the effects of a dependence on former state socialism in the South. The best indicator for such a dependence, in my view, is the extent to which a Third World country imported arms from the three major former Warsaw Pact suppliers: the former USSR, the former CSFR, and Poland. We call their respective share in total Third World arms imports 'Eastern Arms Clientele Status'. On the demand side, we observe a paradoxical effect of military Keynesianism with positive effects on growth precisely in those countries, which are only partially or not at all integrated into the juridical institutions of the capitalist world economy; thus they have not been subjected to the discipline of market forces as were the more open economies with a higher institutional integration. The state classes in the South benefit from militarism in terms of growth; there was a negative effect of dependence under former state socialism on growth in such Third World countries. Furthermore, such dependence did not pay off in social terms. Executive instability and the danger of increasing political violence, however, in conjunction with a better price relation of stockpiled Eastern arms (and, hence, fewer negative consequences for debt ratios), are the cause for Eastern weapons finding clients in the Third World, also after 1989. The dramatic reperipherization of Eastern Europe has manifested itself in indices of infantile underweight at birth as a sign of neglect and under-nourishment, infant and mothers' mortality and rising death rates amongst others in countries like Poland and Hungary. '*Perestroika*' was not a voluntary choice at the crossroads leading to some not too distant socialisms. Rather it was a choice between systems maintenance and the danger of re-peripherization in a changing world economy. All indicators seem to point in the direction of a further authoritarian model in the Russian semi-periphery of the capitalist world system, thus renewing the authoritarian development patterns of Russia during and after a Great Depression, patterns already established under Ivan the Terrible, Michael III, Peter I, Nikolas (the Policeman of Europe) and the imperial expansion in the late nineteenth century. State class control in ageing or socially inflexible environments has produced stagnation in former state socialism, too.

Chapter 9 will look at the global economic implications of the arms-race-induced stagnation path of former state socialism in the former USSR and Eastern Europe in the late 1980s and early 1990s. Soviet style economies and those of their allies in the South have tended to become semi-marginalized in the changing structure of world power, while the former USSR and the other/former socialist nations reveal centrifugal internal tendencies in connection with state class-rule and ethnic heterogeneity. As some former relative top-dogs – defined in Galtung's terms – in the international system lose ground in consequence of the world economic changes in the 1970s and 1980s, Eastern Europe has been challenged by ascending Third World industrializers, especially in East and Southeast Asia.

I also test the validity of the socio-liberal argument *vis-à-vis* corporatist schools. The (neo)corporatists maintain that the institutional integration of organized interest intermediation in capitalist democracies, like Sweden, is good for employment, price stability, fiscal restraint and growth. While I accept that such positive effects might result from the encompassing nature of interest groups in the medium term, I am pessimistic in the long run, predicting narrow group egoism among privileged groups leading to a break up of the corporatist set-up, and to a high rate of social strain. My empirical tests show that corporatism stabilizes short-term capitalist development upwards and increases longer-term growth slightly.

The socio-liberal model presented in Chapter 7 pretty well explains the development in Asian growth economies and European smaller or zero-block nations in terms of residuals and their standard deviations. I aim at a rethinking of adjustment (not exclusively in terms of World Bank thinking) to crises in the shorter term. For Olson, the devastating extent of cyclical downswings comes about by the collusive pressure from secure job holders manifesting itself in the downward stickiness of wages. My politometric evidence, by contrast, suggests that here and only here will a Keynesian strategy be able to boost production in times of crisis. There clearly emerge – as at the time of the Great Depression – two variants of Keynesianism: one more socially oriented, the other leaning towards militarism (vulgar Keynesianism). Such a strategy will be the more successful the less dominant a country already is within the international economy, structured by TNC capital, and the more stable and corporatist is its socio-political environment. But such a strategy can have a heavy longer-term price, while the socio-liberal development strategy (high degree of social equality combined with restraint on the expansion of state sector influence) was already inherent in the Swedish upsurge after 1932; and today it is related to long-term ascent in the world system.

2 World Society Approaches to Development

Ever since the early 1960s, social scientists from very different disciplines tried to explain why some societies grow faster, have a more egalitarian distribution of incomes, a better social development, and more stability than other societies. In the political science and sociology debate in progress in the Western world about the international system, it was – among a variety of possible explanations – dependency and world society arguments that gained considerable acceptance (Russett, 1983a; Weede, 1985a). *Dependencia* and world system/society theories have in common put the main blame for stagnation, inequality and repression in the South on the workings of the international system since its beginnings with the discovery of the American continent in 1492. Small but influential subgroups of international scholarship notwithstanding, whose world society argument is based on military threat from the outside, most of the dependence schools (Roehrich and Zinn, 1983) share some basic agreement on the predominance of economic over other causal development factors, and quite a few accept in principle some categories of Marxist/neo-Marxist political economy, including theories of imperialism.

Why poor people stay poor is explained in these theories by the workings of an exploitative capitalist world economy, which, by its very history and evolution, has structurally thwarted the development chances of the unfortunate rest of the world, not forming part of the centre. Of course, imperialism theory and all the later contributions of Marxist/neo-Marxist development thought pose some very difficult questions to other varieties of development theories: countries like Nicaragua did not choose to produce coffee and bananas; there were decades and centuries of military interventions, colonial rule and decisions from outside shaping a country's and its people's destiny (Raffer, 1987, chap. 8, see also Griffin, 1987: 26–32). Colonialism reduced the indigenous population of Latin America by more than 50 million people, and equally devastating were the human consequences of the slave trade (Wallerstein, 1974/86; Nolte, 1982). Almost the entire population of continents, the North American Indians and the Australian Aborigines lost their lives and the ecological basis of their culture by the march of 'Western civilization'. During the great famine in Bengal in 1943 alone, more than three million people starved to death amidst a war-induced upsurge of industrial production; an entire third of the population of Bengal starved to death between 1769 and 1771 (Griffin, 1987).

The *dependencia* models, which from the mid 1960s onward slowly entered into the international development debate, were an answer both to the inconsistencies of earlier modernization approaches and the limitations of classical Marxist approaches to the theory of imperialism. *Dependencia* thought arose in the Third World precisely because earlier expectations voiced by more optimistic modernization theories (see, especially, Lipset, 1959) about the causal relationship between economic development and democracy were shattered by the rise of authoritarian military regimes in Latin America and elsewhere. *Dependencia* social science first and foremost induced the rewriting of the history of peripheral, or thought to be peripheral, nations (Amin, 1975; Cardoso, 1972–73; Cardoso and Faletto, 1971; Cordova, 1973; Grabendorff, 1973; Mandel, 1973; Marini, 1974; Quijano Obregon, 1974; Roehrich, 1978–86; Senghaas, 1971–77; Sunkel, 1966–74; Raffer, 1979). Let us recall what could be regarded as the essential formulation of modernization theories, for then we can better understand how *dependencia* contrasts with them. Lipset's key model can be summarized and made verifiable in the fashion that Huntington and Nelson proposed: development leads to stability, equality and participation, which, in turn, are enhanced by the 'benign' circle among the last three processes. No vicious circle ensues (Figure 2.1).

Figure 2.1   The liberal model in the Lipset tradition

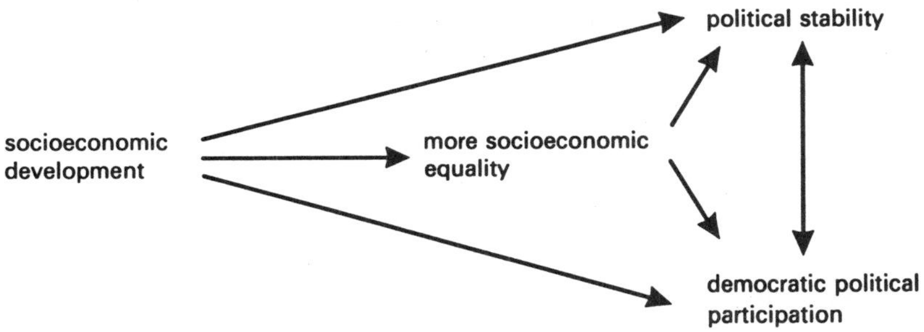

Source: Summarized by Huntington and Nelson, 1976.

What, then, is modernization? According to Huntington it is seen by many modernization theories

as a comprehensive, systemic process in which societies changed fundamentally and across the board from an approximation of the traditional model to an approximation of the modern model. The various components of modernization were associated together, and changes from tradition to modernity in one sector or dimension were related to and reinforced by comparable changes in other sectors (Huntington, 1987: 6–7).

Among the more testable propositions of the pessimistic visions of modernization theories is Deutsch's famous model of political stability (1), linking stability (*st*) to government sector influence over the economy (*g*), social mobilization measured by alphabetization (*L*), political mobilization (*pol*), measured either by electoral participation ratios (*v*) or simply by the percentage of people legally entitled to vote (*ve*), income concentration in the hands of the richest 10 per cent of the population (*y*10) and finally, per capita income (*y*). The model can safely be described as being conservative in political character, Deutsch's later writings on the issue notwithstanding. Government sector influence and income inequality work in favour of stability, while political and social mobilization, as well as 'modernization', i.e. per capita income, are inherently a threat to stability. And let us not forget: this neat little formula was practically the political programme of Brazilian generals after 1964: increase state capitalism and inequality, repress participation in the political and in the social sense, and when growth is fast, perform that authoritarian task even more thoroughly:

$$St = (g/(L * pol)) * (y10/y) \tag{2.1}$$

Huntington's development theory can in its essence be reduced to the following equation and Figure: on the one hand, social mobilization (*sm*) is a threat to stability and works in favour of instability (*ist*), while economic development (*dev*) – in contrast to Deutsch – works in favour of stability and decreases instability:

$$ist = sm/dev \tag{2.2}$$

This formulation, which was proposed by Weede (1985a: 57) in view of the inherent difficulties in finding proper measurement concepts for Huntington's theory, is also compatible with his own causal model, taken from Huntington and Nelson, 1976 (Figure 2.2). Later on Huntington (1987) has vaguely hinted at the possibility of a reconciliatory development theory, i.e. a theory which allows for redistribution with growth. But for Huntington this reconciliation path is culturally predetermined and only feasible in Protestant and Confucian cultures. Lipset (1959: 75) maintained that the more well-to-do a nation, the greater are the chances that it will sustain democracy. A lively debate, which was started by Cardoso and Faletto's ideas in Chile in the middle of the 1960s, soon came to discover that the ups

and downs of authoritarianism and formal democracy and the ups and
downs of the industrialization drive, underway in many periphery countries
since the world economic recession of the 1930s, were within a more general
historical framework of development, which *dependencia* thought described
through such categories as 'outward oriented development', 'inward
oriented development', and 'internationalization of internal markets'.
Third World, especially Latin American, formal democracy, according to
most *dependencia* historians, was closely linked to the rise of import
substitution and the class alliance of populism between the urban wage
earners and the evolving industrial bourgeoisie against the interests of the
traditional export sector (see, especially, Cardoso and Faletto, *passim*). Thus
Cardoso (1977) was right in warning against the linkage between the
dependencia debate in Latin America and the more general attempts to
build macro-quantitatively testable models of world development, started in
Anglo-American literature by Chase-Dunn (1975), Galtung, (1971); and
Rubinson (1976). At a time of the crumbling of the democratic structure,
Cardoso and Faletto envisaged – and indeed practised – the 'concrete
analysis of concrete situations', i.e. of social exclusion and political
repression in countries like Brazil after the military coup of 1964, without
having in mind a formal 'model' of economic growth, income distribution,
let alone democratic stability.

Figure 2.2   The vicious circle of the populist model according to Huntington and
Nelson

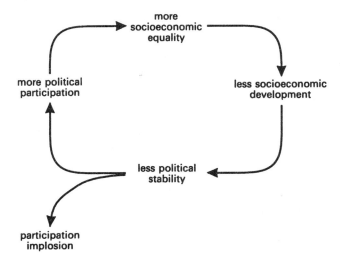

Source: Huntington and Nelson, 1976: 25.

The situation *dependencia* authors were faced with at the end of the 1960s was the precise opposite of Lipset's theory. An obvious industrialization process brought about rising inequality between rich and poor. Democracy and participation by the poorer sectors were brutally suppressed by military dictatorships, as in Brazil (post-1964), or Argentina (post-1966). Brazilian authors wrote extensively on that issue (see also Bresser Pereira (1984); Canak (1984); Cardoso, 1972a–1973c; Cardoso and Faletto (1971); Filgueira (1984); Singer, 1980–1981b; just to mention a few). The 'model' installed in Brazil after the military coup of 1964 was in many ways treated as the symbol of a new tendency on a world-wide scale: disrespect towards human rights, military rule, a powerful alliance between the multinationals, state capital and private capital, and economic growth whose benefits accrued disproportionally to the richest 5–10 per cent of the population, excluding the millions living in the shanty towns around the big cities. The term 'marginality' originally meant those living '*al margen*' (at the margin) of the big cities, but later on that social scientific term was also applied to people living in rural poverty (Cordova, 1973). Tendencies towards land reform in the pre-1964 era were harshly reversed, and the military government carried out a large resettlement programme, pushing millions of landless peasants from the impoverished northeast to the Amazon regions. Such 'concrete analyses of concrete situations' of under-development (a term coined by Cardoso) tremendously enriched the Western development debate, which till then was based on what fellow Westerners wrote about far-away countries. The *dependencia* interpretation of development, causally linking the ongoing repression, social exclusiveness of the 'model', and economic and spiritual 'denationalization' with the growing power of transnational capital and the cumulative weight of centuries of external exploitation, soon entered into Christian circles in Latin America, especially into the thinking of the 'basic communities' in the post-Vatican Council Catholic Church. Liberation theology, up to today so hotly contested the world over, fully accepts and shares the views of the '*dependencia* school' of development and uses it as its own social scientific basis (Zwiefelhofer, 1977; Schoepfer, 1979; Levy, 1989; Zambrano, 1982).

The vacuum into which the then 'new' *dependencia* approaches could thrust in part explains their long-standing success in many social science disciplines in the 1970s. Here was a 'theory' originating in the Third World (Seers, 1981a; Senghaas, 1971, 1972a – hence the English and German terms '*dependency theory*' and '*Dependenztheorie*'), and it was not connected politically in any way with the Vietnam war and other instances of Western foreign policy in the Third World. By contrast, modernization theory, especially in its more pessimistic versions, was alleged again and again to favour Western political interests in the South. Nor did mainstream theoretical justifications for harsh military rule to avert the danger of 'participation implosion' increase the standing of modernization theories among the development and peace research community in the Western world in the 1970s (see also Addicks and Buenning, 1979; Addo, 1981; Chomsky, 1971, 1972; Nohlen *et al.*, 1982–85; Nuscheler, 1974–86; Stauffer, 1985, 1990; Tibi, 1983; Zwiefelhofer, 1977). It is no exaggeration, to call the *dependencia* (and later world system) approach the dominant paradigm in sociological and political science development research for many years, especially in the 1970s and early 1980s (see also Migdal, 1983; Nohlen, 1984; Nuscheler, 1985a; Russett, 1983a; Seers, 1981a; Snidal *et al.*, 1980). The consensus which characterized the new dominant development paradigm (see also Hettne, 1982–89) rested upon the empirically tested assumption, that the degree of dependence from the capitalist world economy creates unequal development. Although an important school within the *dependencia* movement (see especially Hurtienne, 1984; Cardoso; Palma, 1981) precisely maintains that dependent industrialization stimulated economic growth, most cross-national tests on the issue maintain that dependence retarded long-term economic growth. The starting point, and here Almond is correct, of dynamic interpretations is Lenin's famous and very empirically oriented analysis on 'The Development of Capitalism in Russia', subtitled 'The Process of the Creation of an Internal Market for Big Industry', dated 1899 (Lenin, 1973: 3). Lenin's work, directed against the *narodniks* who thought that the immediate collapse of capitalism in Russia at that time, due to underconsumption, was imminent, is used by the 'dynamic' school of Cardoso, Hurtienne and Palma to criticize *narodnik* tendencies in the works of Frank and Marini. Yet given Lenin's extraordinary statistical evidence in his 1899 book, should it not be a motive for dependence literature to take the evidence produced by the 'macro-quantitative school' seriously?

Writing the history of the up to then unwritten 'other side' of development, speaking about marginalization, human rights, dependence, was one point. As social scientists, dependency-theory authors also worked in some way or other on the problem of theory. Cardoso, to be sure, in many instances rejects the notion of a 'general theory' (see especially, 1973b); but other authors from the periphery, most notably Amin (1975), Jaguaribe *et al.* (1972), Gonzales-Casanova (1969–73), and Sunkel (1972, 1978) indeed did think in terms of the more general explanations on why some countries grow/decline economically, politically and socially so differently from others. But these more general approaches do not strictly form part of what later was termed the '*dependencia* debate' started by Cardoso and Faletto's manuscript in Chile during the mid-1960s. Thus, there were attempts – also in Latin America – to formulate more general theories of development. Not only economists, linked closely to the idea of import-substituting industrialization and political populism, so popular from the 1930s onwards, formulated such models (see especially, Prebisch, 1984; Dubiel, 1984; Flechsig, 1987), but also social scientists, who were quite critical about this import substituting populist model in the post-1930 era. Thus, authors like Cordova, Gonzales-Casanova, and Sunkel, all to be categorized as adherents of the more general movement of dependency theory, although they did not contribute to the original *dependencia* debate (Evers and von Wogau, 1973; Palma, 1981), in their writings formulate general hypotheses about the development process, especially the dependence–inequality trade-off. So the metatheoretical debate between Cardoso, Chase-Dunn (1982b), and Ragin (1985) about the impossibility of a more generalized version of 'dependency theory' misses the point, in so far as there are formulations in some original Third World theories which clearly invite the rigorous politometric and econometric testing of developmental propositions, nowadays so common in industrialized country literature. In looking back at the *dependencia* literature, Cardoso himself (1977, and especially 1979) firmly places *dependencia* thought in the tradition of those who, with John Stuart Mill and R. Prebisch, believe that (i) the exchange values of manufactured goods, compared with agriculture and mining, have a tendency to fall in proportion to the increase in population and industry; and that (ii) incomes grow faster at the centre than at the periphery, since the rising productivity in industrial production is not transmitted to prices because the oligopolies defend their profit rate and the labour unions press to keep up wage levels, and thus in international exchange there is a tendency to a relative decline of the price of primary products (Cardoso, 1979: 7; see also Dubiel, 1984; Prebisch, 1983, 1984; Raffer, 1987).

Thus the very foundation for economic equality between nations is denied, while institutional and structural factors beyond the proper sphere of the market explain the tendencies of international trade: labour union struggles, the organizational capacity of workers and employers at the centre, and the effects of monopolies (Cardoso, 1979: 8). There is some parallel in this development theory to that of Kalecki, who explained income distribution by the movements in the degree of monopolization on the one hand and the terms of trade of raw material production on the other. Kalecki's distribution theory predicted that, in order to maintain the share in the distributive struggle, workers would have to benefit from falling raw material terms of trade in order to regain what has been lost in the distributive struggle by the rising degree of monopolization. At a world-wide level, this theory, whose essence practically was established already in the 1930s in his native Poland, integrated many elements of what later became 'dependency theory'. The distributive struggle between wage labour and capital in the centre will be vitally affected by the continued inequality, on a world scale, between raw material producers and the industrial sector (see, especially, Kalecki, 1972; Rothschild, 1966). Sometimes, especially in the United States nowadays, there emerges a harsh and to my mind unjustified critique of dependency-theory literature:

Latin American area studies has not had the sufficient time to develop traditions and professional norms. We should not blink at the fact that the adoption of a dependency perspective was a backward step, a movement away from the hard-won rule of evidence and inference in social studies. It gave up the battle for science in the study of society on the grounds that a complete victory could never be won. It involved the adoption of unfalsifiable concepts of the state as a part of class domination, of politics as struggle and that alone, and of society as a complex of exploiting and exploited economic classes. (Almond, 1987: 454–5)

For a European author, the connections between *dependencia* thought and the heterodoxical traditions of political economy are self-evident and are well documented, especially regarding Prebisch's original formulations of a 'bourgeois' Latin American development theory (Dubiel, 1984, Flechsig, 1989a). Early on, there were several European efforts both at translating texts from the *dependencia* debate and/or at integrating its results into the theory of international relations (see for example Bennholdt-Thomsen, 1980; Boeckh, 1982; Cordova, 1973; Hettne, 1982; Hurtienne, 1974; Palma, 1981; Raffer, 1979; Roehrich and Zinn, 1983; Senghaas, 1971–79; Tausch, 1973–79; von Werlhof, 1975). Imperialism is not just an issue of Leninist theory, it also forms part and parcel of the political thought of European social democrats such as O. Bauer and K. Polanyi, just to mention two. Classical contributions by neo-Marxist political economy, such as Kalecki and Maerz, all dealt with the issue of imperialistic structures, without this justifying the inference of 'Leninist' leanings in their works, as Almond rather sweepingly maintains. For Sunkel, who in many ways must be regarded as a social scientist within the 'structuralist school', reformulating development theory in a *dependencia* perspective first and foremost means analysing the process of capitalist development as a process of 'creative destruction', a term which he borrows from Schumpeter. Development needs changes in the social structure, a redistribution of political power, institutional and cultural transformation. This is not 'Marxism' but simply the continuation of the traditions of classical political economy.

An important intellectual tradition, which contributed to the reception of *dependencia* thought, derives from the Roman Catholic Church and its many private universities throughout Latin America. Catholic social doctrine has unquestionably contributed to the reformist political project on the continent, as Flechsig *et al.* (1989b) quite correctly point out. Leading Church figures, like Archbishop Rivera y Damas (1983) of El Salvador, took a position in the scholarly debate on development and underdevelopment by writing introductions to books compiled by Catholic thinkers or Catholic universities. Almond and other critics of dependency-theory literature overlook this tradition, which found its most coherent expression in the Church documents in Puebla (Zambrano, 1982), all emphasizing dependence as a development block. From a methodological viewpoint, the *dependencia* debate, which developed precisely as a reaction to the failure of the United Nations Commission for Latin America's (ECLA/CEPAL) strategy to reinforce national decision-making centres to absorb technical progress and strengthen domestic markets as part of the Prebisch 'package' (Cardoso, 1979: 9–18), emphasized the historical and structural nature of the situation of underdevelopment and attempted to relate the production of this situation, as well as its reproduction, to the dynamics of capitalism's development on a world scale (Cardoso, 1979: 18). What was new about the '*dependencia* debate' was not the stress laid on 'external dependence' already inherent in the more traditional ECLA/CEPAL-Prebisch approach (see also Dubiel, 1984), but the analysis of these structural patterns which, asymmetrically and regularly, link central and peripheral economies, introducing the notion of domination into the social-scientific debate about development (Cardoso, 1979: 19):

> Thus, the notion of domination was introduced. All stress was laid on the negative: autonomous development is not probable, ceteris paribus. I do not want to discuss here whether this statement was correct or not. I would like simply to remark on the following, at the opposite (and discontinuous) pole from dependency theory: what was glimpsed was not autonomous development but socialism. Of course, this was not made explicit by many writers, but the critique of the possibility of capitalistic 'development', especially as far as 'national development' was concerned, had been the starting point for analyses by Dos Santos, Quijano, Marini, Faletto and Cardoso, to mention only a few. (Cardoso, 1979: 19–20)

Domination was seen not only between nations, but also between classes. Especially relevant here is the linkage between the local industrial elites and transnational enterprise in the era of what Cardoso calls 'new *dependencia*', manifesting itself especially in the industrially advanced countries in Latin America, Brazil, Argentina and Mexico. On the one hand, Cardoso, as already mentioned, drew a sharp distinction between his own thinking and some traditions quantifying *dependencia* arguments – a tradition which

Cardoso treats rather with disdain as 'consumption of *dependencia* literature' (Cardoso, 1977). The reaction of the quantitative profession in the United States, most notably Chase-Dunn (1982a, 1982b) and Ragin (1985), unfortunately did not point out a continuity between their own quantitative attempts and the already mentioned earlier studies in the tradition of political economy, some of them in Latin America, which were quite open to the kind of argumentation used by themselves (see especially the works of Gonzales-Casanova, Kalecki, Lange, Rothschild). Cardoso himself even assents with the (quantifiable) arguments, derived by the 'Yale project' on *dependencia* (Duvall and Freeman, 1981; Snidal *et al.*, 1980; Russett *et al.*, 1983a, 1983b) as constituting the 'essence' of '*dependencia*': (i) there is financial and technological penetration by the developed capitalist centres; (ii) this produces an unbalanced economic structure both within peripheral societies and between them and the centre; (iii) which leads to limitations on self-sustained growth in the periphery; (iv) this favours the appearance of specific patterns of capitalist class relations; and (v) these require modifications in the role of the state to guarantee both the functioning of the economy and the political articulation of a society, which contains, within itself, foci of inarticulateness and structural imbalance.

Cardoso welcomes this synthesis (Cardoso, 1979: 21), proposed by the 'Yale project'. And indeed, Yale's published quantitative results, based on multiple regressions, largely confirm Cardoso's reasoning for a varying amount of some four dozen periphery countries with complete data, in so far as there is indeed – as Cardoso (1979: 21) asserts – a movement in the expansion of capitalism along time limiting self-sustained growth, leading towards (relative) marginalization. Galtung's influence at the start of what should later become known as 'macro-quantitative dependency/world system research' must not be underestimated. Being a pioneering writer in the field of methodology and peace research, he was the first to bring together – in one very influential contribution (1971) – the essence of imperialism and dependency perspectives and quantitative hypothesis testing, made possible by the ever growing number of social science data available on a world level since the publication of the first 'World Handbook of Political and Social Indicators' (Russett *et al.*, 1964). Already Galtung in his famous (1971) contribution had developed and/or applied some measures which could properly catch the essence of dependent insertion into the capitalist world economy: a high concentration of goods among the export products, a high concentration of trading partners, and, above all, a measure which relates imported industrial goods and exported raw materials (a typical periphery characteristic) to exported industrial goods and imported raw materials (a typical centre):

$$\text{Galtung Index} = ((a * d) - (b * c))/((a * d) + (b * c)) \qquad (2.3)$$

a = imported raw materials
b = exported raw materials
c = imported industrial goods
d = exported industrial goods

According to this indicator, Japan is a typical centre (+0.96), Nicaragua a typical periphery country (−0.98). Galtung thus links underdevelopment and inequality to the traditional pattern of the world division of labour, which consisted in the production of manufactured goods by the centres and raw materials by the periphery. This unequal exchange is further extended and stabilized by the imperialist communications pattern, linking isolated 'underdogs' with separate communication channels to the powerful 'top-dog', which means in practice a high trading partner concentration ratio for the periphery. Linkages from the underdogs of one feudal interaction pattern to the top-dogs of another 'bloc' are strictly ruled out; communications, trade, technologies and knowledge flow from a country like Nigeria or Ghana (if at all) to the Ivory Coast via London and Paris. Galtung's cross-national evidence for his famous imperialism theory is relatively simple. If development is measured by GNP per capita, vertical trade by the indicator presented in equation (2.3) above, inequality by the GINI indices of personal incomes or land distribution, and feudal trade by the concentration among a country's trading partners, then the correlations on the basis of the Russett *et al.* 'World Handbook' (1964) do hold up to the expectations of Galtung's theory, just as with vertical trade being measured by the concentration of export commodities. Galtung's simple correlation measure (the dichotomous Yule's Q) and his outdated data can be substituted today by SPSS calculations for the Pearson/Bravais-correlation coefficient on the basis of the 'World Handbook III' (Taylor and Jodice), or other data sets. All the expected correlations are still significant at the 5 per cent level, thus again confirming Galtung's original simple model (Figure 2.3).

A very promising research direction was begun by the Zurich school of world system sociology, founded by the late P. Heintz and continued by his disciples, among them V. Bornschier, T. H. Ballmer Cao; P. Meyer-Fehr and H. Zwicky, just to mention a few. This macrosociology of international society also had some parallels in US quantitative social science. Chase-Dunn (1975), Rubinson (1976), Russett *et al.* (1983b) and especially the works of Bornschier *et al.*, and later on also Bornschier and Chase-Dunn, laid the basis of a theory of international society, in which penetration by transnational capital and the 'imperialism of trade' in the sense of

Figure 2.3   Galtung's model of imperialism (updated)

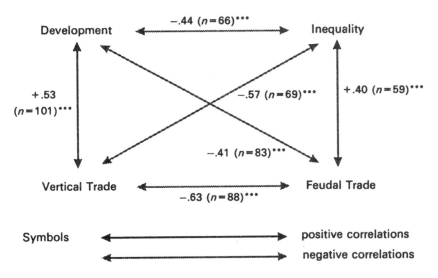

Source: Galtung's original model updated with SPSS-9 correlations, based on Bornshier, Heintz *et al.*

J. Galtung (1971) leads to long-term stagnation and inequality. Further empirical research, using in part the data collection of Bornschier, Heintz *et al.* (1979) has extended the argument and shown the negative consequences of the capitalist dependence for a variety of development 'yardsticks', sometimes including democracy and productive employment (see Bollen, 1983; Bornschier *et al.*, 1980–1985; Delacroix and Ragin, 1981; Evans and Timberlake, 1980; T. H. Johnson *et al.*; Meyer-Fehr (1978); Snidal *et al.* (1980); Timberlake and Williams (1984); Zwicky, 1985a, b). Earlier multiple regression models of dependence and underdevelopment on a world scale, controlling for the curvilenear effects of development level on inequality and growth (see especially, Kuznets, 1955; Jackman, 1982; Jagodzinski/Weede, 1981; Weede, 1980), also found support from the sophisticated model employed by the Yale University research group of Russett *et al.* (1983b), referred to above.

Serious macro-quantitative evidence, published in some of the leading journals of world-wide social science scholarship, further enhanced the paradigmatic 'standing' of dependence arguments *vis-à-vis* contending development theories. Writing in a contribution about empirical international relations research on behalf of the American Political Science

Association, Russett discerns two main areas of research that go on in the discipline: quantitative models of East–West relations, including how armaments affect the national well-being in East and West, and quantitative models of world development along Bornschier and Weede traditions. It should be noted that introductory textbooks in other countries, too, reflect at that time the paradigmatic predominance of the dependency explanation of world development (to mention a few: Roehrich *et al.*, 1978–86; Hettne, 1982; Nohlen, 1984).

Quantitative data, which were reported by such institutions as the World Bank and the United Nations, on file in such compilations as Bornschier, Heintz *et al.* (1979); Taylor and Jodice (1983); or World Bank (1980) also helped to resolve some of the most long standing controversies between two different subgroups within the original dependency school interpretations. On the one hand, authors like Frank, Marini, but also Wallerstein, think that in the long run, stagnation and impoverishment, or as Frank put it, the 'development of underdevelopment' will go on in the periphery, while they do not exclude exploitative industrialization spurts in the semi-periphery, always threatened by the lack of internal demand. On the other hand, the exiled Chilean economist Palma continued the argument brought forward by Brazilian dependency authors in the 1970s (Cardoso, 1972a–1973d). Imperialism and development do not exclude each other, the stagnation-oriented school does nothing more and nothing less than underdevelop our analytical understanding of the development problem. Certainly, the development brought about by imperialism in some periphery countries is a capitalist one, exploitative in character; but exploitation was also present at the time of European industrialization (Hurtienne, 1974; Lenin, 1973, vol. 3).

The dialectical solution to this important controversy (see also Boeckh, 1982; Booth, 1985; Griffin and Gurley, 1985; Palma, 1981; Senghaas, 1977; Tausch, 1976) consists (today) in the empirically quite convincing statement that in the short run fresh 'infusions' of foreign capital dynamize peripheral economies, while in the long run an already existing high degree of foreign capital control over a society leads towards stagnation (Bornschier/Chase-Dunn, 1985; Tausch, 1991a). Empirical estimates about the effects of dependence on national development in the world system have been carried out which correctly estimate these short- and long-term, contradictory effects of foreign capital penetration. In Figures 2.4 and 2.5 I summarize such path models for the determination of economic growth and the absence of structural violence (life expectancy increases) in the world system. For a discussion about the quantitative details of such models and their socio-liberal critique I refer readers to Chapter 7.

Figure 2.4   A dependency-theory path model of economic growth in the world system, 1965–83

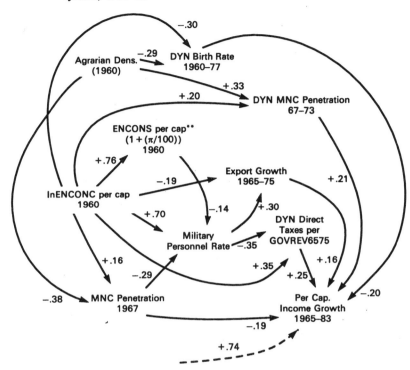

Source: Tausch, 1987b: 574.
Notes: n = 82 countries with complete data, taken from Bornshier, Heintz *et al.*; World Bank, *World Development Report*, 1985; Taylor and Jodice, 1983. Adjusted R**2 = 39.5%. Export Growth = growth in the share of exports per GDP.

Some other important aspects of imperialism theory also received politometric confirmation by Bornschier and his school. As was already asserted by Senghaas (1972a, b and 1974), as well as by Kalecki (1979e) and Rothschild (1966), dependent integration into the capitalist world economy leads towards a considerable decapitalization in the long run. And there can hardly be any doubts about core capital control over the whole of the world economy. Bornschier (1976), Froebel *et al.* (1977a–1986), Hymer (1973) and UN ECOSOC (1978) were among classical attempts to theorize about the power of the transnationals over world industrial production and world trade. Considering the enormous role played by the transnationals in

Figure 2.5 A dependency-theory path model of structural violence in the world system, 1960–77

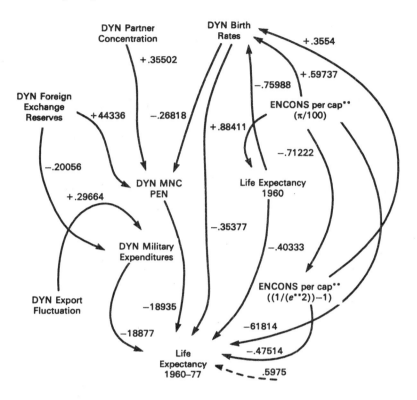

Source: Tausch, 1987b: 386–7.

Notes: *n* = 67 states with complete data; *R***2 = 64.3%. All Pearson Bravais correlations coefficients (◄────►) and path coefficients (────►) significant at the 10% level at least.

North–South and until recently also West–East relations (see Froebel *et al.*, 1977a; 1986; Pinto and Knakal, 1973; Chase-Dunn, 1982c; Szentes, 1982; Tausch, 1979a; 1982c; 1983; 1984a; 1985; 1986b), mainstream social sciences for a long time simply ignored the basic oligopolistic structure of the world system. To the power of the TNCs must be added the financial role played by the transnational banks (Swedberg, 1986b; Raffer, 1986).

3 Neo-Dependency Approaches

The question, then, is not the existence of transnational capitalist penetration, but its effects on world development and the preconditions that this development/decay has on a world level. A number of scholars in the radical and/or neo-Marxist tradition vigorously attacked traditional concepts about the present stage of the division of labour on a world-wide scale. Neoclassical economists in the tradition of Haberler would not deny the necessity for internal, urgent reforms in most LDCs (less developed countries) to make a market economy work, but they maintain that minimal interference with the movements of 'production factors' across national borders will always be the best strategy for a country internationally. They refer to the staggering economic growth rates, achieved even at a time of world recession in such countries as Singapore, and they will argue in favour of many Singapores around the globe. The problem formulation by the world system critics of the evolving new international division of labour is different. What distinguishes the present crisis from former downswings in the Kondratieff cycle? The very idea of the 60-year recurrence of such cataclysmic crises in world capitalist development and their relationship to world hegemony (three Kondratieff cycles add up to one world political hegemony) and world wars (each world war at the end of such world political hegemonies, i.e. the Thirty Years War, the Napoleonic Wars, the long world war of our century, 1914–18/39–45) is deeply disturbing and has been treated in recent literature amongst others by Goldstein (1988), Bornschier (1988), and Tausch (1990a).

What is the human and social cost of the evolving economic world order, and what does it mean in terms of political and social conflicts? Theories in the tradition of Addo, Amin, Frank and Wallerstein have in common that their unit of analysis is the whole capitalist world economy; they want to study its laws of motion, up from the early mercantilistic stage, the so-called 'long sixteenth century' (1450–1640) onwards to the mercantilist stage (1640–1750), the classical capitalist stage (1750–1870), the monopolistic phase (1870–1950) and the transnational stage (1950–) (Addo, 1986: 122–36).

There are two analytical traditions here, which merit special attention: the 'NIDL school' ('*New International Division of Labour*') comprising Froebel, Heinrichs, and Kreye on the one hand, and the feminist critique of the new

27

international division of labour on the other. This approach by a group of authors working then at Bielefeld University (former FRG) is represented in the Bibliography by Bennholdt-Thomsen and von Werlhof. Their approaches have in common the idea that the present crisis in the capitalist world economy, whose beginning they put at around 1967–68, is quite distinct from former minor business cycles in the post-war period and also from former beginnings of the downswing in the long-term Kondratieff cycles (see Goldstein, 1985b). For the 'NIDL group', but also to Goldstein (1985b, 1988), the beginnings of those long-term cyclical downswing periods in the capitalist world economy are closely linked with major upheavals in the international power system and in world culture, as occurred in 1871, 1917 and 1968. But while capitalist development over the last five hundred years created and perpetuated a regionally differentiated development on a world scale since 1450, this regionally differentiated development model now becomes obsolete by the reperipherization of the centres and the rapid industrialization of the semi-periphery, especially on the rim of the Pacific Ocean. Froebel leaves no doubt about his critique of orthodox dependency theory:

Dependency theories arose out of a critique of stages and modernization theories, and, correctly, both stress and demonstrate the polar unity of 'development and underdevelopment' as fundamental elements within capitalism. In addition, however, dependency theories also embrace the politically significant conception that the unity of 'development and underdevelopment' relates primarily to the complementary development of industrial and developing countries and further propose as an absolute tenet that this duality constitutes an inescapable fate which is constantly reproduced in the course of the global development of capitalism, albeit 'at an ever-higher level': the global division of labour as determined by capitalism constantly (re-)produces the subordination of dependent underdeveloped countries which, first, experience a systematic transfer of resources to the benefit of the centre (migration, 'brain drain', unequal exchange of quantities of labour, energy, protein, pollution, etc.), and, second, and more important, a systematic distortion of what may have been autonomous development. In fact, it is even suggested that once any country has been assigned this peripheral status it will retain it as long as it remains integrated into the capitalist world-system. The conclusion that the developing countries are doomed to inescapable and permanent marginalization (within the framework of world capitalism) can be questioned both theoretically and empirically. The likelihood that certain foreseeable tendencies within the capitalist world-system could transform some present developing countries into industrial-capitalist societies, with a corresponding model of accumulation, can no longer be merely dismissed out of hand (Froebel, 1984: 57).

For the NIDL group, some of the most characteristic features of this new world order, emerging around 1967–68 are: (i) major shifts of production not only from one industrial centre to the other or within industrialized countries, as happened during other cycles, but from the capitalist centre to the formerly centrally planned economies and the developing countries; (ii) world market factories for world market oriented manufacture (in contrast to Cardoso's 'model' of the internationalization of the internal markets of the periphery); (iii) structural crises of traditional industries in the centre, such as fibres, textiles, garments, leather and footwear, steel, shipbuilding, watchmaking, optical industries, engineering – all these branches increasingly go 'southwards'; (iv) growth in structural unemployment in industrialized countries, intensification of capitalist exploitation in the LDCs; (v) strengthening of the state apparatuses for legitimation, manipulation and repression.

Closely linked to the question of correctness of those world system approaches is the debate about 'European peripheries' although it would be more appropriate to speak of 'core peripheries'. The industrialization of the periphery and the peripherization of old industrial regions in the centre, like the North of England, West Virginia, the Ruhr, Lorraine, Upper Styria, etc. sharpened regional disparities all over in the OECD countries, disparities that existed already (Froebel *et al.*, 1977a, 1977b; Hoell and Tausch, 1980; Kramer, 1983; Levitt-Polanyi, 1970; Seers, 1978a, 1978b; Tausch, 1977a, 1978a, 1979a; and also US-CIA, 1980). This diverse literature provided evidence regarding the de-industrialization and/or re-peripherization of the centre since the 1967–68 crisis. Some countries adjusted more successfully to the changing world economic conditions than others. The *World Development Report* (World Bank, 1990), dedicated to the issue of 'poverty' contains a wide range of data which let us discern which countries in the 1980s were more successful than the others. Growth rates in GDP of at least 2.5 per cent per annum 1980–88 were to be registered at the level of the West in: Spain, Israel, Australia, United Kingdom, Canada, Finland, United States, Norway, Japan. The following LDCs registered a GDP per annum growth rate during 1980–88 of at least 4.5 per cent: Nepal, Burkina Faso, China, India, Pakistan, Indonesia, Yemen, Egypt, Thailand, Botswana, Cameroon, Turkey, Mauritius, Malaysia, South Korea, Oman, Singapore, Hong Kong.

According to a recent attempt at long-wave Kondratieff cycle research (Bornschier, 1988; see also Goldstein, 1988; Tausch, 1990a, 1991a, 1991b), we are at the closing stage of the third long wave in world capitalist development (1842–83; 1883–1932; 1932–93 (?)). The capitalist world economy has already been through the phases of onswing (1932–45), recovery and prosperity (1945–58), prosperity (1958–66), prosperity-recession (1966–74), and crisis (1974–82), which characterizes any long wave since 1835. The system, according to Bornschier (1988), is now in the final cyclical stage of a temporary recovery before yet another great depression. Each depression (1872–83, 1929–32) was preceded by such a temporary recovery (1866–72; 1920–29). It is the characteristic of any temporary recovery to show who will be the winners and losers in the new wave of capitalist development. It is for this reason that the analysis of the country performance in the early 1980s is so important. Some OECD countries experienced a very painful stagnation in the early 1980s:

Table 3.1   Contraction in the OECD region? The evidence, 1980–85

Country	GDP (%)	Industry (%)	Gross domestic investment (%)
(a) Countries with contracting investment shares			
Spain	+ 1.6	+ 0.6	−2.6
Ireland	+ 1.5	–	−1.0
Italy	+ 0.8	−0.3	−2.3
Belgium	+ 0.7	+ 0.6	−4.2
France	+ 1.1	+ 0.3	−1.2
FRG	+ 1.3	−0.5	−0.8
(b) Countries with stagnating investment shares			
Austria	+ 1.7	+ 1.4	+ 0.2
Netherlands	+ 0.7	+ 0.4	+ 0.9
Australia	+ 2.5	+ 1.0	+ 0.8
Finland	+ 2.7	+ 2.7	+ 0.8
Sweden	+ 2.0	+ 2.8	+ 0.5
Canada	+ 2.4	−0.6	+ 0.4
Switzerland	+ 1.2	–	+ 0.9
(d) Countries with expanding investment shares (> 0.9999)			
New Zealand	+ 3.1	–	+ 8.5
United Kingdom	+ 2.0	+ 0.6	+ 5.3
Denmark	+ 2.4	+ 2.2	+ 4.9
Japan	+ 3.8	+ 5.9	+ 2.4
Norway	+ 3.3	+ 2.4	+ 2.9
United States	+ 2.5	+ 2.4	+ 5.2

Source: Own compilations from World Bank, *World Development Report*, 1987, ranked according to the per capita income.

The growth of export-oriented industrialization at the periphery and the de-industrialization of the centre are thought to be connected with what the NIDL group calls the external subsidy of the reproduction of labour power in the predominantly non-capitalist environment, which makes possible the superexploitation of labour power (Froebel, 1984: 52–71). Feminist perspectives on the capitalist world system have further developed that theme. To begin with, feminist perspectives increasingly questioned the concept of 'marginality' in dependency theories. As Evers and Wogau (1973), Hurtienne (1974), and Bennholdt-Thomsen (1980) showed, ambiguities abound in the original literature, with definitions ranging from the Marxist concept of industrial reserve army to segments of the population whose marginal product of labour is zero or negative, and in between a whole amazing variety of concepts (see also Amin, 1974; Boeckh, 1982; Cardoso, 1973b; Cordova, 1973; Feder, 1972; Ferreira de Camargo *et al.*, 1975; Filgueira, 1984; Frank, 1977a; Gonzales Casanova, 1972; Grabendorff, 1973; Jaguaribe *et al.*, 1972; Nuscheler, 1985b; Palma, 1981; Quijano Obregon, 1974; Raffer, 1979; Russett *et al.*, 1983b; Sandner and Steger, 1973; Schoepfer, 1979; Senghaas, 1977; Singer, 1980; 1981b; Sunkel, 1972, 1978; Tausch, 1979b; Zwiefelhofer, 1977).

To substitute 'marginality' by 'poverty', or simply by the term 'those living in the favelas', misses the point, since poverty and dwelling in shanty towns is also frequent among the industrially working male labour force (Altimir, 1978; Tausch, 1979b). Both in the countryside and in the cities there exist relationships of subordination and exploitation between those who do not receive an industrial or other 'modern' wage, and the dominant capitalist society ('sweat shop workers', see Cardoso, 1973b). And the whole army of those who work under often miserable conditions as housewives, shoeblacks, streetsellers, small-scale criminals, prostitutes in the big cities of the Third World today? Does the marginality of these housewives, shoeblacks, streetsellers, small-scale criminals, and prostitutes in the big cities of the Third World increase during industrialization, as some contend, or does it slowly disappear? Bennholdt-Thomsen maintains that dependency theory's understanding of marginality in particular is oriented towards the predominantly male wage earner, taken from the Marxist textbooks on the industrial reserve army, while the millions of marginalized women in, say, countries such as Mexico and Brazil, are not as yet, by any kind of dependency theory definition, regarded as 'marginal'. Werlhof goes further. For her, the crisis since 1967–68 is not merely a cyclical crisis or a moderate structural change, but the beginning of a totally new phase of capitalist world development:

> It is characterized by the fact (which is exactly what is of primary importance) that it more or less does away with 'free' wage labour. With this development, simultaneously, democracy, human rights, equality, freedom, and brotherhood are also called into question, not to speak of emancipation. (von Werlhof, 1983, engl. transl.: 132)

Primary accumulation (see also Amin, 1975; Maerz, 1976) goes on and on:

> Our freedom rests on the unfreedom of others, our equality on the inequality of others, our non-violence on the violence against others, our wealth on their poverty, our democracy on dictatorship elsewhere. (von Werlhof, 1983, engl. transl.: 136)

On a world-wide scale, it is not the 10 per cent free wage labourers, but the 90 per cent unfree non-wage labourers that are the pillar of accumulation and growth in the capitalist economy, the truly exploited, the real producers, the norm – and they represent the general condition in which human beings find themselves under capitalism. The 'Third World' is coming to 'us' in the capitalist nations, the Third World reveals to us the vision of the future and the real character of our mode of production. According to Werlhof, 'our' economies in the core countries will become marginalized, femalized, naturalized and housewifized. The creation of new hierarchies and the process of violence against women, as with the burning of widows, are part and parcel of the deepening of world capitalist society and not a step backward into the 'middle ages' (von Werlhof, 1983/88, engl. transl.: 120–35; also K. J. Tausch, 1988).

The feminist critique of the capitalist world system undoubtedly unveils the discrimination and injustice against more than half of humanity that development theories, left and right together, all too 'decently' forget (McCormack, 1981). As happens generally with the world system approach, however, the question must be raised as to whether or not the 'unfreedom of others', and here, especially, the marginalization of women, is indeed a precondition of successful capitalist development. To take an extreme case to illustrate my point: Singapore, the 'model case' of liberal development theories today, was characterized not only by a sound growth rate in GDP during 1980–88 (5.7 per cent) but also, in contrast to so many developing countries, a relatively better situation for women. Female life expectancy was 77 years in 1988, 6 years longer than for Singapore males. A very high rate of Singapore girls aged 14–18 attend secondary education (73 per cent), surpassing Singapore boys (70 per cent) (1984). Seventy-four per cent of married women in what the World Bank calls 'reproductive age' practise secure methods of birth control; the number of children per mother averages 1.8 (same as in the United States); maternal mortality is 11 per 100 000 life births and is thus even lower than in France, Italy and Japan (Seager and Olson, 1986: 98–9; World Bank, *World Development Report*, 1990).

It might be somewhat surprising to take notice of the fact that one of the leading authors in the 'modernization' tradition has radically thrown overboard most of his former writings and closely follows an interpretation that is quite similar to that of Froebel and Werlhof. For Apter (1987) the present stage in the evolution of world society is characterized by the ever-increasing contradictions of 'growth', the negative impacts on the labour force, the changing social composition of classes in terms of increasing asymmetrical reciprocities, growing inequalities, and compensatory political controls. The marginalization of industrial wage labour goes on, hand in hand with 'economic efficiency' (Apter, 1987: 16–17). Technological innovations reduce the labour component without opening up equivalent new employment opportunities. Marginality, originally a phenomenon of the LDCs, is beginning to appear in certain highly industrialized countries, with violence becoming an increasing expression of the negative side of development, a 'postmodern' condition (Apter, 1987: 20). Because marginals are difficult to mobilize, many of the most successful movements define marginality in racial, religious, ethnic, linguistic and similar terms to create primordial movements as in Sri Lanka, Lebanon and elsewhere. Innovation generates polarization, marginalization, displacement, dispossession, and with them a growing predisposition to violence in advanced industrial systems. Unemployment in the Western world, such as in the United States, Australia, the United Kingdom or France, becomes marginality; industrial labour becomes marginalized, support for trade unionism declines, racism and discrimination against foreigners such as Arabs, Turks, blacks, Jews, West Indians, Africans and Asians, increases everywhere:

> Indeed, one sees in all parts of the world tendencies toward primordial revivalism, xenophobic, often fascist. And the more that social polarization leads to political polarization, the more extremes of right and left create their own 'discourse' and a common predisposition to violence. (Apter, 1987: 36–7)

Apter defines innovation and marginality in a sociological fashion: innovation has the power to define the functional value of roles, classes and individuals in a community and is central to industrialization. It serves as a legitimizing basis for hierarchies of access to resources and political power. It represents, too, knowledge as science and order, rationally conceived. Marginality is just the opposite. It represents those excluded from participation in that knowledge. It is outside the discourse and the legitimacy it represents. Thus violence on behalf of or in favour of the 'marginals' constitutes an anti-legitimacy; in terms of the modern state it is against the state (Apter, 1987: 37).

For the postmodern theory of development (Apter, 1987), it is the state which becomes less and less effective in handling the problems of marginality and violence. Other authors in the marginality tradition do not blame the state, but the workings of the capitalist world economy for marginality, especially female marginality. I should mention here the essays written by Saffioti (1978), Singer (1981b), or Ward (1985). The latter places her essay well within the politometric tradition and uses data from up to 105 countries. She tests her feminist world economic framework with the aid of multivariate methods, including multiple regressions. With the advent of cash crop farming, women are relegated to subsistence production, without access to new forms of cultivation, technology or credit (Ward, 1985: 564). Males gain control over international and national trading networks, and with the introduction of capital-intensive industries under control of the transnationals, investments result in the long-term female marginalization from the 'official' labour force. Bornschier's capital penetration measure significantly influences the low female shares in industrial and agricultural employment, while the effect on fertility is less clear cut. Males define and control women's work and reproductive roles (Ward, 1985: 567).

Apter defines his understanding of a consensus among those neo-dependency oriented development theories:

> 'Democratic' institutionalization serves as a facade behind which compradore classes, external hegemonies, multinational corporations, and other instrumentalities work for their own interests. Internal efforts to realize internal growth in developing countries result in the partial expropriation of the surplus by external metropoles. Governments and citizens of such countries are less in control of their own resources over time and relatively worse off in terms of real choices. Political development under such circumstances leads to praetorian, bureaucratic, authoritarian, or corporatist regimes. (Apter, 1987: 18–19)

The theories of dependence and the world system which I presented up to now pose some very difficult questions to other varieties of development theory. There were centuries of military interventions, colonial rule and decisions from outside shaping a country and its people's destinies (see also, Raffer, 1987, ch. 8). As I will analyse in more detail in Chapter 9, however, there were dramatic changes in the capitalist world economy over the past three decades which suggest quite different explanations to those proposed by dependency theories (Asche, 1985). As I will also analyse in Chapters 7 and 9, the last three decades brought about a fairly rapid change in the conditions of life of many millions of people around the earth (Holsti, 1986), changes which, paradoxically enough, benefited capitalist semi-peripheries much more than the former socialist countries which, until the early 1960s at least, were largely independent of the logic of international capitalist trade, finance and investment. Two countries/regions achieved spectacular break-throughs in their human development policy under conditions of parliamentary democracy: Costa Rica and Kerala. It is, furthermore, no coincidence that some of the most stagnant societies in the world are countries with a very deficient human capital formation or with a state-class professing a Leninist doctrine in an environment of ethnic tension and warfare. It is no coincidence either that some of the most successful ascenders in the world economy are nations with a relatively egalitarian distribution of land. Talking about dependence and world capitalist exploitation, didn't we all in the development theory profession forget about the different roles that different cultures ascribe to women and children, with the long-term effects that these roles have for labour markets, income distribution, employment, and social change?

With such questions in mind, I should turn to what could yet emerge as one of the more fruitful controversies in development theory over recent years. This controversy leads us to a far-away time and a long-past social order: the social order of the Polish landlords during the Long Sixteenth Century, which according to Wallerstein plays such a crucial role, in so far as it is the first and leading example of how the evolving capitalist world economy with its centre in Amsterdam underdeveloped the most important agrarian periphery at that time. This controversy will show the relevance of internal social conditions in the process of ascent and decline in the world system and has many implications for the new Eastern Europe of today.

4 Poland in the Capitalist World Economy – The Limits of Wallerstein's Approach

Any analysis about the chances of democracy and transformation in the East must start with a more profound understanding of the long-run tendencies of peripherization and stagnation, which are so common in the history of Eastern Europe and Russia since the beginnings of the capitalist world economy. Poland's relationship with the capitalist world economy, to take just one example, does not just date back to the IMF-stabilization plan, it dates back to the so-called Long Sixteenth Century. Central in today's social science debate about these long-run tendencies is Wallerstein's approach. My critique of Wallerstein's world system approach to development which is, in a way, a mere continuation of the Baran/Frank approach to development and in reality has little to do with original dependency thought on the issue (Palma, 1981), is derived from a critique of the very foundation of that approach; i.e., its explanation of the divergence of development in the Long Sixteenth Century in Europe (Wallerstein, 1974: 125ff.; 451).

In his major analysis of the emergence of the capitalist world economy Wallerstein (1974) distinguishes very clearly between the periphery of the capitalist world economy, which produces basic goods for the centre under conditions of unequal exchange, and the external arena, which provides the centre with luxuries (Wallerstein, 1974: 449–50). Labour in the periphery is paid less. Wallerstein does not theorize in detail about this concept of unequal exchange, but he mentions that Poland in the Long Sixteenth Century was a typical periphery, while Russia, at that time, was a typical external arena.

The development theory, inherent in Wallerstein's account of the beginnings of the capitalist world economy, is rather simple, and has been repeated several times (Hopkins, Wallerstein *et al.*, 1982, and Hopkins, 1982): the once existing small differences between the centre and the periphery are tremendously exacerbated by the workings of unequal exchange in the capitalist world economy. The basic variable for political and social processes is the original position in the international division of labour, which tends towards a long-run stability over time since the beginnings of the capitalist world economy. Applied to today's situation, the only variable which would really matter is that position in the world economy. The structures of the international division of labour did not change fundamentally throughout history. The tasks of peripheries and semi-peripheries vary, but the results always are that they do not receive the same economic rewards. The system tends to absorb more and more parts of the 'external arena' into the system over time. The productive specialization changes over time, but the core always specializes in highly mechanized, high-profit, high-wage, high-skill activities against the peripheral opposite, with the semi-periphery showing a mix of both core and periphery activities (see especially Hopkins, Wallerstein *et al.*, 1982: 59).

There is one point where Wallerstein violates his own strict inherent assumptions. For Wallerstein, three conditions are decisive for ascent: a strong state, external expansion and labour control mechanisms (Wallerstein, 1974: 47). But Sweden, whose history Wallerstein debates only briefly, escapes – according to Wallerstein – the threat of peripherization (and thus the fate of a typical periphery like Poland before the partitions in the late eighteenth century) by having a strong peasantry. Why is a strong peasantry responsible for world economic ascent? And is a weak peasantry responsible for or conducive to world economic decline? And what can today's decision makers in Eastern Europe and the agrarian reformers in Russia learn from the strong peasantry in Sweden at that time? Would a thorough land reform be a precondition of rapid subsequent economic growth, just as it happened in South-East Asia centuries later?

And there is another phenomenon that Wallerstein recognizes, but which he cannot explain from the viewpoint of his own theory: the positive trade-off between agricultural density and technological innovation (Wallerstein, 1974: 459 for the debate on Sweden; pp. 50 and 132 for the debate on agricultural density and economic growth). Furthermore, Wallerstein recognizes that the weakness of cities contributes to world economic decline (Wallerstein, 1974: 126–27), just as bureaucracies, centralism and imperial forms of dominance block capitalist economic development (Wallerstein, 1974: 68 and 116). The contradictions of his development theory are exacerbated by the fact, which he clearly states, that state centrality as a precondition of ascent in turn is caused by ascent in the capitalist world economy (Wallerstein, 1974: 457). Wallerstein does not explain, then, the other, more 'internal' preconditions of growth or decline which he anyway recognizes: imperial forms of domination, bureaucracies, weakness of cities, strength of the peasantry, and the effects that agricultural density has on economic growth. Are they all, like his state centrality, in turn explained by his stability of the centre–periphery relationship?

Just as Brazil in the post-1964 era was the 'paradigmatic' case best fitting into the dependency line of argument (see especially Cardoso, 1973a), Poland is considered to represent the best evidence for the validity of Wallerstein's theory (1974) about capitalist ascent and decline during the period 1450–1640 (Denemark and Thomas, 1988). Poland at that time was, by extension, the biggest state in Europe and, in contrast to the colonial powers establishing themselves at that time, it went into decay leading up to the Polish partitions at the end of the eighteenth century. Figure 4.1 outlines the borders of the Polish state at the time of its biggest extension: it ranged from the Black Sea in the south to the Baltic in the north, from the plains along the Wisla river in the west to the Ukraine in the east.

At the time of the onset of Polish decline there was an upsurge in export-oriented grain production, representing between 5 and 20 per cent of total Polish grain harvests (Denemark and Thomas, 1988). For Wallerstein the argument is rather simple: capitalism elsewhere and Poland's inclusion into

Figure 4.1	Poland in the long sixteenth century

Source:	Polsha Akademia Nauk (1979) 'Zarys historii Polski', various charts.

the system via the mechanism of unequal exchange (see also Amin, 1975; O. Braun, 1974; Boeckh, 1982; Dubiel, 1984; Mandel, 1973; Raffer, 1987; A. Schmidt, 1982) determined the specific relations of production in Poland. Among Marxist writers, Brenner (1977) has fundamentally questioned this reasoning, so vital to explaining the 'paradigmatic' case of Polish decline from 1450 to 1640. Brenner must – however we evaluate his arguments – be praised for the straight logic in which he arrives at the very centre of the Wallerstein approach, precisely trying to reduce *ad absurdum* Wallerstein's most favourite paradigmatic example for his own theory. Brenner maintains that export dependence only came about after Polish re-feudalization, and that Polish agriculture did not respond in a 'capitalistic way' to world market price increases by increases in production. For Brenner, Wallerstein's bicausalism in explaining underdevelopment does not hold: not only growth of trade with the capitalist world system and a low labour–land ratio (as is supposed by Wallerstein, 1974: 50, 132) brought about Polish re-enserfment, but (i) the availability of serf labour originally blocked agricultural innovation; (ii) the landlords' surplus extraction meant that the peasants could not establish a market; (iii) restrictions on peasant mobility precluded the growth of the towns in both size and importance, thus foreclosing industrialization; and (iv) the landlords worked to eliminate the merchant class between themselves and foreign traders and encouraged imports from the capitalist world market.

For Brenner, the rise of trade in an economy of serfdom does not necessarily create pressures to develop the productive forces in order to increase incomes, let alone the generalization of innovation. Quite in line with the original Marxist approach, the production of absolute surplus value turns exclusively on the length of the working day, while production of relative surplus value completely revolutionizes the technical progress of labour and the groupings into which society is divided (Brenner, 1977: 45, see also *Das Capital*, vol. III, law of tendential fall of profit rate, Marx and Engels, *Werke*, 25: 221–77). Marx predicts definite limits on the extension of the production of 'absolute surplus value' and precisely formulates his law about the profit rate on the assumptions that Brenner quite correctly reads in Marx's original economic theory: it is the composition of society, the countervailing power of the labour movement and, prior to this, the political weight of the cities, that affect long-term development. To Brenner, the application of the theory of unequal exchange to the conditions of Poland in the Long Sixteenth Century seems to be questionable: it would suppose equal organic composition of capital in all regions and lines of production of the evolving capitalist world economy. He remarks that this premise is highly unrealistic when there is neither free labour nor free land. Furthermore, relative prices of Eastern European agriculture and Western evolving centres, especially Amsterdam, shifted in Poland's favour, so there was a transfer of the surplus not from it to the West, but from the West to the East (Brenner, 1977: 63). For orthodox world system theory, different roles in the world economy lead to different class structures, and the original social structure of the peripheries, like Poland before the long sixteenth century, is not very different from the centres, like France, England or the Netherlands (Brenner, 1977: 80). But for Brenner, very much in line with Elsenhans and Senghaas, the difference between the centre and the periphery is much deeper:

> In the final analysis, however, the whole discussion of unequal exchange leading to the transfer of surplus must be assigned a subordinate place in relationship to the question of the rise of development and under-development. Neither development in the core nor underdevelopment in the periphery was determined by surplus transfer. Economic development was a qualitative process, which did not merely involve an accumulation of wealth in general, but was centrally focused on the development of the productivity of labour of the direct producers of the means of production and the means of subsistence. This development of labour productivity, most significantly in agriculture, which occurred in parts of Western Europe in the early modern period, was dependent in turn upon the emergence of a social system which tended not only to equip the direct producers with capital and skill at the highest level of existing technique, but possessed the capacity to continue to do so on an increasing scale. In short, the uniquely successful development of capitalism in Western Europe was determined by a class system, a property system and a system of surplus extraction, in which the methods the extractors were obliged to use to increase their surplus, corresponded to an unprecedented, though imperfect degree to the needs of development of the productive forces. Capitalism was therefore distinguished from pre-capitalist modes of production to continue to increase their 'profits' (surplus) largely by increasing what we have termed relative, not merely absolute, surplus labour. (Brenner, 1977: 63–8)

It is precisely the non-capitalistic organization in the East which determined that it would not respond in a capitalist manner to growing market opportunities. Polish landlords were not subjected to capitalist type of penalties for failures to do so (Brenner, 1977: 68). As I have already remarked in my debate on the feminist world system approach, exploitation and discrimination in the sense of 'absolute surplus labour' are not always the most successful strategies of capitalist ascent; Brenner maintains that serfdom did not provide an efficient answer in the interest of the capitalist world economy. Gdansk and Krakow–Slask, the two regions in Poland with a relatively more intensive agriculture and less devastating social effects of the big estates, so common in eastern Poland at that time (now all in the Community of Independent States), were the two last Polish regions to experience the general trend of declining productivity and crisis that led up, in the final analysis, to the Polish partitions at the end of the eighteenth century (Brenner, 1977: 70). Polish landlords had lower productivity on their estates than medium-sized agriculture. The growing demand for food in the West in the sixteenth and seventeenth century was responded to only in a sluggish manner by the Polish serf economy. Although exports continued at an impressive level, internal overall production – due to endless wars and low productivity – rather stagnated. Wyczanski and Rostworowski, two leading Polish authors whose statistics are not known in the ongoing debate on the Brenner–Wallerstein exchange initiated by Denemark and Thomas, show that on the one hand, in the crucial period between 1562 and 1599, Polish exports oscillated to regain during 1595–99 only the values already reached during 1562–65, while on the other hand Poland's social structure became increasingly violent, exclusive and repressive. And, after all, the system was not even able to deliver the goods that it was supposed to deliver (see Table 4.1).

Table 4.1   Average yearly grain exports from Poland in the second half of the sixteenth century in thousands of Last

Grain	1562–65	1566–69	1574–79	1580–84	1585–89	1590–94	1595–99
Rye	42.7	35.6	19.8	18.9	27.4	2.8	38.1
Wheat	4.8	2.3	2.1	2.6	2.7	1.8	4.6
Barley	0.5	0.25	0.1	0.15	0.45	0.64	0.55
Flour	4.7	1.4	1.4	1.2	1.6	1.3	1.3

Source: Wyczanski, 1979: 185.

Later increases to 75 000–120 000 Last in the period 1620–50 were brought about by drastically cutting back peasants' subsistence (Denemark/Thomas, 1988: 56–57). An important question in this context is whether the decline in Polish exports came at a time of world economic recession or world economic upsurge. In one of the most comprehensive studies so far on the issue of the world economic and world military cycles, Goldstein (1985b) proposed the following periodization of the Kondratieffs in the world economy since 1495 (see Table 4.2). According to Table 4.2, Poland did not use the increasing opportunities presented by a time of rising world demand;

on the contrary, at the time of the fourth Kondratieff upswing, Poland reduced its grain exports to the centres of the capitalist world economy, while it increased its exports during the upswing of the fifth cycle. If its economic behaviour were to have been determined by world market forces alone, there would be no explanation of this paradox.

Table 4.2   Kondratieff cycles from 1495 onwards

Cycle		Upswing	Downswing
1.	Cycle		1495–1508
2.	Cycle	1509–1528	1529–1538
3.	Cycle	1539–1558	1559–1574
4.	Cycle	1575–1594	1595–1620
5.	Cycle	1621–1649	1650–1688
6.	Cycle	1689–1719	1720–1746
7.	Cycle	1747–1761	1762–1789
8.	Cycle	1790–1813	1814–1847
9.	Cycle	1848–1871	1872–1892
10.	Cycle	1893–1916	1917–1939
11.	Cycle	1940–1967	1968–1975

Source: Goldstein, 1985b: 423.

Certainly, the relationship between the Polish food export economy to the capitalist world market was one of dependence. But the decisive question is whether the capitalist centres at the North Sea coast really needed the Polish serf economy in the first place, or whether Poland could not have produced much more at that time with a more efficient landholding system. Brenner shows that the squeezing of the peasants in the long run brought about a decline of productivity on the lords' own estates, with Polish exports to the world market falling off in the end (Brenner, 1977: 69). While the cities expanded in north-western Europe, and Amsterdam, in particular, was a haven of refuge for persecuted religious minorities of all denominations, including Sephardic Jews from the Iberian peninsula, the Polish social order became increasingly intolerant of Jews and of the Reformation. The landowners were just 2 per cent of total population, with another 0.5 per cent clergy, 6 per cent small landowners, 6 per cent urban non-Jewish middle class, 10 per cent Jews, and 73.5 per cent Polish, Ukrainian and Lithuanian peasants (Rostworowski, 1979: 338). Figure 4.2 shows this class structure.

A more appropriate explanation for Poland's decline in the long sixteenth century, then, would be to search for the effects of the constraints on capitalist development, which Wallerstein himself admits, rather in passing,

Figure 4.2   The Polish class structure, sixteenth century

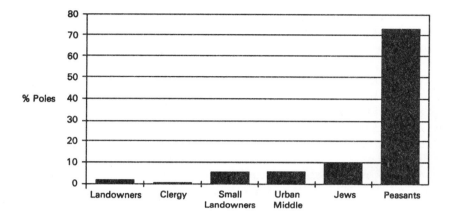

to be at work in other countries: the extensive nature of agriculture, dictated in the first place by the logic of expansion of Poland into the east, while it retreated from world military pressure from the north and the west; the weakness of the Polish cities *vis-à-vis* the land oligarchy, etc.

For Brenner, the development lesson to be drawn from the Polish case in the long sixteenth century is pretty clear:

It was this two sided 'dynamic', under pressure of trade, which constituted at the broadest level the 'structure of underdevelopment' in early modern Poland and elsewhere: the growth of surplus extraction in response to the market, without the transformation of the mode of production which was required to make possible the development of the productive forces so as to increase the productivity of labour. This determines, at the most general level, the intensified use – indeed 'using up' – of labour power, as well as of natural resources, but without an offsetting acceleration of the social productive forces which could make for a correspondingly (or more greatly) increased productiveness of labour power and increasingly effective use of natural resources. Specifically then, the class structure of serfdom in Poland determined underdevelopment by stifling the productivity of the direct peasant producers, thereby undercutting the home market for means of production and means of subsistence, and at the same time determining that what market there was would be largely in luxuries. To the degree, therefore, that Poland was 'incorporated' within the world market, its economy was increasingly strangled; to the degree to which trade (later) declined, the Polish economy stagnated. However, neither of these trends was determined by the rise of trade and the world market, but fundamentally by a class structure of serfdom which precluded the emergence of an 'internal' dynamic of development, while ensuring that any commercially induced dynamic from 'outside' would ultimately lead to retrogression. (Brenner, 1977:71)

This vision of development and underdevelopment was fully developed later on by Elsenhans and Senghaas who, like Brenner (1977: 75–7), did no longer overlook what the latter calls the rise of agrarian capitalism and agrarian demand as a precondition of successful capitalist development. It should be noted, too, that Jenkins, in explaining the decapitalization of periphery countries by the TNCs, arrives pretty much at the same conclusions as the social reformers among the development profession (Jenkins, 1987: 97–101): the lack of mass demand and the corresponding social structures of agriculture, producing wage goods under capitalist conditions are the precondition and not the consequence of the decapitalization of the periphery. H. Elsenhans, however, continued the argumentation put forward by Brenner, and has presented the following hypotheses.

1. Capitalism needs growing mass incomes; capitalist growth requires surplus value for accumulation and a sufficient effective demand. Technological innovations that stimulate enterprises' demand for capital goods without reducing total demand are feasible as long as real wages rise (Elsenhans, 1983: 5, equation (5)).
2. Capitalist growth in England was historically preceded by a far-reaching agrarian modernization. The subsidization of the poor with tax money ('poor laws') was an appropriate strategy geared to increasing employment at the cost of profit (Elsenhans, 1983: 7). Capitalist growth in England was preceded by a considerable decline in the concentration of land ownership. There was a definite improvement in the lot of the masses immediately before the Industrial Revolution (Elsenhans, 1983: 9; see also, Polanyi, 1944). Industrial production offered most of the agrarian population additional incomes; nutrition improved before 1750; innovations could rapidly be introduced because the agrarian population was not subject to guild regulations (Elsenhans, 1983: 11; conversely: Polanyi, 1944, esp. chaps 11–14).
3. Absolutism was the ruling classes' last attempt to install a tributary mode of production (agrarian bureaucracy, oriental despotism, or 'Asiatic' mode of production). In contradiction to Wallerstein, Elsenhans tries to show that only when market opportunities exist, monetary capital will be transformed into real capital. The centralization of the ruling class – the fusion of the feudal nobility with the

commercial and manufacturing classes into one centralized beneficial bureaucracy – is the most persistent development block in the Third World (Elsenhans, 1984) and existed (in contrast to Europe) before the onset of colonialism. The centralization of the ruling class limits competition and hence also the ability to innovate (Elsenhans, 1983: 13). The genesis of capitalism in England is explained by the class conflict after the Black Death and the de-concentration of landowner-ship in favour of a social structure in which the level of exploitation was altogether low (Elsenhans, 1983: 14; see also Polanyi, 1944, *passim*). As a result, English nobility had nothing to expect from absolutist recentralization. Instead, they increased earnings through developing industrial production with a subsequent expansion of mass consump-tion, which created new investment opportunities. From the very beginning, limits on the rule of capital by the resistance of the under-privileged provided a foundation of capitalist growth.

4. The continuous growth and the transition from feudalism to capitalism in north-western Europe were special cases arising from a specific constellation of power. By contrast, the 'normal' case is the develop-ment of bureaucratic systems of domination with centralized state classes.

These systems – in the periphery – are based on the contradiction between agrarian producers and the bureaucratic, urban state class. This class collectively appropriates the greater part of the surplus through the state, and does so at rates of exploitation higher than in Western Europe. In the absence of market competition, this class either invests the surplus or squanders it on luxury.

As a rule, the incorporation of Third World societies into the capitalist world economy did not destroy, but rather strengthened, those structures that impede growth. The periphery initially enjoyed comparative advantages in regard to raw material exports, resulting from the poor industrial development of the periphery, which was caused by the tributary modes of production (Elsenhans, 1983: 24). Specialization in raw materials led to the strengthening of 'reactionary incomes', namely land rents which, unlike profits, do not have to be invested in order to remain competitive. The resulting tendencies to cement inequality (structural heterogeneity) in the periphery make it difficult for resistance movements in the periphery to implement change and reform (Elsenhans, 1983: 25).

Elsenhans and Senghaas certainly introduce some elements of liberal theory into their new development doctrine – elements which are completely absent from the mainstream of world system/dependency theory literature. Both of them presented analyses about the logic of development in the industrialized countries that directly contradict the world system approach. Call this analysis neo-Weberian or not, it is certain that the internal characteristics of the ascending and the declining parts of the world capitalist whole, according to Elsenhans and Senghaas, are closely interrelated with that ascent or decline. Their main variable is mass demand, egalitarian income and land redistributions which – in their view – are necessary for a successful capitalist ascent. Both of them further believe that institutional age and rigidity were a problem in socialism, and that state classes (Elsenhans) and single parties (Senghaas) run the danger of becoming development blocks. The belief in equality as a prime condition for capitalist ascent and the fear of stagnation, resulting from state classes and monopolistic formations, make their theory directly comparable with Olson's development theory, which is also based on these two phenomena.

The political essence of this discussion for contemporary Eastern Europe is the realization that without a strategy of agrarian reform, participation and democracy all attempts to ascend in the world economy will be doomed to failure. 'Iron fist' dictatorships will not be able to create the necessary mass demand in the long run; and raping the peasantry to achieve agricultural hard cash export earnings will not be a long-run successful strategy either. The socio-liberal development theories can claim that they have the historic development policy successes on their side.

It is to these liberal theories that I now turn. Comparative cross-national research devoted considerable attention to the issue of politometric evidence about development blocks to be expected from a dependent insertion into the world market. These comparative quantitative studies concerned growth, income distribution, the position of women in society and the chances for democracy in the periphery. By contrast, systematic studies about the multidimensional development or stagnation effects of state classes, anti-egalitarian patterns of wealth and income and ageing political democracies are relatively new terrain. As in the preceding chapters, it will again be my aim to work out the implications of theories for cross-national, comparative research in Chapter 5.

5 A Socio-Liberal Alternative?

Neoclassical economic theories have always maintained that the market is the most efficient promoter of development. Dependence as a phenomenon practically does not exist, as far as one well-established interpretation of the 'mainstream paradigm' in economics, that of Lord P. T. Bauer, is concerned. Lord Bauer, looking back on his more than four decades of research into the problem of less developed areas, states:

> As I have said, a large part of (i.e. 'enclave') production, and sometimes the entire output, was (and remains) in the hands of the local population. The same applies to the associated activities of trade and transport. Had this been otherwise, the development of export crops could not have transformed the lives of the local people as it has done. In these regions, as in many others, the pervasive economic advance has made it possible for much larger populations to live longer and at much higher standards. (Lord P. T. Bauer, 1984: 30)

Wherever development (in the sense of larger populations, living longer and at much higher standards) occurred, it was

> the result of the individual voluntary responses of millions of people to emerging or expanding opportunities created largely by external contacts and brought to their notice in a variety of ways, primarily through the operation of the market. These developments were made possible by firm but limited government, without large expenditures of public funds and without the receipt of large external subventions. (Lord P. T. Bauer, 1984: 30–31)

Besides the heavily criticized notion of 'group differences' explaining economic success, to Lord Bauer (see Lord Bauer, 1984: 33; for a critique, Lipton, 1984) it is the state and its excessive influence which prolongs the situation of underdevelopment. Especially harmful – according to Lord Bauer's theory – are state marketing boards, which have the right to buy agricultural products for export and to export the controlled products (Lord Bauer, 1984: 39). Originally created to stabilize prices received by producers, and even to improve them, they promptly develop into a system of paying producers far less than the market value of their produce.

The state marketing boards are in reality an instrument of heavy, persistent and discriminatory taxation (Lord Bauer, 1984: 39). This taxation, most notably in Africa, reduces the development of cash crops and private savings, and – according to Lord Bauer – obstructs the emergence of a prosperous peasantry and middle class, and serves as a dominant source of money and patronage for those with political power (Lord Bauer, 1984: 39).

Whether we like such analyses or not, I think that the time has come to reflect more on market distortions, the state and development, independently of whether or not we share such liberal doctrine. Are not there similar statements about the state blocking rural development and benefiting the rich peasants, already present in Kautsky's Marxist agriculture theory, first published in 1899 and practically unknown in the international development debate (save for a French and a Maoist German translation) until Lipton rediscovered it in 1977? And are there not, as has been shown elsewhere (Tausch, 1991a), fundamental insights into the necessity of the price mechanism in the process of capitalist development (and in socialism too), which began to take shape in the Austromarxist debate from 1906–07 onwards?

As that debate very clearly shows, there have always been, within the broader Marxist system of reference, those who sympathize with the idea of the use of state power to the benefit of the oppressed (see also Saage, 1983; Tausch, 1991a). But, of growing importance, there were also those who were, like Bauer, Polanyi and Wigforss, deeply distrustful of mere state power – even under control of a working-class party – and rather thought of self-management within a market framework as a solution to the development problem under socialism (O. Bauer, 1980, see especially, vol. 4, *Introduction to Economics*; Levitt-Polanyi and Mendell, 1986; Maerz, 1983a; Maerz and Szesci, 1984; Polanyi, 1922–44; Rabinbach, 1983; Tausch, 1991a; Tilton, 1979).

The socio-liberal thinkers of the European Social Democracy in the 1920s and 1930s combined in their analysis a thorough understanding of the difficulties to be expected from a state socialist economy with a perspective of how democratic socialism could avoid them. Although Polanyi's ideas are perhaps best known today in the Western world, it is important to emphasize the congruence of thought between Polanyi, Bauer and Wigforss on the issue. Otto Bauer's thoughts on socialist economics are formulated within the framework of his firm belief in political democracy. The socialized sector will be a sector of socialist self-management in direct market competition with the private capitalist sector; the gradual introduction of workers' participation in the decisions of capital will prepare the working class politically and socially to run enterprises for themselves; democracy and self-management will avoid the repetition of errors committed by the Bolshevik revolution.

Polanyi in particular foresaw the difficulties of socialist accounting and socialist strategy in his two important articles published first in Red Vienna in 1922 and 1925. Bauer's critique of the mere substitution of state capitalism for private capitalism, first formulated in his lecture cycle at a Volkshochschule in the academic year 1927–28 (Bauer, vol. 4: 844–76, *Einfuehrung in die Volkswirtschaftslehre*) is as refreshing today as it must have been to his listeners more than sixty years ago: 'If we socialize, and bread becomes more expensive, people will be rather quickly won over in favour of capitalist enterprises' (O. Bauer, 1927–28/1976, *Werke*, vol. IV: 859, my translation). Quite in contrast to Lenin he also foresees: 'The adaptation of state administrative organizations to the economy would be highly dangerous. If one has to accept, for every new machine, to be bought, first a long processing of a file, the economy will be ruined' (O. Bauer, ibid.: 861, my translation).

It would be wrong to assume that liberal thought elements were absent, too, from the theories presented by the pioneering generation of development economics. Prebisch, Lewis and Myrdal were certainly influenced by the intellectual climate and debate in Europe, to which I referred above, which clearly contradicted the assumption of the mutual exclusiveness of socialism and elements of liberal thought. It was the very founder of Latin American bourgeois development theory, R. Prebisch, himself, who wrote in 1984: 'I went over my previous ideas very critically. Although it is true that there were some valid elements in them, they were far from constituting a theoretical system. I arrived at the conclusion that to start building a system it was necessary to enlarge the scope beyond purely economic theory' (Prebisch, 1984: 184). And in which direction did Prebisch want to reconstruct his theory? For Prebisch the idea remains valid that technological progress started at the centres and its fruits remained basically there:

Technological progress started at the centres where its fruits remained. For better or worse, they did not spread to the periphery through a general fall in prices in relation to increases in productivity. Historically, the role of the periphery had been mainly restricted to the supply of primary products. This explains why the growth of income stimulated demand and continuous technological innovations at the centre and gave great impetus to industrialization. The periphery was left behind not because of malicious design but because of the dynamics of the system (Prebisch, 1984: 184).

But there are other elements which seem to be worth considering today, too, which are part of Prebisch's 1984 theory: the imitation of life styles by the elites in the periphery, their importation of ideas and ideologies, their reproduction of institutions; the privileged consumer society, the social power of workers' elites in the periphery, contrasted with the 'marginal sector', all made worse by the alliance between multinational capital and those privileged sectors. The collusion of interests on the part of the permanently employed industrial labour force is made all the worse by the power of the state, due to its spurious absorption of unemployed. Unproductive state consumption tends to rise, including military consumption. The various forms of consumption cannot go on indefinitely, for they encroach on the rate of reproductive capital accumulation (Prebisch, 1984: 183–91).

The time has come, in the view of Prebisch, to arrive at a socio-liberal synthesis: 'I therefore believe the time has come to search for a synthesis of both socialism and genuine economic liberalism, and thereby restore that essential philosophical unity of economic liberalism with political liberalism' (Prebisch, 1984: 191). Socio-liberal thought elements are to be found, then, in the writings of major economists from the 'pioneering' generation in the development studies discipline. Lewis (1984) is particularly aware of the necessity to transform the food-producing sector in LDCs and to provide people with what he terms 'a social wage' (Lewis, 1984: 131) in education, health services, water supplies, unemployment benefits, work-force insurance. Lewis – he calls himself 'a social democrat' (Lewis, 1984: 131) – is also very outspoken about the population problem. It will aggravate the food problem, already acute in semi-arid lands. It puts stress on the balance of payments. It leads to rapid urbanization, which is extremely costly in terms of infrastructure (Lewis, 1984: 133). His position vis-à-vis dependency theory is a reserved one: it seems important for the latter half of the nineteenth century, but can no longer be applied so easily today, since national governments have taken over the place of foreigners in so many countries around the globe (Lewis, 1984: 125). Myrdal is very outspoken about the development blocks to be expected from a high degree of inequality, too. In the 1920s and 1930s he had already observed in his Swedish home country that equalization in favour of the lower-income strata was a productive investment in the quality of people and their productivity (Myrdal, 1984: 154). Higher overall consumption levels are a precondition for overall speedier and more stable growth. In the later 1970s and early 1980s Myrdal developed some views which are quite fitting with a critique of the 'state classes' in the south: it is the governments of Nigeria and Mexico, who have squandered their oil incomes, leaving their large agricultural regions in continuing or even increasing poverty. Population growth goes on, as does deforestation, and it is the military who rule a large number of developing countries (Myrdal, 1984: 160–1). In view of the incapability of the governments and local elites with whom they are allied, aid should be administered more strictly (Myrdal, 1984: 162). Demands for a new economic world order turn into a sort of alibi for not reforming the way that the majority of the LDCs are governed (Myrdal, 1984: 164–5). Among the more pronounced 'reformers' today we find Ehrlich; Elsenhans; Hicks; Kadt; Kalecki; Lipton; Menzel; Myrdal; Olson; Senghaas.

Certainly another major writer in the tradition of political economy, Rothschild, was also well aware of the market distortions that can arise in a peripheral or semi-peripheral economy. Rothschild once remarked in a contribution written almost three decades ago about the situation in a typical small (semi or full) periphery state, that monopolies and cartels are protected by high customs. This enables them to enjoy a comfortable and profitable way of life, protected from outside competition. The main problem of such a society will thus be a very low predisposition to competition in terms of prices and markets (Rothschild, 1963: 247). Liberal theories in the rent-seeking-society tradition (Weede, 1985a, 1988) further developed this point of underdeveloped competitiveness: 'protectionism, provinciality and backwardness' (Rothschild, 1963: 261) in the world economy. Although originally Rothschild seems to have had in mind only small European countries, and especially Austria, when he wrote in a macrosociological fashion about protectionism, provinciality and backwardness as working together in a dependent economy, the argument used by him becomes a central feature of the new development school; it is not necessarily in absolute contradiction, but certainly puts emphasis differently from the dependence/world system argument.

Without question, important thoughts on such a new paradigm are to be found in Lipton and Olson. For Lipton, it is the conflict between the organization and power to be found in the cities on the one hand and the dispersion, the powerlessness of the countryside on the other hand, that is becoming the most important class struggle today. Basic for him is the rediscovery of Kautsky's idea (1899) of state intervention serving the interests of the rich. Organized interests in the cities have a vital interest in low food prices, and it is their socio-economic power and collusion of interests which is to blame for the unfavourable terms of trade for the countryside *vis-à-vis* the city. Subsidies do not reach their target; they primarily aid the bureaucracy and increase corruption. Third World elites consist mainly of bureaucrats and traders, and they do not have the same interest that European elites had in the nineteenth century in increasing mass consumption. The over-valuation of most Third World currencies is another major development block: it increases the price of national exports, and it makes imports of foreign foodstuffs easier, thus limiting agricultural employment and providing no incentives to increase internal food production (Lipton, 1977: 270–327). The Japanese take-off, by contrast, saw quite a considerable rise in agricultural prices in the period 1877–1905. Dependency theory is nothing more than the ideology of the Third World urban elite, providing a foreign scapegoat for the 'home-made' discrimination against their own poor. Lipton advocates the study of the differing experiences of Taiwan, South Korea, China, Cuba, Costa Rica and Kerala (India) regions, which, in the decades after 1960, realized some of the fastest thrusts in human development (Lipton, 1984).

Next, I also refer to Olson's challenging ideas, formulated in 1982; not that Olson presented a socio-political theory and programme similar to my own, but because his theory leads him to two very important conclusions. These are at least compatible, in a way, with the ideas of social reform, pluralism and critique of 'state classes' which the European social democracy of the 1920s and 1930s elaborated: (i) equity will contribute to a capitalist ascent; and (ii) state classes present a problem, especially with the increasing age of the system.

What, then, are Olson's main conclusions relevant to the debate on comparative international development? In many ways, Olson's theory is a challenge both to neo-conservativism and to traditional socialism alike. According to Olson (1987), neo-conservatives and the policies inspired by them in the US and in the UK were wrong because they wanted to increase inequality while capitalism functions best when chances at the start are equal and there are no social rigidities against the poor. Traditional socialism is wrong, too, because it does not differentiate enough between the positive and the negative effects of state action for the life chances of the poor: most economic activities of the state, according to him, benefit not the bottom 40 per cent of the population, but the rich and the middle-income groups. And traditional socialism is wrong, according to this line of thought, because it does not realize how, in ageing institutional frameworks, especially in ageing democracies, state sector influence over the economy leads to the sociological reality of distribution coalitions, which will block further economic growth. For Olson (1982/85) the central features of an explanation of the differing growth rates among (industrial) countries are (a) stable societies within unchanged, stable boundaries tend to accumulate in the course of time organizations and collusions of interests for collective action; (b) such collusions of interests limit the ability of a society to introduce new technologies and to bring about a reallocation of resources as an answer to changing external conditions, which, in the end, lowers the economic growth rate; and (c) as such 'distributional coalitions' increase the complexity of regulation, they increase the importance of the state (Olson, 1982/85: 1–98).

Although Olson recognizes that very big special interest groups, by virtue of their inclusiveness, will be less harmful than smaller ones because they begin to care about global societal development (Olson, 1982/85: 52–61, see also his debate on Sweden, 1982/85: 122–6), recent politometric work by Weede and Tausch confirmed the effects of the joint inclusion of processes (a) and (c) on economic growth in the OECD countries. Olson, who presents only econometric evidence about growth in the different states in the US (Olson, 1982/85: 133–57), would nevertheless expect the following relations to hold: (i) free trade and free mobility of production factors across national borders will weaken distributional coalitions (Olson, 1982/85: 188); (ii) ethnic, racial and social discrimination enhance, and even are the best sign of the existence of 'distributional coalitions', and thus are incompatible with rapid long-term economic growth (Olson, 1982/85: 210–17); (iii) protection-ism and barriers against free factor mobility will in the end increase the existing economic inequalities (Olson, 1982/85: 223), while a 'true' compe-titive capitalist economy needs equal pay for equal abilities and equal efficiency (Olson, 1982/85: 227); and (iv) distributional coalitions, especially the downward inflexibility of wages, are to be held to account for the different degree to which countries are affected by the ups and downs of the business cycle (Olson, 1982/85: 238–309).

Elsenhans and Senghaas would agree with the second point, but not with the first and third. European expansion into the Third World – and here of course I agree with Raffer (1987) – meant in the sixteenth, seventeenth, and eighteenth century extra-economic violence mainly by the following two processes: (i) monopolistic European trading companies and the destruction of Arabic seapower in the Indian Ocean went hand in hand with European accumulation; and (ii) 'native' state classes were often 'substituted' (i.e. killed) by European 'aristocracies'. This process was especially disastrous in Latin America – the introduction of forced labour for the indigenous population and slavery for the Latin American African Americans.

After the long period of such violence, markets in the Third World were opened by military force (Turkey 1840; China 1839). Indian manufacturing was obliterated by the British, and capital exports in the nineteenth century strengthened indigenous ruling classes. Social inequality will limit capitalist growth, when capitalism penetrates a society from outside and labour markets are not changed (Elsenhans, 1979a: 128–49). Thus – in agreement with Amin – capitalist penetration stabilized power relationships in the periphery, which, according to Elsenhans, is incompatible with long-term capitalist growth, mainly because of their institutional inflexibilities and the lack of mass demand (Elsenhans, 1979a: 142–3).

Senghaas (1982–85) would agree with part of Olsonian reasoning in so far as his egalitarian development theories explain rapid socialist growth in the postwar period precisely by the fact that this growth was a catch-up industrialization process in an institutionally new, egalitarian environment; but since the late 1960s the absolute boundaries of extensive industrialization in a state socialist model were reached, and he would argue that there is a very strong need to decentralize, democratize and liberalize Eastern European countries (and hitherto socialist LDCs), and that in the wake of bureaucratic socialism strong interest groups, like the military heavy industrial complex, developed, blocking attempts to reform state socialist systems into true democracies.

It should be emphasized in this context that one of the major thinkers of the 'new social movements' in the periphery, R. Kothari, combines the analysis of ethnic poverty and marginalization with an analysis of state power in periphery development. While millions of rural, tribal and ethnic poor have just been made surplus and therefore dispensable populations by the march of high-tech capitalism (Kothari, 1986: 169), and their traditional access to natural resources and non-commercial products is taken away from them, it is the state which has become the prisoner of the dominant classes (Kothari, 1986: 172) and has increasingly turned anti-people:

The State in the Third World, despite some valiant efforts by dedicated leaders in a few countries, has degenerated into a technocratic machine serving a narrow power group that is kept in power at the top by hordes of security men and a regime of repression and terror at the bottom (Kothari, 1986: 172).

Kothari, who for many years as director of the Centre for the Study of Developing Societies in Delhi has been struggling to keep Gandhian traditions alive, and tries to link 'grass-roots movements' on a world level, went on to say:

Many compromises were effected along the way (i.e. of state power) as for instance in the implementation of land reforms or in establishing truly effective public distribution systems. Concessions were made when entrenched groups and interests put up tough resistance to intended changes. There was too much dependence on the bureaucracy. And finally, there was a considerable degree of corruption and nepotism in high office. These were the inevitable compulsions of the middle class origins of the leadership and the social milieu in which ministers, their secretaries and the technocrats moved. And yet whether it was Lenin or Mao, Nehru or Nkrumah, Nyerere or Nasser, they all pinned their visions of transformation on State power. Only Gandhi did not. But he was, even before India became independent, rendered impotent and irrelevant.

Leaving the Gandhian stream aside – it is necessary to remember that most Gandhians also opted for a model of voluntarism and 'constructive work' which depended heavily on State patronage – there was consensus across the board, from the industrialists to 'left-of-centre' politicians to the radicals including the Marxists, on a positive and interventionist role for the State on behalf of the masses (Kothari, 1986: 171–2, emphasis added).

Even among the 'hard core' of the world systems paradigm, there seems to be a rising awareness that the ruins of socialism are not just a consequence of the rising socialist reintegration into the capitalist world economy, but an expression of the internal bottlenecks of the socialist system (Ost, 1982; see also some remarks by Wallerstein, 1982; Froebel, 1984). Wallerstein's formulation is especially interesting here (1982: 297), since it links the crisis of the communist parties in power with duration, in which these parties retain the most important position in the state. For the 'socio-liberal' world system authors, like Elsenhans or Senghaas, who have all done empirical research of their own into socialist development models (see Elsenhans and Junne, 1974; Senghaas, 1982a; Tausch, 1979a, 1982c, 1983, 1984a, 1984c, 1985, 1986b), it is evident that learning pathologies in a socio-cybernetical sense were in force in Eastern Europe and other socialist models, the longer these models were disconnected from any tangible progress towards pluralism (see also Ehrlich, 1981). Empirically, the time element played a major role: what might still have been compatible with extensive growth in a non-industrialized environment in the postwar period is all the more constraining development today, five decades after the installation of socialist regimes in Eastern Europe.

How are these tendencies to be properly generalized? And how do I measure them? Here I develop Weede's thought: that the best translation of an Olsonian/socio-liberal reasoning into cross-nationally testable research designs will always be the combination of (i) institutional stability and/or rigidity; and (ii) state sector economic influence among the explanatory variables of the regression equations to explain development (Weede, 1986a).

The Olson/Weede process of blocked development through the combined workings of institutional stability/rigidity and state sector economic influence will have to be qualified, though, in the light of recent evidence (Tausch, 1991a, 1989a, 1990b): (i) growth will suffer under the Olson/Weede process, especially when I control properly for the human capital expenditure of the state, the tax structure, the organization of national defence and the long-term logic of foreign capital penetration. The Olson/Weede process will be strongest in ethnically heterogeneous societies with old established constitutions (Hy 1); (ii) the Olson/Weede process will affect distribution and life chances of the great majority of poor in the following way: educational access limitations and female discrimination will to a large extent determine population dynamics and thus long-run distribution patterns, while human development will suffer directly under the joint influence of public investment and ethnic heterogeneity (Hy 2 and Hy 3); (iii) interest collusions will also affect the political stability/political violence dimension of a society: military expenditures are directly related to the political violence potential, as are high government debts (Hy 4); (iv) militarization (indirectly) and low government savings (directly) will contribute towards top level political instability in the form of military *coups d'état*. A functioning competition between political parties will discipline the collusion of established interests, with top-level income concentration and past economic growth spurts as further control variables (Hy 5); (v) allowing for Western orientation of political systems, the collusion of interests in the wake of institutional stability and state sector influence finds it easier to finance the state by credits from Western governments and the transnational banks. Non-traditional exports and direct taxes as the alternatives are overruled because of the social power of landowners and mining companies (Hy 6); and (vi) the Olson/Weede process leads towards an 'internalization' of the social violence potential, manifesting itself in violent death rates according to the WHO classification. Control variables are

(a)   development level,
(b)   organization of national defence as an 'outlet' for male aggressiveness,
(c)   bureaucratization of the occupational structure, mainly affecting female life perspectives, by ascribing to them repetitious, boring and subordinate work, and
(d)   the weight of traditional exports (Hy 7).

To test these contending theories of development in a quantitative fashion presupposes a debate about the methods and statistical data which are used in my analysis.

6 Methods and Data

It will be my task to evaluate the theoretical relevance of the above presented theories in an empirical, cross-national investigation of world development from 1960 onwards. Modernization, dependence/world system approaches and socio-liberal traditions will be submitted to politometric testing on the basis of cross-national data. The standard statistical technique of ordinary least square multiple regression, as installed in the standard statistical social science package SPSS IX is applied to test for the quantitative relationship between various explanatory variables X_1 to X_n and the explained variable Y, with 'a' being the intercept and b_1 to b_n the unstandardized regression coefficients:

$$Y = a + b_1 * X_1 + b_2 * X_2 + b_3 * X_3 + b_n * X_n + e \qquad (6.1)$$

In my equation, e is the error term. When we z-standardize my equation, $beta_1$ to $beta_n$ are the standardized regression coefficients. Significance is the measure, according to which a relationship falls within the boundaries of what must be expected by simple random, or, due to its extraordinary strength, is something not to be explained by random: i.e., it is significant. The level of significance can be interpreted in terms of the statistical probability of a relationship given the numbers of cases and explanatory independent variables, and is designated by p, the probability. Adjusted for the number of variables and cases ('degrees of freedom') we arrive also at a measure, which compares the 'band spread' of the explained variable, $\hat{Y}$, (variance), as predicted by my equation, compared to Y, observed in the real world. The resulting ratio of variances of $\hat{Y}$ to variances of Y we call '$R**2$': i.e., the variance accounted for.

It ranges, logically, between 0 per cent and 100 per cent, but in macro-quantitative relationships of variables on the level of nation states, 2/5 or 3/5 of 'variance explained' is already something good. F and p of the whole regression estimate relate to the quality of the relationship in terms of randomness versus significance (very high and rather unusual influences). My statistical programme package, the SPSS IX, of course contains the multiple regression procedure: stepwise OLS (ordinary least squares)

57

regression. SPSS IX makes these results reproducible at many research institutions; all the more so since my data are standard statistical data files available either on computer tape (for larger computing centres) on floppy disk or in book form (for the personal computer user). The data used were the Ballmer-Cao/Scheidegger Zuerich data file; the Taylor and Jodice 'World Handbook of Political and Social Indicators III'; and data series from the World Bank, either available as 'World Data Tape' from the Economic Analysis and Projections Department of the Bank or in book form (*World Tables*, updated each year by the *World Development Reports*).

Not all statistical relationships are linear, of course, and for that reason some transformations had to be used, which are indicated whenever they occur in this text. Most quantitative studies of world development introduced such non-linear formulations to explain economic growth and income inequality at some stage. Both phenomena (growth: Jackman, 1982; inequality: Kuznets, 1955; M. S. Ahluwalia, 1974) are weakest at very low and very high levels of development, with each peaking somewhere in the middle. I can do nothing practical about it, but these effects have been named 'Matthew's effect' and 'Kuznets' curve', although a careful reading of both Matthew 13: 12 in the Bible and of Kuznets (1955) would certainly not justify any link of the empirically observable realities with these two pieces of literature.

Bornschier in particular developed his world system approach using such non-linear dependencies of growth and inequality on the development level in the preceding period. How, then, is such a Bornschierian development theory formulated? 'MNC PEN' is the stock of foreign direct investment related to total capital stock and to total population, 1967; 'MNC INVEST' denotes fresh investments by the transnationals in the period 1968–73 weighted by GDP in 1968; 'INCOME' is the logged income per capita 1965 converted at official exchange rates into US$; 'INCOME SQUARED' is the squared term; 'CAP FORM' denotes averaged gross domestic investment rates 1965–1970–1973; 'EXPORTS' are averaged for the same years; 'SIZE' is the absolute size of the 'modern' market segment, measured by logged total energy consumption; 'GROWTH' is measured by the average annual per cent growth rate of GNP per capita between end 1965 and end 1977 from World Bank figures. Since each given coefficient in the parameter estimate is well above double the size of the standard error of the estimate, I report Bornschier's results (1982) in an abbreviated fashion, and interested readers are referred to Bornschier's original publication for the more exact details:

GROWTH = − 20.48 − 0.0263 * MNC PEN

$\qquad$ + 0.0076 * MNC INVEST + 13.81 * INCOME

$\qquad$ − 2.49 * INCOME SQUARED

$\qquad$ + 0.0664 * CAP FORM + 0.0444 * EXPORTS

$\qquad$ + 0.8856 * SIZE $\qquad$ (6.2)

$n = 103$ countries with complete data, $R^{**}2 = 39$ per cent
Source: computed by Bornschier, 1982: 62.

To account for income inequality ('INEQUAL'), measured by the GINI index of personal income inequality as reported in Jain (1975), reanalysed by Bornschier, he introduces another explanatory variable, called 'SYSTEM TYPE', measuring simply the extent of state control over total investments:

INEQUAL = + 1.21 + 0.0829 * MNC PEN + 42.97 * INCOME

$\qquad$ − 8.97 * INCOME SQUARED

$\qquad$ − 0.1739 * SYSTEM TYPE $\qquad$ (6.3)

$n = 72$ countries with complete data, $R^{**}2 = 50$ per cent
Source: calculated by Bornschier, 1982: 67.

As we shall see in Chapter 7, however, Jackman is quite right in warning against too sweeping a generalization in the trade-off between development level and development performance in the successive period, since in Jackman's work (1982) the 'Matthew's effect' was dropped after the introduction of other proper control variables. The 'Plateau curve' of basic human needs (Goldstein, 1985a; Tausch, 1991a) is up to now resistant to such tests.

What is this Plateau curve all about? Some social scientists (Srinivasan *et al.*, 1986) are particularly aware of the problems of life expectancy as an indicator, both cross-nationally and over time, of the conditions under which the majorities of populations have to live in different regions of a country or in different countries. Although there is an infinite list of possible determinants of life expectancy both cross-nationally as well as over time, there are attempts in recent literature to relate life expectancy and its dynamics to a parsimonious model with only a few variables, starting from the question of how many inputs a social system (a nation) has to provide in order to produce a resulting basic human needs satisfaction.

One such attempt, by Goldstein (1985a), formulates the Plateau curve of basic human needs attainment in a society, and tries to show that, with rising per capita incomes, at first basic human needs satisfaction increases quicker, but then slower, until a stagnation point is reached. Considering this non-linear trade-off, Goldstein (1985a) replicates the results already attained by Woolhandler and Himmelstein that there are still huge differences in the basic human needs satisfaction of countries. Woolhandler and Himmelstein, in their challenging piece quite overlooked by social scientists, identify militarism (military expenditures per GNP) as the basic block against higher life expectancies irrespective of the already achieved development level. Linking life expectancies or infant mortalities to development level (either in terms of real GDP/GNP per capita in US$ or purchasing parity rates or energy consumption rates) has some published evidence already in its favour (Birdsall, 1980; Cornia, 1984; Goldstein, 1985a; Hicks, 1979, 1982; Hicks/Streeten, 1979; McGranahan *et al.*, 1982; Rodgers, 1979; Russett, 1978; Tausch, 1984b, 1984c, 1986a, 1986b, 1987a, 1991a, 1991b; Woolhandler/ Himmelstein) with some formulations allowing for a downturn in life expectancy increases/infant mortality decreases after a certain level in the development of productive forces has been reached (Goldstein, 1985a; Rodgers, 1979; Tausch, 1990b).

In the dark days of the Second World War two authors – who inspired generations to come – had practically at the same time the same idea about this. Polanyi wrote in his 'Great Transformation' of 1944 about the 'progress' of the capitalist mode of production, which in the end undermines biological life on earth. He was the most important Western socialist writer to take up anew the 'green' problem already inherent in the socialist classics of the nineteenth century. But now, after the Chernobyl accident, I venture to assert that J. Nehru in his 'Discovery of India' was even more correct when he warned about the dangers of industrialization in the following way:

A deficient diet, alcoholism, neurotic conditions or poor health generally, mental or physical [is the result of industrialization]. Perhaps [also] the strain and stress of modern life, the ceaseless competition and worry. It would seem that the kind of modern civilization that developed first in the West and spread elsewhere, and especially metropolitan life that has been its chief feature, produces an unstable society which gradually loses its vitality. Life advances in many fields and yet it loses its grip; it becomes more artificial and slowly ebbs away. More and more stimulants are needed – drugs to enable us to sleep or to perform our other natural functions, foods and drinks that tickle the palate and produce a momentary exhilaration at the cost of weakening the system, and special devices to give us a temporary sensation of pleasure and excitement – and after the stimulation comes the reaction and a sense of emptiness. With all its splendid manifestations and real achievements, we have created a civilization which has something counterfeit about it. We eat ersatz foods produced with the help of ersatz fertilizers; we indulge in ersatz emotions and our human relations seldom go below the superficial plane. (J. Nehru, 1944: 554)

In order further to clarify my concept of a Plateau curve, let me schematically reproduce its shape in the cross-national static dimension for 1977 and in the incremental dimension, with life expectancy increases 1960–77, as in Figure 6.1.

By looking at Figure 6.1 we get a better understanding of what Galtung had in mind when he spoke in his contributions in the 1970s about 'structural violence' as the relationship between the 'actual' and the

Figure 6.1a   The Plateau curve of basic human needs

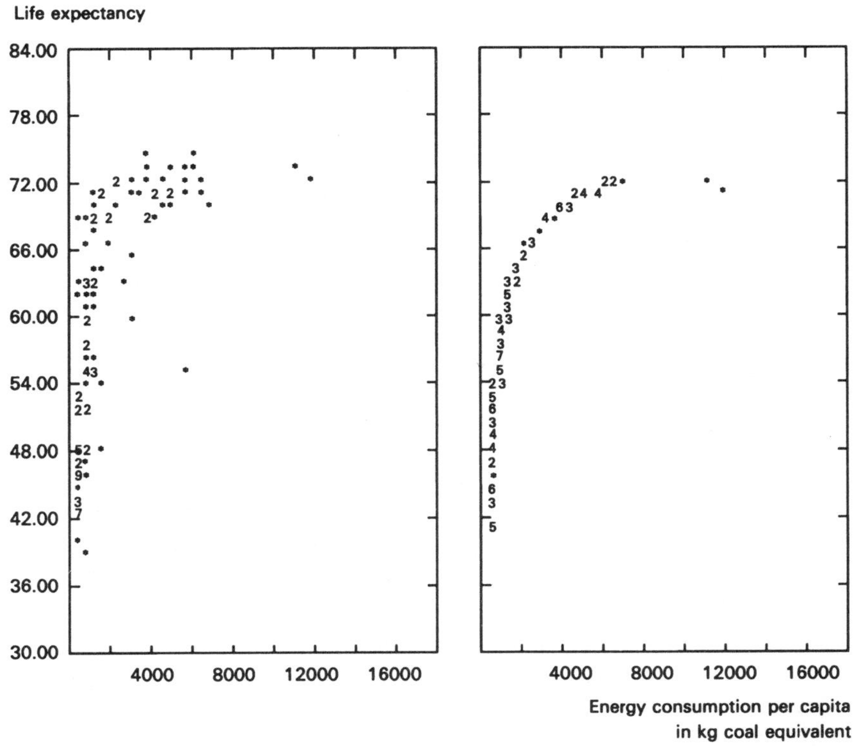

Life expectancy

Energy consumption per capita
in kg coal equivalent

Figure 6.1b The Plateau curve of basic human needs – dynamic aspects

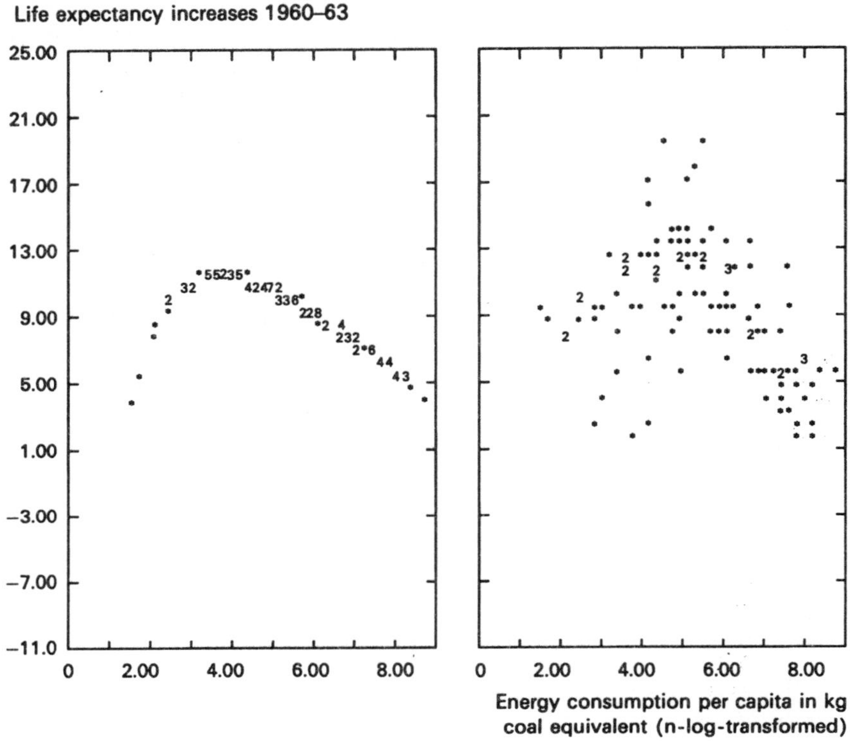
Life expectancy increases 1960–63
25.00
21.00
17.00
13.00
9.00
5.00
1.00
−3.00
−7.00
−11.0
0
2.00
4.00
6.00
8.00
Energy consumption per capita in kg coal equivalent (n-log-transformed)

Source: Tausch (1987a).

'potential'. The stable relationship (across data sets, time points, choice of subgroups) between the level of development of industrial productive forces with today's technologies and the quantity of life gives us a fair indicator of how much entire countries are characterized by the existence of structural violence: the higher the level of energy use and the lower the life expectancy achieved, the greater the level of structural violence. Or to put it in even simpler terms: countries below the two curves are characterized by the actual falling below the potential; i.e., they are characterized by structural violence.

My formulation of the Plateau curve of basic human needs would allow for the ecologically sound idea, that – above certain limits of primary energy consumption of a given society at present technologies employed – there are relative boundaries of health development to be observed, the higher the energy consumption becomes (i.e. the dirt from factories, automobiles, aeroplanes, etc.) due to emission of SO_2, CO, CO_2 and other poisonous substances (Michelsen, 1984). My function, to give expression to this phenomenon, is based on two very well-known natural constants, the numbers e (2.7) and π (3.14) and their derivates, quite frequently used in the natural sciences, $1/(e**2)$ and the natural logarithm of π, i.e., $\ln(\pi)$ (see also, Martinez-Allier, 1987, on the rediscovery of the economic writings of Chemistry Nobel Laureate F. Soddy, Oxford University, on the issue of the social and ecological limits of energy consumption). These mathematical/natural constants were taken from Bronstein and Semendjajew, and they do fit the data better than any other formulation used up to now (see Tausch, 1991a, chap. V). Equation 6.4 relates life expectancy to energy consumption (parameter estimates with a short time lag for life expectancy in 1977, explained by energy consumption in kg coal equivalent per capita in 1973) while Equation 6.5 relates the difference in the natural logarithms of life expectancies 1977–60 to the already achieved level of life expectancy in 1960 (natural logarithm) and the first derivates of Equation 6.4, using exponentials only. All predictors are significant at the 5 per cent level. Thus we have:

$$\text{Life Expectancy} = a + b_1 * \text{Energy Cons. per cap} ** (1/(e**2))$$

$$- b_2 * \text{Energy Cons. per cap} ** (\ln(\pi)) \qquad (6.4)$$

Parameter Estimate:
$n = 121$; adj. $R**2 = 73.8$ per cent, $F = 170.18$, $p = .0000$
$y = 12.16 + 20.42 * X_1 - .00027536 * X_2$

DYN Life Expectancy $60 - 77$

$$= a - b_1 * \ln \text{Life Expectancy 1960}$$

$$- b_2 * \text{Energy Cons. 1960} ** ((1/(e**2)) - 1)$$

$$- b_3 * \text{Energy Cons. 1960} ** (\ln(\pi) - 1)) \qquad (6.5)$$

Parameter Estimate:
$n = 112$; adj $R**2 = 54.7$ per cent, $F = 45.77$, $p = .0000$
$y = 1.21 - .24 * X_1 - .60 * X_2 - .03 * X_3$

Source: own calculations, SPSS IX (stepwise new regression) on the basis of World Bank *World Development Report* and *World Tables* data, contained on the *World Data Tape* (1980) and the Ballmer-Cao and Scheidegger figures on primary energy consumption rates per capita, 1960–73. All countries with available data were entered into the regression estimates, except for the high energy consumption 'enclaves' Luxembourg, United Arab Emirates, Qatar, Bahrain, Kuwait, Bermuda, New Caledonia, Netherlands Antilles, Brunei, Guam, which would bias results in my favour. DYN Life expectancy is calculated as the difference in natural logarithms following Jackman (1980).

These equations thus tell us how much primary energy input a society needs in order to achieve a certain 'life quality' or, to be philosophically more precise, a certain life quantity, and how all this looks in time perspective. I will then be able to define the basic human development efficiency of a system in terms of the earth's limited available energy resources and environment. Human development efficiency is defined accordingly in terms of the residuals from the regression, established in Equations 6.4 and 6.5. My pessimistic results for the former socialist countries are presented in Table 6.1 as a test of the exactness of the measurement concept.

Table 6.1   Human development efficiency of socialist systems, 1960–77

Country	Residuals ('Efficiencies') for	
	Equation 6.4	Equation 6.5
	Life expectancy 1977	Growth rate life expectancy 1960–77 (%)
Bulgaria	+ .41 years	−5.1
CSFR	−1.82 years	−5.5
former GDR	−.10 years	−4.8
Hungary	−1.08 years	−4.7
Poland	−.78 years	−1.2
Romania	−.53 years	−0.0

Computations: Residual plots, SPSS IX new regression text above, notes to Equations 6.4 and 6.5.

From a perspective of world-wide comparisons, the use of energy consumption instead of gross product (however it is measured and converted) must seem especially attractive. Measurement bias for energy consumption in non-capitalist societies and in underdeveloped countries cannot but be lower than the measurement bias for gross product; and although economists have been trying very hard in recent years to overcome these problems and to solve the question of the proper conversion of national products into some international unit, e.g., the dollar, or into purchasing power parities, it is evident that, for the measurement of the degree of classical industrialization and 'northern' consumption styles patterned around the private car, energy consumption is a much superior indicator, being a constant of relevance in the natural sciences (Michelsen, 1984; see also: Myrdal, 1956, 1984; Nohlen and Nuscheler, 1982) directly connected to the degradation of our environment. In graphic terms, the development efficiency of the now defunct socialist systems can be presented as follows (Figure 6.2).

Figure 6.2   Human development deficiency of socialism

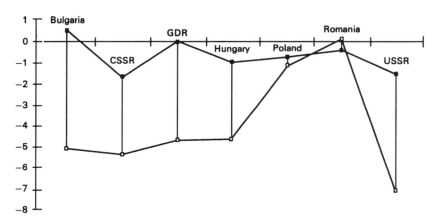

A further methodological note should concern my operationalization of liberal and socio-liberal theories on the negative influence of state classes on socio-economic development. For one, my measurement concept provides a test about these theories regarding their ability to explain (the growth of) basic human needs satisfaction. There is a well-known bias concerning per capita income growth and income distribution as the two most common yardsticks of development (M. S. Ahluwalia, 1974; Jain, 1975; Paukert, 1973; Tausch, 1982c, 1986b; McGranahan and Hong, 1979). Second, to test (socio-)liberal theories properly, there must be a joint inclusion of institutional framework and state class influence. Such institutional frameworks are democratic age, systems age, the composition of the population allowing for ethno-social stratification and distribution coalitions, and the role that the disciplining effect of the world market has on the power of the state classes (see especially Chapter 8). Third, it must always be clearly stated that during a long economic cycle the influence of state expenditures on growth might vary. Fourth, the relationship between growth and state sector activity might vary in different socio-economic systems, while the relationship between public investments, ethnic heterogeneity and deficient basic human needs satisfaction will be quite stable across systems.

Introducing both parts of Olson's growth theory into a regression explaining OECD country growth for the period 1960–82, we get:

$$\text{Economic Growth} = a - b_1 * \text{Age of Democracy}$$
$$- b_2 * \text{State Sector Influence} \qquad (6.6)$$

Estimate:

Growth Predictor 1960–82	Beta weight	Significance
Age of democracy in 1965	−.92711	.000
State sector expenditures per BIP in 1965	−.64189	.000

$n = 20$ stable OECD democracies according to Weede (1986a); adj $R**2 = 70.3$ per cent; pairwise deletion of missing values; democratic age for Finland and Austria in 1965 coded as 20 years; all other data: Weede (1986a). Based on calculations, SPSS IX, reported in Tausch (1991a).

The time horizon of my empirical studies is chosen in such a way as to cover the beginning long-wave downswing of the third Kondratieff cycle from 1967 onwards (Bornschier, 1988; Goldstein, 1988; Tausch, 1990a). If not specified otherwise, my unit of analysis is the totality of the states of the world system, the only constraint being formed by missing values among the dependent or independent variables. To further clarify the socio-liberal character of my regression results, I should specify how I operationalized 'stable institutional conditions' and 'state influence' over the economy (see Table 6.2).

Systematic exclusions of predictors, which for other theories are relevant in explaining income distribution, life expectancy, economic growth or political instability, can be detected. For one I re-checked the systematic patterns of the correlations of residuals from regression equations with the rest of the variables from my cross-national data sets. Correlation results were compared with the results of former theoretical debates, and new analyses were performed within the socio-liberal frame of reference about the influence on long-term socio-economic development by (i) the state sector and its economic activities; (ii) international trade and capitalist dependence; (iii) political structure and political stability; (iv) socio-economic structure, employment, inequality; and (v) the satisfaction of basic human needs, including human rights.

Furthermore, the main predictor variables of other quantitative development theories were all tested regarding their effects on my explanatory variables. Insignificant results which only refute established theories are not

Table 6.2   Measurement concepts for socio-liberal development theories

---

(a) Stable institutional conditions ('institutional sclerosis') likely to appear in political systems with:
(i) high constitutional age; (ii) ethnic heterogeneity; (iii) traditional export structure; (iv) lack of political party competition; (v) bureaucratization of the professional structure; (vi) high political systems stability index

(b) State sector influence benefiting collusion of economic interests with increasing 'institutional sclerosis' likely to appear in political systems with:
(i) high government expenditures or (ii) high public investment shares or (iii) tax revenues relying on indirect taxes or (iv) deficit 'finance' or (v) low government share in total savings rate (hence high government deficits) or (vi) high government consumption rates or (vii) high military expenditures

(c) Possibilities for the state to counteract the joint influence of 'institutional sclerosis' and the collusion of interests in the wake of high government influence over the economy mainly consisting of:
 (i) organizing national defence by conscription; (ii) raising direct taxes; (iii) spending public money on education

---

reported here for reasons of space and because I want to present new perspectives. Further quantitative development research, though, will need to decide on the appropriateness of my chosen explanations *vis-à-vis* established theories.

In the following chapters I shall propose new explanations of the development process developed from a socio-liberal perspective and thoroughly tested for any possible omissions of relevant, but still excluded, predictor variables in the regression equations.

7 Recent Research, New Results and Discussion

My empirical results on a world level will now be presented in the following order: first, I shall deal with the determinants of economic growth and – related – income distribution. I shall then move on to a discussion of the determinants of basic human needs (life expectancy and employment). Political violence and political instability will also figure on the agenda for this chapter, and I shall look into the implications of a socio-liberal development theory regarding the analysis of debt and social decay. The correct analysis of the forces shaping capitalist ascent and decline in the world system becomes all the more important since Eastern Europe and the former USSR have become the testing ground for all kinds of political and economic strategies, and a thorough knowledge of its determinants can help to shorten the necessary search time for new democratic models.

Jodice, Taylor and Deutsch (1980) and Deutsch (1978b) clearly see the advantage of a macro-quantitative approach in the cumulative character of its results. Thus, *vis-à-vis* the well-established quantitative dependence/ world systems approach, 'internally oriented' arguments are not new. Jackman, Jagodzinski and Weede were the first empirically to challenge the established paradigmatic dominance of quantitative dependence interpretations. While the former two tended to concentrate on the methodological problems of the proper specification of the multiple regressions used by Bornschier and his school (see also Equations 6.2 and 6.3), Weede proposed, from 1980 onwards, a methodologically very sophisticated but certainly provocative explanation of economic growth and redistribution of incomes. Poor countries become richer and more egalitarian, if they are militarily threatened from abroad. They will start building up large conscript armies, which lend importance to the great mass of the population in the eyes of the elites. The masses will be rewarded by redistribution, and military training will bring about a greater discipline of the (male) work-force, thus having its own effects on long-term economic growth. Weede was able to show that measures of dependence, such as capital penetration, absence of 'vertical trade' or feudal interaction patterns with the world's leading trading powers, never eliminate the significant effect exerted by military personnel rates per population on economic growth. To further highlight the issue, it must be recognized that Weede used Bornschier's own data set. As a leading writer in the field of macro-quantitative methodology he was particularly careful to avoid specification errors, such as the exclusion of the 'Matthew's effect' or the 'Kuznets curve' without testing for their influence on growth and income redistribution. Those countries relying on conscription, such as Taiwan, Israel or South Korea, are fairly egalitarian developing countries, and they recorded very rapid growth in the last four decades, while regions like Latin America suffered precisely from the lack of an external challenge, according to the logic of that theory (Deutsch, 1978a; Szentes, 1984; Tausch, 1979b, 1982a).

Let us be clear: Weede, first of all, talks about military personnel and not about military expenditures. For many LDCs conscription would be a cost-saving device to achieve some measure of 'national defence', whatever is understood by that. Thus the argument that personnel will lead to expenditures is not valid for every case. Secondly, Weede carefully includes other control variables, also those of the quantitative dependency theories. Thirdly, he does not manipulate his sample by excluding/including just a few outliers as he sees fit. On the contrary, he is the author who up to now most carefully integrated into his empirical research designs explanatory variables which are common to the econometrician (M. S. Ahluwalia, 1972; Chenery, 1975; Jodice *et al.*, 1980; Kuznets, 1955; Russett, 1983a). And fourthly, adherents of the world systems approach should be reminded that authors from their own side of the spectrum, like Ramirez and Thomas, were among the first to introduce the very related concept of state centrality as an agency of capitalist ascent. Mass armies, furthermore, were an old popular tenet of the social democratic left in Europe in the 1920s and 1930s of this century. And, to extend the reasoning still further, it was Elsenhans who has shown that, historically, in the sixteenth century the English Crown had seen fit in the sixteenth century to issue the 'depopulation acts' and to introduce conscription, and both worked against tendencies towards a more extensive land use (Elsenhans, 1979a: 116–17). At that crucial time before the industrial revolution England was just too poor to have a professional army (Elsenhans, 1979a: 117).

Another theoretical/empirical innovation against the mainstream of the macro-quantitative world system approach is directly connected with the Brenner/Wallerstein debate. What is the role of the labour to land ratio in development, and how is it to be interpreted? Both Wallerstein and Brenner agree that, for the Polish case in the Long Sixteenth Century, extensive agriculture (a low ratio of labour to land) constitutes a development block. In the macro-quantitative debate it is a long time since Russett (1967) linked extensive agriculture and stagnation empirically. Tausch (1991a) has taken up the issue again, confronting scattered elements of existing theory about the development block constituted by extensive agriculture with new evidence based on the Taylor and Jodice data set. Among the theories chosen to explain that phenomenon, it is especially important to mention J. C. Mariategui (1894–1930), whose writings are well known only to a small circle of Latin American specialists, but whose theories up to now were never debated in macro-quantitative development research. Mariategui is well aware in his Marxist approach about the particular character of Iberian colonialism (in Latin America, the Philippines and elsewhere) as its very distinctness, compared with the English and French colonies in North America, is extensive use of production factors, especially land. Mariategui recognizes the importance of human capital formation for growth. The use of 'unlimited supplies' of land and fresh, unqualified labour thwarts technological progress. Other formulations about this so important trade-off are to be found in Feder, Hein, Mahar, Simon and Sandner and Steger. Again, the contrast between the East Asian 'dragons', including Japan, and Latin America, is striking: indeed, the Asian 'dragons' have some of the highest density rates in the world, while Latin America is characterized by extensive land use in the *latifundista* institutional framework.

Mariategui's development theory deserves more than passing attention, in so far as he was very familiar, too, via his journalistic work in Europe, with the social democracy of the European continent, and had a deep understanding of the need for reform to bring about a more stable capitalist development. Mariategui's cultural critique of Spanish influence in Latin America is certainly one of the most challenging chapters that a Marxist has ever written on cultural patterns and socio-economic development (Mariategui, posth., 1986: esp. pp. 53ff.). His analysis of the ancient Inca civilizations in many ways brings him into the vicinity of Polanyi's theory of ancient society (Polanyi, 1979).

On the basis of the Taylor and Jodice data file, Tausch (1991a) explains, in a multiple regression of economic growth per capita 1960–75 on rural density, the absence of high birth rates and the 'Matthew's effect', 43.9 per cent of the growth rate in the 92 countries with complete data. Other regression designs, including for the period 1965–83, again confirm the basic validity of the Mariategui/Russett (1967) argument about stagnation in an 'extensive institutional setting'. It should be emphasized, furthermore, that intensive and extensive landholding systems are to be found in countries with high and low population dynamics, and the correlation between the two variables is even a negative one, as suggested by Figure 7.1, based on Taylor and Jodice (1983).

An extensive landholding system is always highly correlated with a high ratio of concentration in landholdings (Tausch, 1991a). In Mariategui's theory a rapidly growing labour force in scattered tiny settlements in conjunction with extensive land use and high land concentration is precisely the predicament of regions like the Peruvian Sierra which is, even today, six

Figure 7.1 Crude live birth rates (*x*) and intensiveness of agriculture

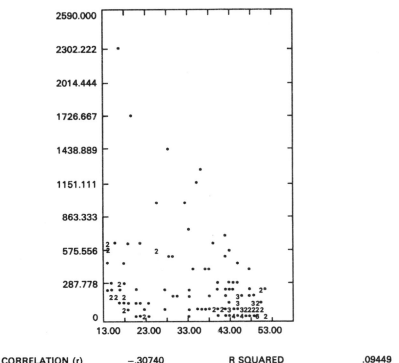

CORRELATION (r)	−.30740	R SQUARED	.09449
SIGNIFICANCE R	.00009	STD ERR OF EST	319.47000
INTERCEPT (A)	525.70068	STD ERROR OF A	82.00397
SIGNIFICANCE A	.00001	SLOPE (B)	−8.21760
STD ERROR OF B	2.13474	SIGNIFICANCE B	.00009
PLOTTED VALUES	144	EXCLUDED VALUES 0	MISSING VALUES 7

decades after Mariategui's death, a region of misery and violence. And all three phenomena do allow landholders to continue with the system under practically no compulsion towards technical innovation (see also von Oertzen, 1988).

A modern econometric investigation into the patterns of growth (Reynolds, 1985: 413) by contrast erroneously estimated the effect of density on growth. To begin with, there is a high multicollinearity among his one-dimensional predictor variables (agricultural production growth, export growth, investment growth), which will render the effect of density spurious, at any rate. Worse, Reynolds in his widely circulated work defines 'population density' as 'hectares of arable land per head of population' (Reynolds, 1985: 413), which could be formulated as:

$$DENS~(1) = LAND/POP \qquad (7.1)$$

which in reality measures extensive land use (DENS (1)), while density (2) is

$$DENS(2) = POP/LAND \qquad (7.2)$$

Reynolds, however, confounds the two concepts: the regression coefficient of DENS (1) on growth is $-.005$ in his regression ($t = -0.8$), which would mean that there is a slight negative effect of the disposability of land per population (DENS (1)) on economic growth. However, Reynolds (1985: 413) interprets as follows: I surmised that a country with less arable land per capita [i.e. DENS (1)] might on this account have a lower growth rate. He claims that his hypothesis is weakly supported here.

Tausch (1991a) on the other hand has shown the connection between culture, land use patterns and growth. In the Middle East extensive land use is often being favoured, too, while protestant countries, irrespective of development level, favour a much lower birth rate, thus affecting growth. Properly considering further influences on the birth rate, like alphabetization, protein availability, population density, and agricultural employment, a catholic culture, too, tends towards a faster population growth.

Of course I would agree with Raffer's recent reformulation and development of the world systems argument in so far as this extensive landholding system was implanted in many parts of the world by brute force. But what about the cultural consequences for development? Whether implanted from the outside – as in most colonies of Spain and Portugal or corresponding to a millennium tradition – extensive landholding will create its own socio-cultural dynamics, which must be taken into account by future development research.

Although Jackman (1982) has shown in his critique of Bornschier's works that population does play a major role in blocking growth, systematic comparative studies about the different effects of population and dependence on development were quite overlooked in the 'classical' macro-quantitative literature on the world system. Economic, social and political demography is, however, a major discipline within the larger framework of comparative social research, and relevant titles about the linkages between population, blocked growth and/or inequality and instability now include Ahluwalia (1974); Anker and Farooq, 1978; Birdsall (1980, 1984); Bollen and Jackman, 1985; Bulatao, 1984; de Carvalho and Wood, 1981; Choucri, 1974; Cornia, 1984; Demos Lee, 1980; Deutsch (1979a); Goldscheid, 1924, 1983; Khalatbari, 1984; Gwatkin, 1984; Kurup, 1986; Kuznets, 1955; Lewis (1978a–1984); Lindert, 1986; Mahadevan, 1986; Myrdal (1972); Nayar, 1986; Rodgers (1978a-1979); Rodgers and Standing, 1981; Russett *et al.*

(1981); Schattat, 1976; J. Schmid (1976a–1984); Schultz, 1982; Singer (1971); Spengler, 1976; Srinivasan, 1986; Standing, 1978; Tausch (1984c, 1985, 1986a, 1986c, 1987a); Trussell and Pebley, 1984; Visaria, 1979.

All these many studies suggest the developmental importance of an early demographic transition for growth, redistribution, health and basic human needs. Pronouncedly pro-natalist views, such as those of Simon today, are rather an exception, with some (neo)Marxist authors, like Khalatbari or K. B. Ward expressing their belief in a hypothesis of retarded demographic transition brought about by transnational capital penetration.

The World Bank's *World Development Report* 1984 has done much to popularize the anti-natalist viewpoint. The emphasis today is of course not on food availability versus population, but on development quality (life expectancy, low infant mortality, human capital formation, equity and quality of the environment), which suffers from too rapid population growth on the macrosocietal level. But even growth suffers directly from too rapid demographic dynamics. On the basis of Taylor and Jodice, Tausch (1991a) could demonstrate a correlation coefficient of −.40633 between crude live birth rates in 1960 and subsequent economic growth per capita in real terms (1960–75) in 100 countries of the world with complete data. Multivariate analysis supports the view that extensive use of land and population are major growth impasses (Tausch, 1991a: 554–74). If development is understood in terms of basic human needs, the balance becomes all the clearer in favour of anti-natalist theories of development (Birdsall *et al.*, 1984; Bulatao, 1984; Gwatkin, 1984; Hicks, 1979–82; Hicks and Streeten, 1979; Trussell and Pebley). Re-analysis of such approaches has again confirmed the basic validity of the argument in favour of early demographic transition (Tausch, 1991a).

A further problem for 'classical' and 'neo'-dependency traditions is their treatment of the trade-off between equity, pluralism, social reform and development. While extensive landholding and population growth might still be somehow integrated into dependence/world system approaches, the problem with equity, pluralism and social reform is much trickier. Wallerstein (1976), and with him most of the world system/dependency school, believes that capitalism works by a 'dog eat dog' principle, allowing states to ascend by (i) nationalism; (ii) state interventionism; and (iii) curbing workers' demands.

This strategy (Wallerstein, 1976: 476) corresponds to classical Marxist positions which stress the impossibility of redistribution within the framework of capitalism (see Lange, 1964; Maerz, 1976; Rothschild, 1966; Sweezy, 1971; Tausch, 1976). But ever since Boehm-Bawerk (1914, especially pp. 258–9) discovered that with rising real wages population growth will diminish and capitalists will be forced to introduce innovations, thus stimulating reforms, the 'reformists' have again and again challenged the preponderance of the views, left and right alike, which causally link capitalist success with inequality and material sacrifice among the under-privileged. Support for the socio-liberal interpretation of world development now does not come only from R. Prebisch, the founder of economic 'dependence analysis', but interestingly enough also from Bornschier's account of the European experience (1988), whose analysis of the equality legitimation growth trade-off arrives at the same conclusions. The Japanese post-war history of land reform, economic and educational social access equality especially receives proper empirical attention (Bornschier, 1988: 348–66).

Social democratic and liberal reformers will maintain that inequality and discrimination are not good preconditions for long-term growth. What is the evidence, beside the fact that some of the most persistent 'miracle countries' of the 1980s, like Finland, Japan, Hong Kong and Norway show egalitarian income distribution patterns (World Bank, *World Development Report*, 1987; M. S. Ahluwalia, 1974; Ahluwalia *et al.*, 1978; Tausch, 1991a) and even social minimum programmes regardless of past work experience (G. Kent, 1989)?

The range of available indicators from the Taylor and Jodice data set for such a test includes GINI indices for incomes, land and sectors; it includes education, political and economic discrimination as measured by area specialists in the United States and indices of basic human needs. My re-analysis of earlier optimistic results uses the 'Matthew's effect' as control variable (see Equation (6.2)). I report these results mentioning partial correlation coefficients, degrees of freedom and levels of significance. Since conservatives and the traditional Marxists alike (Seers, 1981a, b) would expect a strong negative correlation between 'redistribution', pluralism and growth, because growth is built on the misery of human beings, I also mention coefficients which are not significant, but are opposed to these conservative (non-Marxist and Marxist) interpretations (see Table 7.1).

It emerges again that equity, basic needs satisfaction and indicators of the degree of democracy and pluralism, like the absence of political or economic discrimination and the unionization of the labour force, enhance subsequent economic growth. Here my empirical results must be interpreted within the framework of Menzel and Senghaas (1986) who maintain that societies with a low level of income and land concentration and a free peasantry are especially adaptive to the development process. At later stages of develop-ment, especially, changes in the political power-relationships and the rise of new elites, and often an alliance between social democracy and peasant groups (as happened in Scandinavia), became decisive.

Table 7.1   Partial correlation coefficients of the redistribution with growth process

(a) Explaining growth 1960–75 on the basis of Taylor and Jodice data

Growth predictor (if not specified otherwise, measured around 1960)	Partial corr with growth	DF	Error probability
Intensity of discrimination against political minorities	−.2250	77	.023
Voters per adult population (65)	+.3205	51	.010
Proportion of people affected by economic discrimination	−.0232	77	.420
Intensity of economic discrimination against minorities	−.2734	77	.007
GINI index of personal income inequality (mainly Jain/World Bank data for around 1968)	−.3103	69	.004
GINI index of sectorial income inequality	−.1197	91	.127
GINI index of land inequality	−.4881	47	.001
Daily average calorie intake	+.0042	90	.484
Daily average protein intake	+.1219	90	.123
Female life expectancy	+.2629	52	.027
Infant mortality	−.1628	48	.129
Doctors per million inhabitants	+.1616	113	.042
Crude death rates	−.2962	76	.004
Access to safe water in per cent of total population, end 60s	+.1189	66	.167
School enrolment 1st level	+.1048	116	.129
Literacy	+.0817	113	.193
Unionization of labour force	+.0637	88	.276

(b) Explaining growth 1965–83 on the basis of Bornschier, Heintz *et al.* data

(Predictor variables, if not specified otherwise, measured around 1965)			
GINI income inequality (see above)	−.3543	60	.002
Literacy, 1960	+.2253	70	.029
Secondary school enrolment r.	+.2247	82	.020
Social Security programme experience index, 1967	+.0041	89	.485
Land inequality (GINI)	−.4641	42	< .001

Source of per capita income per population real growth rates: World Bank, *World Development Report*, 1985.

With the greater attention paid to distributional factors, the distribution process itself has been re-analysed by many authors, including M. S. Ahluwalia, who presented the first conclusive econometric evidence on a world scale in 1974, maintaining that redistribution does not exclude economic growth. Interestingly enough Griffin, a development theorist in the radical tradition, has joined the ranks of those advocating redistribution as a strategy of growth:

> The true division between orthodox and radical economists centres on distributive issues. Radicals are usually egalitarians. They give high priority to greater equality for its own sake and often affirm that there is no necessary conflict between faster growth and a more equal distribution of wealth and income. Orthodox economists give priority to increasing production ('you can't redistribute nothing') and postulate a trade-off between growth and equity. (Griffin, 1987: 42)

According to M. S. Ahluwalia, education and population play a major role in the determination of income distribution. Although his important essay was published in 1974, his results were somehow overlooked by the macro-quantitative debate about income distribution and the world system from the late 1970s onwards. Discrimination against women plays an important role in the underlying demographic process. Tausch (1991a), based on World Bank machine readable data, maintained that access of females to secondary education is a decisive factor in the demographic transition. This approach, which is extended also by some politometric evidence regarding the relationships between religion and the demographic process, would expect that by decisive government action it is possible to break up traditional domination patterns in the family and the village, even when world economic conditions are adverse (Tausch, 1986a). As the Costa Rica case study shows, the benefits of such a strategy are immense in terms of gains in health and democratic stability, an argument, which later on was further developed by Tausch (1991a), showing the population dynamic/democratic quality trade-off.

Distribution, in my view, is determined to a large degree by the demographic process. Not just 'youthful population', as in Bollen and Jackman (1985) or Muller (1988), but the dynamics of population have a profound influence on the distribution process. Owing to the well-known difficulties of data incomparability in the field of income distribution, especially due to the outdated and rather limited figures for Eastern Europe in both the data collections Bornschier, Heintz *et al.* and Taylor and Jodice (see also Tausch, 1986b), I limited my sample to the capitalist world economy with some degree of (unweighted) MNC penetration (>.0099).

Thus, results by M. S. Ahluwalia are again confirmed when I introduce – according to Rodgers (1978b) – a variable measuring the change in the long-term supply of labour (see also Rodgers and Standing, 1981). It will suffice here to use the increase/decrease in crude live birth rates over time 1960–77, although a better time fit of this variable would be desirable for future research. Further explanatory variables are the Kuznets curve, access of the population to secondary education, and crude live birth rates in 1960. Again, a larger time span between these explanatory variables and the dependent variable would be a future research requirement, but there are severe problems of data availability before 1960, when so many nations around the globe were still colonies:

GINI Income Inequality $*$ 100

$$= - 20.33 + .52 * \text{Crude Live Birth Rate 1960}$$

$$+ 14.88 * (\ln \text{Energy Cons. p.c.65})$$

$$+ .60 * \text{DYN Crude Live Birth Rates } 60-77$$

$$- .93 * (\ln \text{Energy Cons. p.c.65}) **2$$

$$- .13 * \text{Secondary Enrolment R 1960} \qquad (7.3)$$

$n = 63$ countries with complete data and an integration factor into the capitalist world economy (MNC PEN) 'ge 0.01', calculated with SPSS IX and Bornschier, Heintz *et al.* data set
adj. $R**2 = 58.3$ per cent; $F = 18.06$; $p = .0000$
All predictors except education significant at least at one per cent level, p for education $= 11$ per cent z-standardized residuals > 1.499 for Tanzania, Zambia($+$); Pakistan, Ghana, Taiwan(-)
Regression results without these outliers:
$n = 58$; adj. $R**2 = 75.0$ per cent; $F = 35.19$; p $= .0000$
Secondary Enrolment: error $p. > 5$ per cent.

The predictor 'school enrolment ratio' at the secondary level achieves, unfortunately, only insignificant results for the reduced sample which excludes the outlaying cases. Thus, only population dynamics and the Kuznets curve are really stable *vis-à-vis* the necessary controls for outlaying cases, a result which further increases in weight when regarding the evidence for changes in income distribution over time (see below). Criticism of existing data sets on income distribution is of course highly relevant. Later data collections by the World Bank, published in the *World Development Reports*, have been trying very hard to eliminate outdated or untenable results and to make the few available data more comparable. Also, the

International Labour Office (ILO) in its *World Labour Report* (1984) published data with good data comparability, and the *World Data Tapes* contain also new, more restrictive and more comparable figures (see also Table 8.5). Only a few authors attempted to use these new materials, and they drew conclusions from the changes in income distribution over time in the few countries with reliable estimates calculated with the same methodology for both around 1960 and 1970. One of them is H. Zwicky, who, together with P. Heintz, had already successfully questioned some basic propositions of research on political instability and violence, developing a socio-liberal interpretation of the causes for pro-*status quo* conflicts. Inequality increases such conflicts, while demands from 'below' and a functioning competition between political parties dampen them (Zwicky and Heintz, 1982, esp. p. 276). On the other hand, Zwicky shows in his essay, dated 1985a, that the increase in repression over time 1960–70 and the increase in income inequality are closely associated with each other (Zwicky, 1985a: 18ff.)

Tausch (1991a), for his part, maintained that if the GINI index of inequality is a curvilinear function of development level, then the changes in income distribution over time must be predicted upon the first derivate of the Kuznets curve (Tausch, 1991a). For the 34 countries of the capitalist world economy with reliable data on income distribution patterns in both around 1960 and 1970, the change in the share of the poorest 20 per cent indeed is a function of 1/Energy Cons. p.c. 1960 (the first derivate of ln Energy Cons. p.c. 1960) and it is also a function of the change in the percentage of the population aged < 15 years from 1960 to 1970. With a rise in the industrialization level and, very likely, Energy Cons. p.c., chances for redistribution deteriorate quickly, and an unimpeded demographic dynamic further decreases the share of the poorest 20 per cent in total incomes over time. The relationship, however, is not too strong: $R**2 = 26.9$ per cent; adj. $R**2 = 16.9$ per cent; $F = 2.67$; $p = .05$

Nevertheless, this exercise shows something politically important: to achieve income redistribution over time a country has to work in the direction of changing the supply structure within the labour force, thus being able to change the long-run distribution of earnings. Increasing industrialization will create demand for skilled labour. When the supply of unskilled, unorganized, youthful labour goes on and on, no redistribution of incomes will come about, even when higher levels of industrialization are reached (see especially the World Bank Country Report on Brazil, 1979). It is no coincidence, then, that the European labour movement before the Second World War vigorously demanded free access of all population strata to birth control and the legalization of abortion upon indication for precisely such reasons (Goldscheid, 1924).

There is another factor of influence on development, too, that deserves more than a mention in view of recent advances in development theory: the state. Most dependence theories of world development would share Raffer's recent view that peripheral countries should provide domestic markets for their own industries, and establish a strong state. Protectionism and government intervention can be good – depending on the circumstances and the goals one wants to achieve (Raffer, 1987). Some of the literature up to now has presented only preliminary evidence (Heitger, 1985; Landau, 1983, 1986; Marsden, 1983) while theory, formulated at a cross-national level, abounds (Andreae, 1985, 1986; Canak, 1984; Deutsch, 1979b; Duvall and Freeman, 1981; Elsenhans, 1985a, 1985b; Filgueira, 1984; Kalecki, 1979c, 1979d; Lal, 1985; Lipton, 1977; Migdal, 1983; Nitsch, 1979; Nuscheler, 1985a; Ossadtschaja, 1983; Ramirez and Thomas, 1981; Remner and Merkx, 1982; Rueland and Werz, 1985; Saage, 1983; Schuett, 1986; Therborn, 1985). While some empirical studies, using cross-national macro-quantitative evidence, like Heitger (1985), Landau (1986), Marsden (1983) and especially Weede (1983a, 1985a, 1985b, 1986a–1986d) generally confirmed neoliberal tenets about the development block, constituted by a too predominant state, there are other serious studies, like Katz *et al.* (1983) which did not confirm a negative development effect constituted by economic state power. There are two elements which up to now have not been properly treated in macro-quantitative development research.

1. Lipton's and Olson's correct insistence on the fact that often economic measures by the state do redistribute 'upwards'; i.e. to the benefit of the rich, especially in LDCs. Brazil, one of the most anti-egalitarian countries in the world, is predominantly a state capitalist country, with the government controlling 50 per cent of capital in 1984 through state firms (Frieden, 1987: 115).
2. Some countries, like Japan, show a very high measure of state centrality and a restrictive state sector at the same time: more than 68 per cent of Japanese government revenue comes from direct taxes on incomes and property (World Bank, *World Development Report*, 1987: 273), while typically 'drifting' developed and developing countries have excessive government consumption rates, large deficits in relation to their GNP and a large public debt/export earnings ratio.

As for the capitalist world economy (penetration MNC PEN > .01), no clear picture emerges as to the effect of state power on income distribution. Keeping constant the Kuznets curve and time-fitted population dynamics (birth rates, increases in birth rates), note some interesting relationships in Table 7.2:

Table 7.2   Government influence and income distribution

Government size and income inequality keeping constant the Kuznets curve and demographic dynamics	Government expenditures	Government consumption
	per GDP	
Top 20 per cent	−.12	−.06
Next 20–40 per cent	+.10	+.23
Middle 40–60 per cent	+.20	+.20
Lower 60–80 per cent	+.11	+.14
Poorest 20 per cent	−.05	−.06

Source: Partial correlation coefficients with the data from Bornschier, Heintz *et al.*, keeping constant Kuznets curve and demographic process as specified in equation 7.3 (demographic data: World Bank, *World Tables*, 1980) degrees of freedom: 58 (GOVEX); 57 (GOVCONS).

Thus the middle-income groups can be shown to benefit most from government 'redistribution' on the basis of my admittedly limited data source. More profound effects, which really benefit the poorest groups, come from land redistribution, population and educational policy, directed to change the long-run asset distribution (including human capital distribution) .

My final explanation of growth, however, just as in the case of employment dynamics, must make one concession to existing world systems approaches. In a short-term perspective, penetration dynamizes growth and employment, while the long-term perspectives of MNC penetration (weighted by population and proxy capital stock according to Bornschier, Heintz *et al.*) and its effects on growth are negative. Furthermore, there is an interesting interplay between agricultural density, penetration and growth. Tausch (1991a) showed in a path model of economic growth (1965–83 for 82 countries with complete data) that density (intensive agriculture) stabilizes population dynamics and attracts an inflow of foreign capital, while originally MNC penetration 1967 was lower in countries with intensive agriculture. Thus there has been a shift in the penetrating presence of the transnationals, away from the nations with extensive landholding systems, like in Latin America, to the more dynamic areas of the world with intensive agriculture. I also should note the path coefficient of −.29 from density to DYN birth rate, compatible also with the correlation coefficient of −.405 between the two variables in 114 countries with complete data. Density is square rooted to correct for outliers like Hong Kong.

Consistent with Bornschier's approach, my growth explanation now expects a positive association between flows of TNC capital and growth, and a negative association between foreign capital stocks and subsequent economic performance. Consistent with the path model Figure 2.4, the effect of intensive/extensive agriculture is not direct, but via the 'dialectics' of transnational capital penetration, at least in the period in question. The human capital formation effort by the governments concerned will enter the institutional rigidity/state control cycle, in so far as public expenditure on education should have a very large positive association with growth, even when overall increases of state expenditure over time block growth in ageing political systems. Systems age, i.e., the reciprocal date when constitution was given, will affect growth negatively (i.e., date will have a positive B and Beta). Consistent with the re-analysis and critique of the quantitative literature on the state and development, I expect furthermore that direct taxes will have a positive effect on growth, especially in the dynamic perspective (Tausch, 1991a). I would also anticipate a positive association between logged military personnel ratios (adding one to the original values across the whole scale to avoid indeterminate natural logarithms of military personnel ratios per 1000 inhabitants < 1.0) and economic growth. Drifting states tend towards higher government consumption, indirect taxes, growing deficit spending, etc. (Ramirez and Thomas; Tausch, 1991a) (see Table 7.3).

I should not avoid drawing a clear development policy lesson from that equation. Olson's contention about distribution coalitions, ageing political systems and growing state sector influence as a retarding effect on growth is right, but this contention has to be qualified in an important respect. State centrality, a variable which also plays some role in world systems approaches and which is to be measured by direct taxes, the organization of defence (military personnel service ratio), and public educational efforts, strongly favours growth, while dependence on transnational capital first dynamizes growth but later leads towards stagnation, just as predicted by Bornschier in his growth theory. Thus, present-day growth theories, stressing single aspects of the growth process, like Olson's distribution coalition argument, and Bornschier's sophisticated dependency theory, not to forget Weede's long-standing results about defence structure and development, all catch important but isolated aspects of the process, which must be analysed from a more general and inclusive perspective. This perspective, indeed, is the historical effort during the 1920s and 1930s of our century to reform capitalist society with a maximum of social justice and a minimum of state capitalism. It should be noted that my equation explains almost 50 per cent of the economic growth process without any reference to investments and exports, so prominent in other accounts of economic growth. In order to stimulate growth, thus, state sector influence contributing to state centrality must be enhanced, and state sector influence, contributing towards a weakening of state centrality, must be avoided,

Table 7.3   Explaining economic growth, 1965–83

MULTIPLE R	.73257				
R SQUARE	.53666				
ADJUSTED R SQUARE	.48261				
STANDARD ERROR	1.44462				

$n = 68$ countries with complete data

$F = 9.92795$ SIGNIF $F = .0000$

—————————— VARIABLES IN THE EQUATION ——————————

VARIABLE	B	SE B	BETA	T	SIG T
V501	.83483	.22917	.39165	3.643	.0006
(ln (Military Personnel Ratio per 1000 inhabitants + 1)					
DYN14	−.16590	.04581	−.39107	−3.621	.0006
(Increase in government expenditure per GDP 1965–73)					
V232	.62205	.17443	.40368	3.566	.0007
(Public expenditure on education, 1970, as per cent of GNP)					
DYN12	.08312	.02614	.28649	3.180	.0023
(Increase in the share of direct taxes per GDP 1965–73)					
v603	−.09415	.03780	−.22970	−2.490	.0155
(Square root of Bornschier's Capital Penetration Indicator, 1967)					
OL1	.00819	.00371	.21701	2.208	.0310
(Year during which today's constitution went into effect)					
V605	.16773	.07884	.19496	2.128	.0375
(Increase in Capital Penetration Indicators, 1965–73 (square roots))					
(CONSTANT)	−16.12187	7.38025		−2.184	.0328

Data Sources: Bornschier, Heintz et al.; Taylor and Hudson (year of constitution).
Note: At a later date, government expenditure figures should be used, which specifically refer to non-educational government expenditure data only.
z-standardized residuals > 1.499 Jordan, Saudi Arabia, Brazil (+); Nicaragua, Ghana, Senegal, El Salvador (−)
Regression results without these outliers:
$n = 61$; adj. $R**2 = 61$ per cent; $F = 14.41$; $p = .0000$
All predictors retain or improve significance.

especially in ageing political systems within stable boundaries or constitutional frames of reference. World systems ascent is still connected with the logic of world capitalist penetration by its contradictory effect on short-term dynamism and long-term stagnation, but state centrality plays an important and overlooked role in that world system ascent.

My growth explanation 1965–83 accounts very well for certain developments in some nations that cannot be accounted for by other approaches. Let me illustrate the point here: I predicted a 6.4 per cent growth rate per annum in South Korea; in reality it was 6.7 per cent. I expected 4.0 per cent growth in Japan; in reality it was 4.8 per cent. Also, for OECD countries with more dynamic economies in the period in question, like Norway, Greece, Spain, Portugal, Austria, my explanations come off well (residuals < 1.0 per cent growth rate; see also Chapter 10, Table 10.7).

Life expectancy research and research on energy consumption patterns as the main indicator of industrialization level received less attention in quantitative world system research than variables like income distribution or economic growth. However, there is at least one attempt in the literature to develop this theme from a world system theory – the essay by Bunker (1984). This author, who earlier on did research on the Amazon region, radically questions the wisdom of economistic measures of development:

> Conventional economic measures can only capture the exchanges or flows between classes and systems in the monetary terms of wages, prices, and profits, or in the ultimately nonquantifiable notions of abstract labor value. Wages can be shown to create consumption capacity and thence the market demand that makes production and return to capital possible. By focusing on the flows and conversions of matter and energy, however, we can extend these measures directly to the accretion of humanly useful forms of knowledge and social organization, modifications of the physical environment, and the environmental costs of matter-energy transformations, as well as to the production and exchange of commodities. (Bunker, 1984: 62)

In the tradition of Soddy (Martinez-Allier, 1987) I think that any energy use to date is connected with changes in the natural environment of our planet. On the other hand, life expectancy is the indicator which – together with infant mortality – uniquely measures the overall conditions with which human beings are faced in a given society. According to Bunker, there will be crucial differences in the way in which different societies around the globe master the vital problems of energy and life preservation:

Although all conversions of matter and energy heighten entropy, this rate is also highly variable. Human intervention in the conversion of energy and matter accelerates entropy, but it may also direct or embody energy and matter in forms that are both more durable and more humanly useful. Genetic manipulation of plants, the storage of food products, or the treatment of wood are all possible examples. At a more abstract level, human memory and learning – and thus social organization – also involve the partial conservation of experiences that required the consumption of energy but that may make future uses of energy and matter more humanly useful. As well, the capital plant and physical infrastructure of articulated production systems require and embody energy that has been consumed but is being dissipated in ways and at rates that preserve its human utility. (Bunker, 1984: 63)

From such reasoning Bunker develops the notion of the articulated society, the flexible society, and, on the other hand, the extractive region. Flexibility in terms of by-products of energy and articulateness in terms of the ability to produce for internal consumption will be the characteristics of the capitalist centre, while the periphery will become an extractive region, which

loses energy and matter, becomes increasingly simplified, both ecologically and socially, and less adaptive or flexible, both through its simplification and its loss of resources and through the disruption of the natural energy transformation process related to or dependent on the extracted resource. Unable to embody energy in either durable physical infrastructure or in complex and adaptive social organization and technology, it becomes increasingly vulnerable to penetration by and subordination to the productive economies that can concentrate control over nonhuman energies and effectively coordinate much larger and more complex organizations of human energy. (Bunker, 1984: 63)

Socialism, in my view, was characterized precisely by becoming an unproductive economy in that sense. The rising capital intensity of the economic process is but a part of the rising energy intensity of economic growth under socialism. Socialism will be the social formation where the rising secular trend in life expectancy in the world economy will be reversed due to the extractive character of the economic growth process at 'home' and due to the rising subordination to the Western centres in terms of raw energy exports (see also Chapter 8). Natural gas, coal and crude oil will dominate the export structure of what there remains in terms of former world socialism. Basic industries dominated life and architecture and economic structure in the 'internal arena' of Eastern Europe.

There is, of course, a very large number of predictors which are recurrently mentioned in the literature as wielding an influence on life expectancy (Mahadevan, 1986; Srinivasan, 1986; as well as the quantitative life expectancy research by Hicks, 1979, 1981; Rodgers, 1978a, b, 1979; World Bank, *World Development Report*, 1984, Tausch, 1991a). A quantitative re-analysis of this literature on basic human needs resulted in a regression equation, which determines 88.9 per cent of life expectancy in the year 1977 for 103 countries with complete data contained in the World Bank's World Data Tape. The six predictors are: (i) the trade-off between energy consumption per capita and basic human needs satisfaction; (ii) the negative effects of dependence on rural employment; (iii) interestingly enough, also the negative effect of industrial employment; (iv) the negative effect of a high birth rate (time lagged); (v) the negative effect of a lack of doctors (population per medical personnel); and (vi) density affects overall life expectancy in a slightly positive fashion (error $p = 6.97$ per cent), although the influence might very well be non-linear (very high and very low population densities with a negative effect on life expectancy).

The dynamic changes of life expectancy over time were also predicted on the rates of change of the above mentioned predictors and Equations 6.4 and 6.5 of this book. For 102 countries, adjusted $R^{**}2$ is still 52 per cent; all predictors are stable in their effect on life expectancy. The only exception is the effect of the increase of density on the increase of life expectancy over time (Tausch, 1991a). A number of other predictors, quite often mentioned in the literature (Mahadevan, 1986), did not achieve the required statistical significance, among them (i) urbanization level; (ii) calorie consumption per capita; (iii) lack of density of hospital services (population per hospital bed); and (iv) time-lagged female secondary school enrolment ratios.

It was also attempted to estimate a path model of life expectancy increase over time (1960–77) for 67 countries of the world with complete data (Tausch, 1991a). The model determines 64.3 per cent of life expectancy increases over time; besides the 'Plateau curve' of basic human needs the significant predictors are: (i) the negative effects of increases in military expenditures; (ii) the negative effects of an increase in capitalist penetration; and (iii) the negative effects of an increase in birth rates.

Militarism, demographic dynamics and world capitalist penetration thus determine structural violence in the world system (see also Figure 2.5). But this model must be compared with a socio-liberal account of the determinants of life expectancy (over time); and the results of this comparison show the insignificance of that model *vis-à-vis* a socio-liberal explanation.

Deprivation in terms of human development, measured by life expectancy, will be determined here by the absence of a rapid demographic transition (Birdsall, 1980, 1984) and by the joint effect of the state class and the ethnically heterogeneous environment. This idea, which is a continuation of hypotheses voiced by such different authors as R. Kothari (ethnic relative deprivation in the world society) or M. Olson (social discrimination in relatively immobile environments, in conjunction with the effects of state power) finds its explosive illustration by the ethnic tensions in heterogeneous societies with strong state power, such as in the Transcaucasian parts of the former USSR, in Sri Lanka, Ethiopia, or the Indian Punjab. For the cross-national determination of life expectancy, military expenditures lose their significance *vis-à-vis* the negative effect of public investment.

My estimate was calculated for 94 countries with complete data, adjusted $R^{**}2$ reaching 84.2 per cent, and F level being at 99.9 (see Table 7.4).

Here, again, Olson's contention about state sector influence on development in an environment of institutional rigidity is shown to be relevant. In advanced capitalist countries it is institutional age that allows distribution coalitions to emerge, especially in the wake of strong state classes. In world society, ethnic heterogeneity is the institutional background which in a most destructive way contributes to the negative development effects of 'state classes'. Under the condition of an increasing extent of industrialization – in itself first a blessing, and then a threat for the satisfaction of basic human needs – it is the market, and not former state socialism, which still proves to be most successful. This result, however, has to be qualified again in a decisively socio-liberal way. Especially in the LDCs, the position (or rather subjugation) of women in society to a great extent determines the possibility for basic human needs attainment. The position of women in society is measured relatively well by the crude birth rate per 1000 inhabitants, although in future research the validity of alternative measures for that process cannot be excluded. Thus demographic transition is important for two further dimensions of development: redistribution and basic human needs. And I shall analyse its importance for still a third dimension of development: political stability.

The demographic effect also holds over time, although, under the present formulation, the significance of the last two predictors attains > 10 per cent error probability. Without level of life expectancy reached in 1960 as a further control variable, the Beta-weight above 1.0 would disappear (see Table 7.5).

Still more sophisticated politometric research is needed in future, especially regarding the association between changes over time in public investment, ethnic heterogeneity and the life chances of the population as measured by life expectancy. This modelling effort could also shed some light on the causes of political violence in ethnically heterogeneous nations, such as on the Indian subcontinent or in the former USSR. Other indicators

Table 7.4 Explaining life expectancy in 1977

MULTIPLE R	.92207				
R SQUARE	.85022				
ADJUSTED R SQUARE	.84171				
STANDARD ERROR	4.28608				

$n = 94$ countries with complete data

$F = 99.90641$ SIGNIF $F = .0000$

——————————— VARIABLES IN THE EQUATION ———————————

VARIABLE	B	SE B	BETA	T	SIG T
DYN8	10.76153	1.80875	.56358	5.950	.0000
(Energy consumption per capita, 1973 ** ($1/(e^{**}2)$))					
BI1	−.39656	.06165	−.47630	−6.433	.0000
(Crude live birth rate, 1960)					
V245	−4.87947	1.69236	−.13439	−2.883	.0049
(Ethno-linguistic fractionalization index)					
V44	−.07402	.02213	−.13947	−3.344	.0012
(Public investment per total investment, around 1965)					
RJ14	−.22290E−03	.9233E−04	−.18919	−2.414	.0178
(Energy consumption per capita, 1973 ** ($\ln(\pi)$))					
(CONSTANT)	55.46959	6.00210		9.242	.0000

Data Sources: Bornschier, Heintz *et al.*; World Bank, *World Development Reports* and *World Data Tape* (edition 1980) (Life Expectancies, Population Dynamics)
z-standardized residuals > 1.499 Sri Lanka, Costa Rica, Malaysia, Singapore, Panama, Canada(+); Saudi Arabia, Mauritania, Senegal, Libya(−)
Regression results without these outliers:
$n = 84$; adj. $R^{**}2 = 91.9$ per cent; $F = 189.77$; $p = 0$
All predictors retain or improve significance.

of basic human needs confirm the relevance of this socio-liberal model. Here, I analyse employment. My explanation is quite in line here with the more 'dynamic' views of dependence theories (Palma, 1981). Where transnational capital was not tied to an import substitution process but to export-oriented industrialization and 'free zones', employment rates increased considerably. Furthermore, I have to control for population dynamics and its negative effects on employment growth measured in

Table 7.5   Explaining the percentage change in life expectancy, 1960–83

MULTIPLE R	.86696
R SQUARE	.75162
ADJUSTED R SQUARE	.73429
STANDARD ERROR	.04683

$n = 93$ countries with complete data

F = 43.37407   SIGNIF F = .0000

———————— VARIABLES IN THE EQUATION ————————

VARIABLE	B	SE B	BETA	T	SIG T
RJ2	−.42013	.05105	−1.11156	−8.230	.0000
(ln life expectancy, 1960)					
DYN6	−.90521	.21679	−.31287	−4.176	.0001
(Energy cons per capita, 1960 ** $(((1/(e**2))−1))$					
V245	−.06187	.01927	−.20301	−3.212	.0019
(Ethno-linguistic fractionalization index)					
V44	−.47096E−03	.2588E−03	−.10579	−1.820	.0723
(Public investment per total investment, around 1965)					
RJ12	−.05911	.03716	−.11258	−1.591	.1153
(Increase in n-logged crude live birth rates, 1960–77)					
RJ13	−.01229	.01979	−.07871	−.621	.5363
(Energy cons per capita, 1960 ** $(((\ln(\pi))−1))$					
(CONSTANT)	1.90606	.17241		11.055	.0000

Data Sources: See Table 7.4.

Note: Percentage changes were calculated by the difference between the two life expectancies: DYN LEX = $(ln(\text{LEX83})) − (ln(\text{LEX60}))$

z-standardized residuals > 1.499 Syria, Cameroon, Jordan(+); Sierra Leone, Morocco, Pakistan, Malawi(−)

Regression results without these outliers:

$n = 86$; adj. $R**2 = 88.3$ per cent; $F = 108.22$; $p = .0000$

All predictors retain or improve their significance, including population dynamics (error p .002), and the second part of the first derivate of the 'Plateau'-curve (error p .104).

terms of labour force participation rates (LFPRs). Let me summarize the relationship between development level and subsequent growth of the LFPRs: at very early levels of industrialization, employment per total population is lost, a process which continues quite negatively until we reach a stage of around 1100 kg energy cons. per capita for 1960, when employment growth reaches a positive value, continuing thereafter – *ceteris paribus* – at a smooth pace of growth of employment per total population. The most critical stage is between 100 and 1100 kg energy cons. per capita industrialization level, where the other influencing factors become of crucial relevance: an early demographic transition, and a policy *vis-à-vis* the multinationals that avoids import substitution but rather stresses export-oriented investment in 'free zones'. Employment growth was calculated by relating labour force in 1975 and 1965 each to total population, thus yielding overall Labour Force Participation Ratios 1975 and 1965. (LFPR75 − LFPR60) * 100 was then the variable predicted in my regression equation (see Table 7.6).

Politically, it thus emerges that over the time period in question, those countries that most successfully expanded their employment record did exactly what neo-dependency theories describe; i.e., opening their 'human resources' towards the expansion of the model of 'free zones' (see especially Froebel *et al.*, since 1974). Allowing for the trade-off between development level and subsequent employment expansion, demographic pressure played an important further role in the overall determination of employment rates, which in good part explains the different experiences of countries like Taiwan on the one hand and the Philippines on the other.

My thesis was that the demographic process and export-oriented production in 'free zones' dynamizes employment growth, properly allowing for the effects of the level of the development of productive forces on employment.

Next, I aim to explain political violence. Violence and *coups d'état* will be fundamentally related in my approach to the militarization of development and to the strains that this military burden causes for the ability of the government to control the savings rate. This theory of instability has already been presented by Tausch (1991a and 1989a) with a path model and regression analyses on the causes of *coups d'état* 1963–77. Here the reasoning goes further, now including political violence, a theme that was very popular among political science writers especially in the United States in the 1960s and 1970s. Government savings is a central concept here: the more debt that a government has, the lower the government savings rate will be.

Political violence has at last emerged anew as a major theme of cross-national comparative research. After a certain period of stagnation (see also

Table 7.6   Explaining the overall employment rate increases, 1965–75

MULTIPLE R	.78852				
R SQUARE	.62176				
ADJUSTED R SQUARE	.59774				
STANDARD ERROR	1.09403				

$n = 68$ countries with complete data

$F = 25.88993$ SIGNIF $F = .0000$

———————— VARIABLES IN THE EQUATION ————————

VARIABLE	B	SE B	BETA	T	SIG T
RJ12	−3.97923	1.00685	−.41560	−3.952	.0002
(Increase in n-logged crude live birth rates, 1960–77)					
V167	.03648	.01034	.32872	3.528	.0008
(Workforce, employed in free production zones, around 1975, as per mill. of the total labour force)					
RJ13	1.69873	.50108	.41600	3.390	.0012
(Energy cons per capita, 1960 ** $(((\ln(\pi))-1))$					
DYN6	10.19897	3.38996	.33965	3.009	.0038
(Energy cons per capita, 1960 ** $(((1/(e^{**}2))-1))$					
(CONSTANT)	−5.64518	1.06903		−5.281	.0000

Source: Calculated from Bornschier, Heintz *et al.*
Note: Unfortunately, no data about free production zones are available for earlier years. The data about 'free zones' on the Bornschier, Heintz *et al.* data tape are taken from the 'NIDL group' publication (F. Froebel *et al.*, 1977a)
z-standardized residuals > 1.499 Hong Kong, Paraguay(+); Jamaica, Haiti, Burma, Tunisia, Thailand, Philippines(−)
Regression results without these outliers:
$n = 60$; adj. $R^{**}2 = 76.9$ per cent; $F = 50.02$; $p = .0000$
All predictors retain or improve their significance.

literature surveys in Muller, 1985a; Powell, 1981; Tausch, 1991a; Weede, 1975, 1977a, 1987) the availability of new data in Taylor and Jodice has stimulated that research. Muller, having proposed (in 1985a) an approach emphasizing democratic breakdown as a consequence of United States direct military aid, finds (1985b) support for the hypothesis about a causal relationship between inequality and political violence (logged death rate from the cumulated number of the victims of political violence per million population). Still, Muller's account is in an Hibbsian tradition (see also, Weede, 1975, 1977a), explaining the logged political death rate (to which I must add the number 1, because natural logarithms of numbers below 1.0 are indefinite) by: (i) coercion, which first increases, but then deters violence; (ii) past experiences of violence, which still enhance the potential; (iii) communism, which generally deters violence; and (iv) separatism and ethnic fractionalization, which work in favour of violence.

There is, as Muller maintains, a positive trade-off between violence and development (Muller, 1985b: 58), suggesting an increasing potential of violence with ongoing industrialization. Muller explains roughly 50 per cent of variance in his equations by including in his models government sanctions and regime repressiveness. Muller and Seligson further develop the argument by maintaining that not land reform but redistribution will stabilize political systems. Indices of the number of landless peasants showed no sign of being related in a systematic way to violence potential in the course of development (for an excellent account of political violence in contrast to such a thesis, see Rivera y Damas *et al.*, 1984). Their method of estimation of landlessness is based on the following procedure for the some 60 countries of their varying samples:

> Agricultural households without land as a proportion of the total labour force are estimated by multiplying the proportion of agricultural families that are not owner-operators or state farmers by the percentage of the labour force employed in agriculture circa 1970. (from the data file of the *World Handbook of Political and Social Indicators*, see Taylor and Jodice, 1983) (Muller and Seligson, 1987: 447)

The basic fallacy of their estimate consists in overlooking the fact that among the agricultural labour force not registered as 'owner operators' or 'state farmers' there is, at least in industrialized countries, a whole variety of workers and employees registered under 'agriculture' but in fact not differing politically or economically from wage labour in other 'industrial sectors'. Since one-third of the sample are industrialized countries, this has serious effects for the results. Let us look at some of their figures: landless peasants are alleged to comprise 3.6 per cent of the total labour force in Austria, but only 2.9 per cent in the Congo. The 3.6 per cent 'landless peasants' in Austria (and very probably their colleagues in Kent or Michigan as well) must include – else this figure would be sheer nonsense – a high share of workers and employees of large, export-oriented, high-tech, high-profit and high-skill dairy factories owned by companies like the transnational Raiffeisen banking group and other capitalist or mixed economy enterprises, whose workers and employees are not differentiated in any way *vis-à-vis* other workers and employees of a highly developed country. Whatever those 'landless peasants' do economically, they cannot reasonably be compared with landless peasants as development research knows them in the Third World (Feder, 1972).

Although Muller and Seligson derive their political death rates in a similar fashion as in my approach, they work with shorter periods (1968–77) and they *a priori* exclude such violent nations as Kampuchea, Laos, South Vietnam, Pakistan and the Irish Republic (spill-over from the Northern Ireland conflict) from their investigation. Furthermore, they virtually cut off the violence scale (death rate per million population), simply recoding all countries with values > 50 per million as being equal to 50 per million. Thus Zimbabwe (then Rhodesia) and Argentina figure with the same coding, although their rates differ considerably (544 versus 177). Muller and Seligson arrive at the following explanation of the political violence phenomenon. The process of: (i) inequality; (ii) industrialization level; (iii) separatism; (iv) a semi-repressive regime; and (v) past violence experience will increase violence in a country, while government sanctions, like closing down news media of the opposition, preventing them from assembling in public, imprisoning or even killing them, first increase and then deter the growth of violence (Muller and Seligson, 1987: 437). In an essay published in 1988, Muller further develops his insights into the inequality↔violence trade-off by regressing inequality on level and experience of democracy, level of development, and world system status. For varying samples of some five dozen countries with complete data, Muller explains some 25 to 50 per cent of the GINI coefficient. In a way, Muller departs from earlier studies in so far as he uses the variable 'per cent of population under 15 years of age' already used by Bollen and Jackman in their essay published in 1985. This demographic approach to the explanation of inequality is quite in line with other recent published research on income inequality (Tausch, 1991a). But the departure is also in the direction of research on distribution coalitions, since his indicators – years of constitutional rule and years of full democracy – are good indicators of the Olson and Weede process. 'Level and experience of democracy' both affect redistribution in a positive way (Muller, 1988: equation 4.3b, p. 60). Muller again maintains that inequality brings about democratic instability (esp. Muller, 1988: fig. 1: 64).

Bollen and Jackman take up in their essay specification problems of earlier published stability research. They especially reconsider the adequate expression of the functional form of the development→inequality relationship, and the consequences to be drawn from the different types of inequality data used; i.e., household versus individual units. The major result of their study is that political democracy, in contrast to Muller, has no meaningful effect on inequality and vice versa (Bollen and Jackman, 1985: 448). Instead of relying on a 'pure' world systems argument, explaining the absence of democracy by peripheral or semi-peripheral status (Bollen, 1983), they introduce protestant culture (logged per cent of protestants) and British colonial heritage as further explanatory variables and explain about 56 per cent of the variance of democratic performance, based on Bollen's index, 1980. Thus, Third World democracy is a legacy of Protestantism and British colonial influence. Muller's earlier studies, especially 1985a and 1985b, came under criticism in recent literature. Both Weede (1986a–e, 1987) and Tausch (1989a) questioned methodological aspects of Muller's studies. Weede has shown that for the period chosen by Muller, the atypical case of Zimbabwe plays an enormous role and that, without the political system that was then called Rhodesia, Muller's results change quite considerably. Tausch, on the other hand, questioned Muller's account of democratic breakdowns in the Third World by developing a model that is within the growing current of socio-liberal development thought, contrasting with Muller's monocausal explanation of democratic breakdowns by US military influence (Muller, 1985a). Weede summarizes:

Taken together the macro-relationships give little comfort to deprivation theorists. Neither the level of development which is, of course, closely related to average incomes and standards of living, nor income inequality seem to affect violence. Neither average nor relative deprivation seems to matter. (Weede, 1987: 107)

The Muller and Seligson essay (1987) in a way multiplies the difficulties inherent in Muller's earlier contributions. Government sanctions without any plausible cause are weighted by population. Sanctions appear in his equations, 1968–72 (enhancing level of violence, but deterring increases) and 1973–77 (deterring violence). And above all, there is still a broader issue: separatism, regime repressiveness, sanctions and past experience of political violence are all, strictly speaking, part of the dimension of an already violent political system, and hence tautological.

My explanation is the following: state centrality – measured by the capacity of the government to share positively in the savings process – will be enhancing political tranquility, while military expenditures act in favour of political violence. My explanation accounts for 43.3 per cent of political violence in 70 countries under the exclusion of outliers. Muller's results considerably diminish in their explanatory power when taking outliers properly into account. My explanation increases its theoretical power, however, under exclusion of outlying cases. The theoretical direction of this explanation again is socio-liberal in character: state sector debt and military

Keynesianism increase the potential for civil violence in a country. It again emerges that state class influence is detrimental to stability. The socio-liberal character of my explanation emerges from the role assigned to state centrality: government saving increases not only growth but also political stability.

Table 7.7   Explaining log-transformed political death rate, 1963–77

MULTIPLE R	.51241				
R SQUARE	.26256				
ADJUSTED R SQUARE	.24315				
STANDARD ERROR	.62473				

$n = 79$ countries with complete data

$F = 13.52965$ SIGNIF $F = .0000$

───────────────── VARIABLES IN THE EQUATION ─────────────────

VARIABLE	B	SE B	BETA	T	SIG T
V46	−.00796	.00350	−.28538	−2.272	.0259
(General government saving per total saving, around 1965)					
V257	.01151	.00509	.28389	2.260	.0267
(Military expenditures per total government expenditure, around 1965)					
(CONSTANT)	.11725	.13571	.864	.3903	

Data Sources: Bornschier, Heintz *et al.*; Taylor and Jodice (deaths from political violence)

Notes: Deaths from political violence were cumulated from 1948–62 and from 1963–77. Those cumulative numbers were related then to respective population size (1960 and 1970). From these population-weighted figures natural logarithms were taken, first adding the number '1' to the original scores in order to avoid the indefinite expression in case of ln (< 1.0)

z-standardized residuals > 1.49 Nigeria, Lebanon, Rwanda, South Vietnam(+)
Regression results without these 4 outliers:
$n = 75$; adj. $R**2 = 15.2$ per cent; $p = .0010$; $F = 7.64$
Predictor 'government savings' error p. 15.6 per cent
Regression results without all outliers > 0.99 (Egypt, Cameroon, Syria, Taiwan, Dahomey plus Nigeria, Lebanon, Rwanda, South Vietnam):
$n = 70$; adj. $R**2 = 43.3$ per cent; $F = 27.34$; $p = .0000$; Beta-Weights and significance T for the two predictors:

Military Expenditures	+ .57	.00
Government Saving	− .22	.02

Outliers are a problem of all analysis of political violence, since results will be determined by the record of such outlier countries as Zimbabwe, Kampuchea, South Vietnam, Indonesia, Nigeria, even after the log transformation of the original scales. But I think that this approach is well within the range of further results presented in Table 7.8, on the one hand, and secondly Table 7.7 also holds when I exclude all outliers whose z-standardized residual is greater or equal 1.0 above and below the regression prediction. According to the reasoning first put forward in Tausch (1989a), the government savings' dimension can also be taken as a sign about the state classes' freedom of action and room for manoeuvre, to avoid political instability.

In line with Zwicky and Heintz (1982), I do not regard stability as being threatened by party competition. On the contrary, in accordance with some more optimistic formulations of modernization theory (Jodice *et al.*, 1980), past economic dynamic will furthermore enhance stability, while income inequality concentrated at the very top 5 per cent of the social pyramid will increase instability, mainly by alienating the following 15 per cent to 25 per cent of the population (Tausch, 1991a). I developed a path model which includes crude live birth rates and military spending as further model variables. In Figure 7.2, the path model is presented in graphical form:

Figure 7.2   Determinants of illegal executive transfers, 1963–77

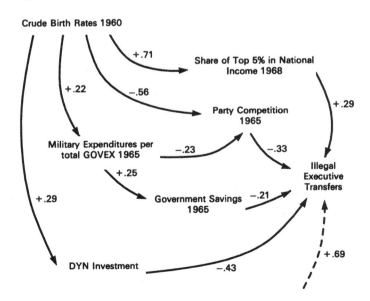

Military spending negatively influences government savings – and through the socio-political might of the military apparatus – also party competition. Birth rates influence income concentration at the top 5 per cent; and – in accordance with Choucri – contribute towards increasing military burden ratios. The regression model confirms these explanations of the direct influence on executive instability 1963–77:

Table 7.8   Explaining the number of illegal executive transfers, 1963–77

MULTIPLE R		.66885			
R SQUARE		.44735			
ADJUSTED R SQUARE		.40130			
STANDARD ERROR		1.37759			

$n = 53$ countries with complete data

$F = 9.71375$ SIGNIF $F = .0000$

—————————— VARIABLES IN THE EQUATION ——————————

VARIABLE	B	SE B	BETA	T	SIG T
V209	.05877	.02759	.24819	2.130	.0384
(Income share of the top 5 per cent in total (household) Incomes, around 1968)					
V42	−.11831	.03853	−.33861	−3.070	.0035
(Growth of domestic investments in the period 1960–65)					
V248	−.14661	.05329	−.32264	−2.751	.0084
(A.S. Bank's indicator of party competition, around 1965)					
V46	−.02246	.00938	−.26220	−2.395	.0206
(General government saving per total saving, around 1965)					
(CONSTANT)	1.84589	1.00648		1.834	.0729

Data Sources: Bornschier, Heintz *et al.*; Taylor and Jodice (for executive transfers in the period 1963–77)
z-standardized residuals > 1.49: Pakistan, Iraq, Thailand, Dahomey, Greece(+);
Chad, Morocco, Brazil, Mexico(−)
Regression results without these outliers:
$n = 44$; adj. $R^{**}2 = 58.7$ per cent; $F = 16.26$; $p = .0000$
All predictors retain or increase their significance.

My rather simple model of political violence also receives some confirmation in a dynamic perspective: the growth of violence over time in the periods 1948–62/63–77 correlates with the predictors in a way expected by my theory. A socio-liberal policy must be based on an appropriate tax structure, relying on direct taxation and a low government sector debt in order to be compatible with long-term political stability. This policy will both increase growth and will avoid too high military expenditures. Growth and low military expenditures in turn directly reduce the increases in political violence over time:

Table 7.9 The growth of political violence

Correlation of . . . with	*Growth of political violence, 1948–77*	*n =* 103	*p =* .070
DYN military expenditures per GOVEX, 1965–73	+.3358	95	.001
Income growth 1960–75	−.1678	103	.045
Government deficit per GDP 1960	+.2107	71	.039
Direct taxes per GDP 1960	−.1784	70	.070

Source: PEARSON CORR, SPSS IX, with the data Bornschier, Heintz *et al.* (predictors) and Taylor and Jodice, 1983. Government deficits calculated by us from the original values about GOVEX and GOVREVENUE; taxes per GDP calculated from the data about DIR TAX per GOVREV and GOVREV per GDP; DYN MILEX per GOVEX 1973–65 is calculated by a simple subtraction; income growth is the difference in real per capita in US$1960–75.

These research results are quite optimistic regarding the development efficiency of a liberal democracy. Weede (1988) in his empirical investigation has shown that democracy is compatible with long-term economic growth, and that average regime repressiveness has a spurious effect on economic growth, once we control for other influencing variables, such as price distortions, the 'Matthew's effect', and the military personnel ratio. Price distortions are operationalized either by the World Bank *World Development Report* 1983 index of price distortions or by Lipton's urban/rural disparity rate. Liberal democracy does not block economic growth, once we take the negative growth effects of price distortions and small professional armies into account. Thus, there might emerge a consensus regarding development alternatives: early and rapid demographic transition will enhance low-key approaches to military expenditures, in turn positively influencing the fiscal soundness of the state. By its effect on distribution, stability will be enhanced, and the state will be less tempted to run large deficits due to the very process of labour supply-induced changes in income distribution. Changing distribution patterns will be in mutual interaction with a change in the organization of national defence (conscription). By avoiding state consumption-oriented government sector deficits, the state can concentrate on the prime task of widening the stock of people of both sexes with higher vocational and non-vocational education, the proper 'mix' being determined largely by the demand on the labour market. State centrality (an expanding tax revenue, direct taxes, conscription, state efforts in human capital formation) too will avoid a large dependence on multinational capital; what TNC investment there is must not be guided towards an import-substituting process, which allies the national elites with transnational capital and builds up barriers against redistribution and employment growth. The market will be especially important in ethnically heterogeneous societies to discipline economically discriminating dominant groups which find easier access to state power. A sweeping land reform and high agricultural prices for family-based production at the very start will assure the success of this 'model'.

An important argument could now assert that such reformist ideas are totally irrelevant *vis-à-vis* the debt crisis in the eastern and southern world periphery. But a careful reading of both neoclassical or dependency oriented accounts of the debt crisis, especially in Latin America, will confirm the central role played by the national peripheral state in determining the degree of indebtedness (Holthus, 1987; Raffer, 1986, 1990; Swedberg, 1986b). The results of this debt crisis are all too clear: investment ratios per GDP decreased over the last decade from 22.6 per cent to 16.3 per cent in Africa and from 21.4 per cent to 14.7 per cent in Latin America. Some observers, most notably Raffer (1990), advocated the application of *Chapter 9* of the *United States insolvency laws* on an international level to come to terms with a crisis that has by now lowered the quality of life for almost 900 million people and led to an increase of infant mortality by 18 million per year. My empirical account of the differing growth of indebtedness in the periphery and semi-periphery (for which the World Bank mentions the data in the *World Development Reports*) again confirms the basic validity of the socio-liberal argument: in stable institutional environments, *it will be unproductive government (consumption) which will enhance the growth of debt*. Countries allied ideologically with the West were particular prone to debt growth due to the ease of access to credit from the transnational private banks after 1973 (Swedberg, 1986b).

Up to now, my indicators of development were relatively familiar in international research on the subject. I now present results which throw some light on the phenomenon of culture in the process of development. Without such an analysis, development theory will become meaningless in an age of growing religious fundamentalism and ethno-religious intolerance.

Table 7.10   Explaining the percentage change in debt service ratios, 1970–83

MULTIPLE R	.51881
R SQUARE	.26916
ADJUSTED R SQUARE	.22442
STANDARD ERROR	3.08304

$n = 53$ countries with complete data

$F = 6.01552$ SIGNIF $F = .0014$

—————————— VARIABLES IN THE EQUATION ——————————

VARIABLE	B	SE B	BETA	T	SIG T
V267	1.05492	.33489	.39449	3.150	.0028
(Degree of 'Westernization' of political UN General Assembly votes, 1970)					
V35	.15804	.07840	.25674	2.016	.0493
(General government consumption per GDP, 1970)					
V254	.41485	.22441	.23129	1.849	.0705
(Haendel *et al.*'s Index of Political Systems Stability, based on 15 indirect measures, 1961–66. Index ranges from -5.98 (very unstable) to +4.56 (very stable)					
CONSTANT	−6.40540	1.93959		−3.302	.0018

Data Sources: Bornschier, Heintz *et al.*; World Bank, *World Development Reports*; *World Data Tape* (various issues) (debt service ratios).
Note: In order not to bias the estimate, increases/decreases of debt service ratios are the residuals from the regression:
DEBT R (1983) $= a + b_1 *$ DEBT R (1970)
z-standardized residuals > 1.499 Costa Rica, Morocco, Ivory Coast($+$); Liberia($-$)
Regression results without these outliers:
$n = 49$; adj. $R**2 = 33.4$ per cent; $F = 9.01$; $p = .0001$. Levels of significance for the first two predictors improve; third predictor (systems stability) still significant at 11.7 per cent level.

Considering the growing evidence of the fact that development in many countries means not only environmental degradation but also forms of social decay (Seager and Olson), it is especially important to consider with all necessary statistical caution the preliminary cross-national evidence about violent death rates and their association with the development process. Certainly, my indicators do not measure intra-family violence, rape and persistent mental violence against women as expressed in divorce case court proceedings. Nevertheless, violent death rates are a serious

indicator of an important aspect of life quality in a country and should not be easily dismissed, especially since psychology lays particular emphasis on data of that kind (Caruso, 1972).

My explanation of violent male death rates starts out from the assumption that commodity concentration could mitigate the all too often occurring outbreaks of politically motivated violence in the narrower sense, while it is strongly associated with violent death rates of males in many ways: by appallingly unsafe work conditions especially in Third World mining, but also by the culture of violence *('machismo')* which is part and parcel of the social reality of the export-oriented classical plantation economy. Conscription lowers violent male death rates significantly (*'ersatz'* character and outlet for potentially aggressive male behaviour), while both development level and public investment are associated in a positive way with that indicator of social decay.

In different degrees, violence against women is a constant feature of life in practically all countries of the world. Apart from the violent death rates according to the WHO classification, a reliable indicator of this process is longer life expectancy for males than for females, as is to be observed in parts of the Indian subcontinent. This is mainly due to overt or covert infanticide committed on girls and the poor nutritional character of food left over for women in the household (Benard and Schlaffer, 1985). Instead of glorifying 'traditional Third World culture' Benard and Schlaffer propose a radical programme of change, directed to female needs, which in a way continues the struggle of social democratic and liberal oriented women in developed countries in the nineteenth and twentieth centuries: i.e., higher legal minimum marriage age, legal protection against all kinds of intra- and extra-family violence, voting rights for women, free access to education and medical care, the right to divorce, etc. World system theories either expect antisystemic movements precisely from traditionalist forces opposed to 'Westernization' (Wallerstein, 1986; Amin, 1986) or specifically endorse 'self reliance' and the strengthening of autochthonous cultures (Raffer, 1987) as a strategy to overcome dependence.

Such diametrically opposed views of Third World culture will be submitted to an empirical test. Is it the process of industrialization that, in conjunction with bureaucratization and the economic power of state classes, leads towards a high level of violent death rates among women, as liberal approaches will contend, or are such death rates a consequence of dependent insertion into the capitalist world economy? Again, my socio-liberal approach to development survives the empirical test: it is not MNC penetration, nor any other form of dependence, but – as socio-liberals expect – the interaction between the state and an immobile and stable institutional environment, which discriminates against population groups

Table 7.11   Explaining violent male death rates (around 1970)

MULTIPLE R	.69850
R SQUARE	.48790
ADJUSTED R SQUARE	.39036
STANDARD ERROR	13.40830

$n = 26$ countries with complete data

$F = 5.00189$ SIGNIF $F = .0054$

————————————— VARIABLES IN THE EQUATION —————————————

VARIABLE	B	SE B	BETA	T	SIG T
V88	.75893	.21575	.67885	3.518	.0020
(Commodity concentration in exports, 1970)					
V44	.29913	.14216	.33809	2.104	.0476
(Public investment per total investment, around 1965)					
V506	10.90949	4.47865	.51944	2.436	.0238
(ln energy consumption per capita, 1970)					
V501	−6.97029	3.53802	−.35031	−1.970	.0622
(ln (Military personnel rate + 1))					
(CONSTANT)	−22.03042	36.17464		−.609	.5491

Data Sources: Bornschier, Heintz *et al.*; UN *Compendium of Social Statistics,* 1980
Note: Violent death rates from motor vehicle accidents, other transport accidents, accidental poisoning, falls, fires, drowning and submersion, accidents caused by industrial work, by firearms missiles, suicide and self-inflicted injury, all other accidents, homicide, war deaths, and from undetermined injuries are cumulated here, following the United Nations practice (AE 138–AE 150 UN WHO classification).
z-standardized residuals > 1.499 Austria, France(+); New Zealand(−)
Regression results without these outliers:
$n = 23$; adj. $R^{**}2 = 72.9$ per cent; $F = 15.78$; $p = .0000$
All predictors retain or improve their significance.

and in the long run endangers growth. The level of development, which increases violence and self-destruction among both sexes, brings about high violent female death rates. This effect is increased by the bureaucratization of the labour force structure: that is, the ever-growing self-repetitious exercise of work on behalf of others (mostly males) in conjunction with economic state power, measured by government expenditures.

Thus, feminist views of the world system, as discussed above (Chapter 3) have to be qualified in one important respect. It is the dependent insertion of a society into the world market as a raw materials exporter, which indeed is very strongly connected with the process of inter- and intra-personal violence, that leads to a high male violent death rate; but at the same time the state machinery and the bureaucratic structure, built up by males, discriminate heavily against socially weaker groups, such as women.

Table 7.12　Explaining violent female death rates (around 1970)

MULTIPLE R	.81814				
R SQUARE	.66935				
ADJUSTED R SQUARE	.62802				
STANDARD ERROR	7.57215				

$n = 29$ countries with complete data

$F = 16.19453$　　　SIGNIF $F = .0000$

————————— VARIABLES IN THE EQUATION —————————

VARIABLE	B	SE B	BETA	T	SIG T
V506	4.85957	2.36844	.32848	2.052	.0513
(ln energy consumption per capita, 1970)					
V203	1.49075	.51318	.42175	2.905	.0078
(Bornschier's Bureaucratization Index measures, at the time point of available data about income concentration, the organizational power distribution in non-agricultural sectors)					
V30	.39008	.20365	.26024	1.915	.0674
(General government expenditure by GDP, 1965)					
(CONSTANT)	−25.39743	14.44294		−1.758	.0914

Data Sources: See Table 7.11.
Note: The bureaucratization index is measured as follows:
BUR = (clerical workers * 100)/(EA population outside agriculture)
Labour Force Data are taken from the various ILO Yearbooks of Labour Statistics
z-standardized residuals > 1.499 France(+); Bulgaria(−)
Regression results without these outliers:
$n = 27$; adj. $R**2 = 69.3$ per cent; $F = 30.32$; $p = .0000$
The first two predictors retain/increase their significance, while GOVEX per GDP attains error probability 15.7 per cent.

Socio-liberals expect that discrimination against population groups and differential wage rates at practically the same productivity for different groups block long-term development (Olson, 1982/85, chap. 6). Thus, as an alternative to feminist world systems theories, I postulate that indicators of discrimination against women will correlate very negatively with long-term economic growth, while feminist world systems analyses maintain that this kind of marginality and repression is necessary within the framework of the logic of capitalist accumulation. My empirical test will be the partial correlation of male privileges in terms of life expectancy *vis-à-vis* female life chances (and hence: structural violence against women in a Galtungian sense) for the year 1960 with economic growth rates 1960–75, keeping constant the 'Matthew's effect' introduced in Equation 6.2, calculated for the year 1960 (ln energy cons. per capita, and ln energy cons. per capita squared). On the basis of Taylor and Jodice I get Table 7.13.

Table 7.13   Structural violence against women and economic growth

	Partial correlation of growth with
Structural violence against Women (1960)	−.3899 (48 DF) $p = .003$

Source: My own calculations from Taylor and Jodice (1983).

I should note that, due to its extraordinary outlying statistic on the Taylor and Jodice data file, I excluded Gabon from this analysis. For the 52 countries with complete data, these three explanatory variables account for adjusted 33.7 per cent of the variance of growth rates 1960–77. To put it in simplest terms: the most blatant form of discrimination against women to be observed in world society, constituted by the lag in life expectancy *vis-à-vis* male life chances, is morally wrong and is economically, like any discrimination, simply counterproductive.

8 A Transition That Never Happened

Eastern Europe and the USSR were capitalist peripheries and semi-peripheries before 1917/1939, and they started being that again in recent months (Chase-Dunn, 1992; Juchler, 1992; Tausch, 1991b). Socialism once was described by some dependency theories as the alternative to periphery capitalism (Amin, 1975). Most dependency theories and later world system approaches do indeed endorse some kind of socialism or other, even if only by implication (Cardoso, 1979). When penetration by transnational capital inhibits long-term economic growth, it is logical to have less dependence from transnational capital, or none at all. Romania had less core capital penetration than Malaysia, and yet its long-term performance compares miserably with Malaysia. When public investment is beneficial for income redistribution, let us enjoy its benefits and expand it while we can; maybe people in the GDR voted with their feet when the mere opportunity arose to go Westward. When peripheral capitalism in the end means stagnation and inequality and the political repression that we saw in countries like South America, it is necessary to think about alternatives. But what can we learn from socialism? The implicit option for socialism that was inherent in most dependency theories, and from which we cannot escape, was spelt out most clearly in Cardoso (1979). That precisely those societies that once were thought by many to be the alternative to periphery capitalism have rejoined the capitalist camp must have the most profound repercussions for dependency theory and all approaches that were inspired by it. The harsh realities of 'real existing socialism' were implicitly or explicitly criticized by many who advocated a socialist alternative, but these arguments were moralistic in nature and avoided the most difficult question: why have these models failed again and again in their development? It might be convenient for the former believer to sigh with almost stoic resignation:

> The economic failure of communism is a failure only relative to the wholly unrealistic expectations and promises of the communists themselves, who thought that they could uplift large demographic masses to match the standards of wealth of the West through a systematic delinking from the global circuits of capital. However, by no stretch of the imagination can this failure be called a failure relative to what has been achieved by regimes that ruled over regions at levels of income

comparable to those of the regions under communist rule, and that did not delink from the global circuits of capital. (Arrighi, 1990: 28)

Wallerstein, to be sure, has gone even further than Arrighi in delinking the crisis of former world socialism from its own, home-made development constraints. Instead of talking about the extensive agriculture systems under former state socialism, the lack of participation and democracy, the fatal interaction between state class control and ethnic heterogeneity, the indirect taxes collected by the state bureaucracies in the former socialist bloc, the historically high population growth in countries like Mongolia, Poland and Albania, the neglected human capital formation and health care systems that in the end had a very heavy price in terms of forgone economic growth, Wallerstein blames liberalism and the West for the collapse of communism in Europe: it is our, and not their defeat, for they were our disciples: 'The true meaning of the collapse of the Communisms is the final collapse of liberalism as a hegemonic ideology.' (Wallerstein, 1991a: 13) Was socialism really that better than periphery capitalism? My approach (see also the earlier studies Tausch, 1989b, 1989c, 1991b) will precisely consist in trying to find out empirically which development tendencies characterized former world socialism in the 1970s and 1980s by international comparison. What effects did socialism have on income distribution, human development, economic growth? The resulting tendencies could be called warning lights because, according to our analysis, the disaster had already taken shape in the two decades before the 1989 revolution; furthermore, it can be shown in this *post mortem* that socialism and the arms race formed an integral unit of world politics which in the end overstretched the system and finally brought it down.

Today, former state socialism has crumbled (at least in Europe), nationalism eroded the process of *perestroika* and of building democracy in the East, and the remaining leaderships committed to maintaining 'socialism' (iron-fist rule), like the one in China (Dittmer, 1989) have not hesitated to use brutal force against their own populations. For some more conservative authors, like Rummel (1990), the record of 'socialism' in China and the former USSR amounts ultimately to the biggest democide in human history with 90 million victims – from forced labour, famine, mass executions and the disrespect of fundamental human rights. Others do not go as far as Rummel, but still would agree that both in China and the former USSR there were millions of victims in mass famines, executions and labour camps. Most analysts – in contrast to many European politicians – were rather sceptical from the outset about the long-term prospects for *perestroika* in the former USSR, mainly because the reforms never did plan to overcome the limitations of Leninism and restrictive democracy (Bialer,

1988; Braun and Day, 1990; Chase-Dunn, 1992; Frank, 1990; Hasegawa and Pravda, 1990; Holloway, 1989; Juchler, 1992; Leante, 1989; Nolte, 1990; Tausch, 1989a–1991b; White, 1990; just to mention a few). The fate of Soviet Central Asia with its rapidly growing population – nearly half the conscripts in the CIS Army are already of Central Asian origin – will determine to a large extent the world political orientation of the CIS, and the clash between Leninist and now Great Russian nationalism with nationalism and religious fundamentalism in the Southern parts of the CIS is only at its beginning (Roí, 1990).

But not everybody shared this view of former world socialism. One of the most current approaches within the radical political economic tradition to former world socialism is Griffin's attempt to formulate a theory of alternative development. For Griffin, communal tenure systems are the key towards understanding that

> it is not coincidental that countries with well developed communal tenure systems have tended to perform better than the average. In fact, there are good reasons to believe that communal tenure systems have an advantage by: (i) ensuring that labour is fully employed, (ii) achieving a more equal distribution of income, (iii) sustaining a high rate of capital accumulation, (iv) providing a framework for industrializing the countryside and (v) promoting grass-root participation in the organization and delivery at the local level of a wide range of social services, including educational, family planning and health facilities. (Griffin, 1987: 12–13)

On another occasion, Griffin's hypothesis sounds even more far-reaching:

> communal systems are characterized by a set of features which makes them attractive to those concerned with combining sustained growth of output, the alleviation of poverty, the provision of basic needs and the creation of an egalitarian society. The adoption of a communal land tenure system does not guarantee that any of these objectives will be attained, but it does make their attainment somewhat easier. (Griffin, 1987: 80)

This optimism regarding the development efficiency of socialism also characterized other currents of development research in the 1970s and 1980s, especially in Scandinavia and in German-speaking European countries (Brundenius, 1979; Flechsig, 1985–89; Senghaas, 1977; Tausch, 1976). Adherents of the world systems approach were more cautious from the beginning in advocating 'real socialism' as a strategy for world economic ascent (Froebel *et al.*, 1977a, b).

Eastern Europe before the convulsions of what Wallerstein (1984) called the long world war in our century 1914–45, constituted part of the world periphery and semi-periphery with the notable exception of what would later become the CSFR and the former GDR. For Wallerstein, exploitation and the lack of political and civil liberties, sexism and racism in the societies that often called themselves 'real socialist', were a consequence of the fact that those societies until today formed part of the peripheral and semi-peripheral areas of the world economy (Wallerstein, 1984: 94–5). To illustrate what Wallerstein had in mind when he spoke of the semi-peripheral status of most socialist economies in the international division of labour, I need only recall that products of mining, food and fuels made up 85 per cent of Soviet and 54 per cent of other Eastern European exports to the developed OECD economies in 1986, before the onset of the revolutionary upheavals of the late 1980s (UN ECE, 1988: 294). Equally important, imports from the developed capitalist centres just looked like those in any country of the periphery: 81 per cent of former USSR imports and 77 per cent of other Eastern European imports from the West were final products, one third of the total consisting of products of advanced technology. Trading coal, iron, food and natural gas for machines and machine-making-machines was the world economic role of Eastern Europe yesterday, and it continues so today (UN ECE, 1988: 296–300). Needless to say, semi-peripheral status increases economic long-term vulnerabilities: the terms of trade for Eastern Europe and the former USSR have quite dramatically moved against the East from about 1982–83 onwards. Total net debts now amount to well over US$ 170 billion, and net debt service payments to the West in its dealings with the East fatten Western balances to the tune of yearly US$ 6–8 billion, almost a third carried by Poland alone (UN ECE, 1988: 305). Poverty rapidly increased in the socialist world during the late 1980s and affected 14 per cent of the population in China (1988), 23 per cent of the population in Poland, and 25 per cent of the population in Yugoslavia (1987) (World Bank, *World Development Report*, 1990: 43). In a way, this kind of dependency theory analysis of Soviet socialism was already inherent in Polanyi's 'Great Transformation', where its author said:

Seemingly in the twenties Russia stood apart from Europe and was working out her own salvation. A closer analysis might disprove this appearance. For among the factors which forced upon her a decision [in the direction of authoritarian rule] in the years between the two revolutions [the destruction of absolutism in 1917 and the the establishment of a socialist economy in the thirties] was the failure of the international system. By 1924 'War Communism' was a forgotten incident and Russia had re-established a free domestic grain market, while maintaining state control of foreign trade and key industries. She was now bent on increasing her foreign trade, which depended mainly on exports of grain, timber, furs, and some other organic raw materials, the prices of which were slumping heavily in the course of the agrarian depression which preceded the general break in trade. Russia's inability to develop an export trade on favorable terms restricted her imports of machinery and hence the establishment of a national industry; this, again, affected the terms of barter between town and countryside – the so-called 'scissors' – unfavorably, thus increasing the antagonism of the peasantry to the rule of the urban workers. In this way the disintegration of world economy increased the strain on the makeshift solutions of the agrarian question in Russia, and hastened the coming of the kolkhoz. The failure of the traditional political system of Europe to provide safety and security worked in the same direction since it induced the need for armaments, thus enhancing the burdens of high-pressure industrialization. (Polanyi, 1944: 247–8)

Polanyi's thesis about the interaction between the capitalist world economy and the chances for reform in the Russian/Soviet semi-periphery can be extended well back into the sixteenth century. There was a constant recurrence of repression and tyranny in Russia before 1917 during a Kondratieff depression (see also Tausch, 1991b, for more politometric evidence on the Kondratieff cycles since the eighteenth century). The new model emerging out of a depression and developing the productive forces each time was an authoritarian one (Iwan IV; Michael III; Peter I; Elisabeth; Nikolas I; the imperialist expansion of Russia 1883–92 and finally Stalin), while during the end of Kondratieff cycles, especially during temporary recoveries before depressions, the regime in Russia/the former USSR tends towards indecision, crisis and often also reform (Boris Godunow; the split in the Orthodox Church; the Nobility's Victory 1730; Katharina's Constituent Assembly; the Great Reforms after 1861; Lenin's New Economic Policy, and finally Gorbachev).

There is an increasing awareness among social scientists from all quarters about the parallels between the Eastern European and the capitalist southern peripheries (Poznanski, 1986; Tyson, 1986). That parallel was the reason why even early on world systems research took up a far-reaching debate on socialism, which was dominated by three basic approaches. This debate is all the more important because the reform communist tradition, like Afanassjew, Aganbegjan, Gorbachev and Mlynar, not only neglected this topic in their writings, but even welcomed further integration into the capitalist world economy.

The first, a dependency theory model of socialism, would assert with authors like Chase-Dunn and Frank, presented in the Bibliography, that, whatever the reasons for the re-opening of the once ascending nations of the East to the capitalist world market, this renewed world market linkage blocked a fruitful development to the benefit of large sections of the population because:

> they (i.e. socialist states) challenge the cultural hegemony of capital, but not very effectively, because their political ideas and institutions reflect their defensive position in the capitalist world-economy ... Our discussion and critique of previous Marxist conceptions of socialism focuses on the lack of attention paid to the importance of the scope of capitalism as a system ... In a strong dynamic capitalist world-economy, the transition to socialism requires political organization on a scale capable of overcoming, rather than simply responding defensively to, the market forces and political-military exigencies of capitalism. (Chase-Dunn, 1982c: 48–9)

> All the talk about the 'economic crisis' in the Soviet Union proving that state-led economic development is a flop is completely wrong. The current economic crisis has political, not economic causes. The state-led model of development was a great success by most of the standard measures of 'development' both within the Soviet Union and in Eastern Europe. Stalinism rapidly industrialized, urbanized, and educated these societies. Their rates of growth in the 1950's and 1960's were among the highest in the world . . ., and the levels they achieved were high, especially if we compare them with other semiperipheral countries. (Chase-Dunn, 1992: 35)

This hypothesis about the defensive position of former world socialism will be challenged in this chapter mainly on the grounds that former world socialism constituted a world-wide military power system allied with different distribution coalitions, accounting for roughly half the world arms transfers to the South in the 1980s (US ACDA, 1988: 127).

There has been a small current of opinion in the world-system tradition, most prominently represented by A. Szymanski, which maintained the former, pre-*perestroika* 'official' Eastern European view. The former USSR presented for him a model of growth with equity. Some others discern such a model only in socialist LDCs (see Brundenius's now classical essay on Cuba, 1979). There was, according to Szymanski, some USSR reopening to the world market, but at least for the USSR it was not significant; growth had been more rapid than in the West, and its fruits were distributed more equally than in Western capitalism. Grain imports were mainly caused by positive changes in consumer behaviour (meat), there was no such thing as USSR exploitation by direct investment or unequal exchange with the south and, last but not least, former USSR foreign policy, by and large, was class conscious and supported the progressive forces around the world. There was nothing like an alarming dependence of the East on the West, at best only linkages like those between Europe and the Arabic world in medieval times before the emergence of the world capitalist system. Eastern Europe was not a periphery, but an external arena to world capitalism, just as, for Wallerstein, Russia was such an external arena during the sixteenth century (Wallerstein, 1974):

> The long-term tendency of the socialist world system is toward increasing differentiation from the world capitalist system in terms of values, social institutions, political processes, and economic forms. Once the Soviet Union overtakes the United States in terms of living standards, which at current rates of growth will occur in about a generation, Soviet society can be expected to become even more insulated from the economic and ideological influence of the West. The temptations of the West that have been principally responsible for the minor Soviet emigration and a certain prestige of Western lifestyles in the USSR should then disappear, perhaps to be replaced by a counterflow of emigrants and the attraction of the now higher (and more humane) life-style of the East for the West. (A. Szymanski, 1982: 82)

Amen. The third position, still within the framework of a world systems approach, stressed the need for internal reforms and the danger of learning pathologies in (former) socialist countries. This position is a link between the world systems debate and the reform communist movement, represented internationally by authors like Z. Mlynar. The clear counter-position to the other two approaches above is best represented in the quotation from A. Abonyi:

> In addition to the economic imperatives, the efficiencies and economic growth afforded by the reassimilation into the capitalist world-economy have political requisites. The contradictions associated with post-1945 development have enveloped most East European regimes in a continuing battle for legitimation that reached crisis proportions during the 1970s in countries such as Poland. To be sure, the crisis situation was exacerbated by the re-establishment of production and trade linkages with a turbulent and recession-prone capitalist world economy. However, roots of present difficulties can be traced back to the principles of Soviet-type industrialization and the inflexibility they have produced in resolving the enduring

economic problems in the region. The problem of legitimacy arose at the outset, in the 1940s, when these regimes were installed to initiate a Soviet-type socioeconomic transformation for which there was little indigenous support. (A. Abonyi, 1982: 193–4)

Since both the requisites of intensive industrialization and the growing consumer demands, squeezed out by increasing investment funds, could not be met simultaneously, Eastern Europe turned towards the West.

But even the most massive infusions of Western finance and technology in the 1970s could not make the Eastern European economies more effective, basically because the need to conform to former USSR norms and values within the Eastern economic bloc, CMEA, provided few opportunities for reforms in central planning (see Abonyi, 1982: 195–6). For Abonyi, the 'socialist world' is withering rather than emerging, and the problems are made even worse by recession in the West and increased competition from the South.

For socio-liberal approaches to socialist development, on the other hand, the problems of socialism increased with a system's age and with the already achieved development level (Senghaas, 1981). Their explanation of the downfall of socialism integrates elements of social cybernetics theory in the tradition of K. W. Deutsch:

> Wherever power is monopolized, there is an imminent risk of self-isolation of leadership groups from their own societies. Precisely in a society without private enterprise, the resulting social distance has considerable negative consequences with respect to the effectiveness of self-steering mechanisms. Such self-isolation results in the weakening of reality-testing as shown theoretically by social cybernetics and in practice by socialist societies. Without participation, publicly relevant communication atrophies, information sources run dry and motivations wither. In consequence, the basis for a down-to-earth assessment of reality by leadership groups shrinks and their chance of controlling political, social and economic processes rationally is impaired. The more they lay claim to infallibility, the more their loss of reality is translated into pathological learning. How uncertain such leadership groups are objectively, or feel subjectively, is revealed by the expansion of the internal security machine and the militarization of society. (Senghaas, 1981: 298)

A transition from the despotic phase of socialist development to social emancipatory socialism seemed to be improbable under such conditions. Rather, the maximum reform possible would consist in the establishment of a 'mature' socialist class society, with 'mature' patterns of institutionalized conflict settlement. The contradictions of socialist development would have to be freely admitted, and the political organization of the differing interests conceded to be legitimate.

The implications for development theory are omnipresent. Most of the Left, in developed and underdeveloped countries alike, recall J. Galtung's article on imperialism and structural violence (1971), which pronounced that imperialism causes the disparities of life chances. But what happens, then, when the life chances – owing to alcoholism, double or even triple work, environmental pollution – of entire segments of the population began to stagnate, and even medium developing market economies threatened to overtake the once so rapidly developing Eastern European nations?

Table 8.1   Health in Eastern Europe, 1965–86, as a central indicator of development performance

Country	Life expectancies at birth (years)			
	Male		Female	
	1965	1986	1965	1986
Hungary	67	67	72	75
Bulgaria	66	69	73	75
former CSFR	64	66	73	75
former GDR	67	68	74	75
Poland	67	69	72	76
Romania	66	68	70	73
former USSR	66	64	74	73

Source: Own compilation from *World Development Report*, 1988.

I represent the empirically observable patterns of female and male life expectancy in Eastern Europe from 1965 to 1986 in Figure 8.1 and Figure 8.2, on the basis of World Bank data, contained in the *World Development Report* (1988).

The outbursts of ethnic violence in the southern parts of the former USSR have drawn world-wide attention to the patterns of socialist development prevailing in that region, once regarded as an excellent performer in the context of the whole of West Asia (McAuley, 1985). *Glasnost* helped to give a more realistic picture of Russian realities. On the basis of the Russian debate, carried out in such media as *Prawda, Izvestija, Turkemnskaya iskra* etc., Bohr (1988) put the figure for infant mortality in the Karakalpak region, the poorest region of the whole CIS, at 83 per 1000 live births, i.e. higher than the average in Brazil, Kenya or Honduras in 1983 (Grant, 1986:

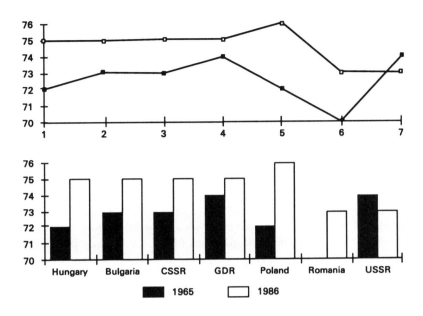

Figure 8.1   Female life expectancy in Eastern Europe, 1965–86

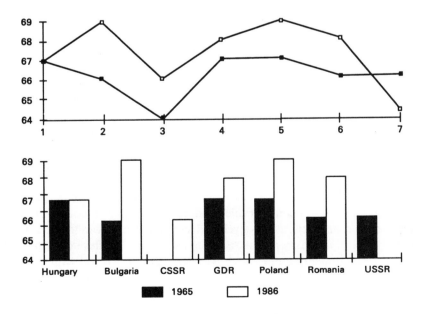

Figure 8.2   Male life expectancy in Eastern Europe, 1965–86

154). Owing to the environmental degradation caused by the massive use of chemicals such as Butifos in the cotton-growing regions, 8 out of 10 children born in the Karakalpak region on the southern shore of Lake Aral are already ill, in one form or another, from their infancy onwards. Some 104 major cities in the former USSR are heavily polluted, and there are no less than 4.5 million registered alcoholics and a further 'normal' 22 million alcoholics. More than 20 per cent of the population live below the official poverty line; each year there are more than 8 million registered abortions due to the lack of available contraceptives (Trehub, 1987–89; Bohr, 1988; Tausch, 1989b).

Only Soviet Armenia (before the earthquake and the influx of thousands of refugees from the pogroms in 1988) had any life expectancy pattern similar to advanced Western countries, i.e., a male life expectancy of 70.5 years and a female life expectancy of 75.7 years in 1985–86 (G. Meyer, 1989: 602). Other regions of the former USSR, among them the entire Republic of Turkmenistan, had a mortality pattern typical of a developing country. The importance of cross-national comparisons of life expectancy patterns also emerges from an analysis, written in the radical political economy tradition, quoted at the beginning of this chapter:

> Yet is clear that even the poorest countries are in principle capable of alleviating the worst forms of poverty. China demonstrates this beyond any shadow of a doubt. For example, life expectancy in China is 67 years whereas it is 52 in India; the infant mortality rate is 71 per thousand in China whereas it is 121 in India (Griffin, 1987: 43).

Senghaas (1981) in a similarly worded and dramatic comparison outlined his hypothesis of the beneficial effects of the first phase of socialist development. What would have happened to the (former) socialist countries without any socialist transformation? His answer, then, was that those countries would all belong to the problem cases of international development policy. China would not differ fundamentally from Brazil or India. The entire non-coastal hinterland of China would be an enormous poverty-stricken region like the north-east of Brazil. Without socialism, China's agriculture would be disaster-prone, as in the past; North Korea, for its part, would still be an enclave economy specialized in the exports of minerals, dependent on considerable food imports; Albania would certainly be numbered among the least-developed countries, and would have sunk more or less to the status of a recipient of charitable development aid: 'Socialist development cannot work wonders. But peripheral capitalism is no alternative to the socialist development of former peripheral-capitalistic societies' (Senghaas, 1981: 297–8).

Compelling as such a comparison might sound, another 'hypothetical scenario' (Senghaas, 1981: 297) must be sketched here. This scenario does not compare countries across continents, but rather starts out from the region about which the original Brenner–Wallerstein debate was all about (see Chapter 4'); i.e., the Baltic and its relations with the capitalist world economy (see also the map in Figure 8.3).

Figure 8.3 Life quality under different development models: the case of the Baltic states (infant mortality, 1986)

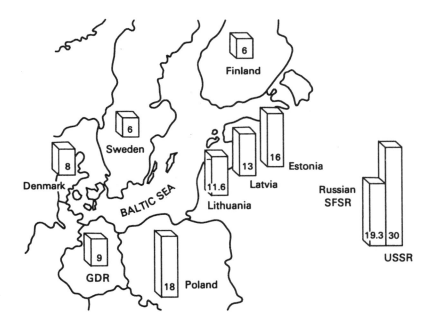

Source: World Bank data; Bohr, 1988; Trehub, 1987a, b. Figure designed with the help of the Department of Geography, University of Hawaii.

Some parts of the former socialist countries (Mecklenburg in the former GDR, large parts of Poland and the Baltic coast of the former USSR) were for some period part of the Swedish empire; on the other hand, Finland from 1809 to 1917 was a poor and underdeveloped part of Russia. Could Western capitalism, welfare style, have developed the Baltic states in a more rapid and equitable way? The comparison between the socialist and capitalist nations around the Baltic becomes all the more important, since the three Baltic republics joined the USSR only as a consequence of the Hitler-Stalin Pact in 1940, and thus did not share the socialist project of the former USSR for the difficult twenty-two years during the period 1917–39, with their civil war and the hunger years of the 1930s. My comparison, it must be emphasized, is just a beginning; it raises a question which I hope will be taken up by historically oriented regional geography in the not too distant future. The potential results of comparative research into the development patterns of the Baltic states, however, are very important from a theoretical point of view – therefore the comparison of development indicators looks at all the coastal states of the Baltic sea: Denmark, the former GDR, Sweden, Poland, Finland, the former USSR, from west to east (see Table 8.2).

Table 8.2   Development performance in the Baltic region

Development indicator	Denmark	Sweden	SF	Former GDR	Poland			Former USSR
Infants born with abnormally low weight	6%	4%	4%	6%	8%			8%
Infant mortality per 1000	8	6	6	9	18	Estonia:	16	
						Lithuania:	11.6	
						Latvia:	13	
						all USSR:	30	
Maternal mortality	4	4	5	17	12			—
University education rate	29	38	33	31	17			21
Female life expectancy	78	80	79	75	76	Estonia:	74.9	
						Lithuania:	75.9	
						Latvia:	74.5	
						all USSR:	73.3	
Male life expectancy	73	74	72	68	68	Estonia:	65.5	
						Lithuania:	66.8	
						Latvia:	65.5	
						all USSR:	64.2	

Source: Own compilations from Trehub, 1987a; Grant, 1986; World Bank, *World Development Report*, 1988; Meyer, 1989.

Finland's development performance would merit very special attention here. In the nineteenth century it was the only country of the Western world ever to have continuously belonged to the Czarist empire, and after 1917 it was torn apart by civil war and political instability. After the Second World War the country did not receive Marshall Plan aid and yet followed a market-oriented development path under strong influence of a social democratic party and the trade unions (Senghaas, 1982f). Its world political status was specially attractive to countries like Poland and the Baltic republics for some years, since the security interests of the former USSR were satisfied by a friendship and defence treaty while, internally, the basic guiding principle of Finland's political economy is a capitalist system with strong elements of a social welfare state in the framework of a pluralist Western democracy. Back in 1965, the country was still more dependent on agricultural employment than the former GDR or the ex-CSFR, and was not too distant from the former USSR in its low degree of 'modernization' (24 per cent of agricultural employment in 1965 *vis-à-vis* 34 per cent in the whole former USSR). On nearly all social and economic accounts, Finland has overtaken its socialist Baltic neighbours, thus offering a model that is neither periphery capitalist nor state socialist, but politically pluralistic and economically liberalist in the framework of world political neutrality and a social welfare state. The data from Table 8.2 become all the more impressive since the former GDR, before the Second World War, was an integral part of a capitalist centre, the German Reich, including the industrial metropoles Berlin, Leipzig and Dresden. By contrast, on all accounts, Finland as an entire nation was poor (Senghaas, 1982f) and a typical semi-periphery. But in all three Baltic republics of the former USSR, infant mortality was almost double or even higher than in Finland.

I also think that a good way of comparing Soviet social performance consists in looking at social welfare achieved in countries directly neighbouring the European part of the former USSR. The results of such a comparison are reported in Table 8.3.

In terms of life expectancy, all European republics of the former USSR ranked poorer than their socialist or capitalist neighbours, and in terms of infant mortality only the Ukraine performed better than Poland and Hungary. It was quite typical that, between 1971–72 and 1985–86, the Central Statistical Administration simply suspended the publication of figures on life expectancy, because these were showing a trend downwards. If there is a problem, 'cover it up' was the policy of the Brezhnev years (Trehub, 1987b).

Throughout the former USSR there were for many years no doctors, only nurses, on duty in maternity homes at night, which is precisely the time when most women give birth. No wonder, then, that in the former USSR infant mortality was higher than in 50 other industrialized and semi-periphery countries of the world. Population-weighted averages for Eastern Europe tell an even more striking story about the stagnation that crept into Eastern European development from the middle 1960s onwards until the

Table 8.3   Social performance in the different former Soviet republics and their neighbouring countries in Europe

SSR/Neighbours	Male life expec.	Female life expec.	Infant mortality
(a) Northern Europe			
RSFSR (aggregate)	63.8	74.0	19.3
Lithuanian SSR	66.8	75.9	11.6
Latvian SSR	65.5	74.5	13.0
Estonian SSR	65.5	74.9	16.0
Belorussian SSR	66.7	75.5	13.4
Norway	74	80	9
Finland	72	79	6
Poland (aggregate)	68	76	18
Sweden	74	80	6
(b) East Central Europe			
Ukrainian SSR	65.9	74.5	14.8
Poland (aggregate)	68	76	18
CSFR	66	75	14
Hungary	67	75	19
(c) Southeastern Europe			
Moldavian SSR	63.1	69.5	26.4
Romania	68	73	26

Source: G. Meyer, 1989 (USSR data); World Bank (1988) World Development Report.

final onset of the crisis of socialism in the late 1980s. In graphic terms, the results of this comparison are presented in Figure 8.4.

A. Szymanski's world systems approach to socialism maintains that the socialist world system was characterized by social development. 'Soviet internal economic, social, and political processes are qualitatively different from those of the West. For example, their income distributions, especially in their higher and lower reaches, are qualitatively more equalitarian than those of the West' (Szymanski, 1982: 79). But income distribution in the (former) socialist countries was not qualitatively very different, even according to estimates based on the official data, from advanced capitalist or more egalitarian underdeveloped countries. The 'second' economy was not covered by the data reported in Table 8.5. The share of the poorest 20 per cent in total net household per capita incomes was, in comparison with the share of the rich 20 per cent (see Table 8.5).

Figure 8.4   Life quality under different development models: the USSR and its European neighbours (infant mortality, 1986)

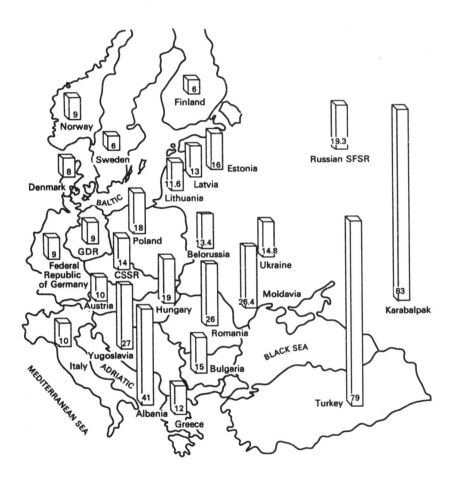

Source: World Bank data, Bohr, 1988; Trehub, 1987a, b. Figure designed with the help of the Department of Geography, University of Hawaii.

Table 8.4   The challenge to socialist social performance: life expectancies, infant mortalities

World region	Population weighted averages for					
	Life expectancies				Infant mortality	
	Male		Female		1965	1986
	1965	1986	1965	1986		
PR China	50	68	56	70	90	34
India	46	57	44	56	151	86
Low income countries, including China and India	47	60	50	61	122	69
Lower middle income countries	47	57	50	61	133	77
Upper middle income countries, among them:	58	64	62	70	83	50
South Korea	55	66	58	73	63	25
Western capitalist countries	68	73	74	79	24	9
High income oil exporters	48	62	51	66	138	62
Socialist non-member countries of World Bank	65	65	72	73	33	30

Source: Own compilations from World Bank, *World Development Report*, 1988: 324–5.
Note: Categories established by the World Bank:
Low income < 450 $GNP per cap. in 1986
Lower middle-income 451–1750 $
Upper middle-income 1751 + (excluding Western capitalist)
High income oil exporters: Libya, Saudi Arabia, Kuwait, U.A.E.
Western capitalist: Spain, Ireland, Italy, NZ, Belgium, UK, Austria, NL, Japan, France, Finland, FRG, Australia, Denmark, CND, Sweden, Norway, US, Switzerland.

Table 8.5 The challenge to socialist social performance: share of the poorest 20 per cent in total per capita household incomes in comparison with the top 20 per cent in all countries of the world with available data

Country	Income share of the Poorest 20% (%)	Richest 20% (%)
Bangladesh (1981–82)	6.6	45.3
India (1975–76)	7.0	49.4
Kenya (1976)	2.6	60.4
Zambia (1976)	3.4	61.1
Sri Lanka (1980–81)	5.8	49.8
Indonesia (1976)	6.6	49.4
Philippines (1985)	5.2	52.5
Ivory Coast (1985–86)	2.4	61.4
Egypt (1974)	5.8	48.0
Thailand (1975–76)	5.6	49.8
El Salvador (1976–77)	5.5	47.3
Peru (1972)	1.9	61.0
Turkey (1973)	3.5	56.5
Mauritius (1980–81)	4.0	60.5
Costa Rica (1971)	3.3	54.8
Brazil (1972)	2.0	66.6
Malaysia (1973)	3.5	56.1
Mexico (1977)	2.9	57.7
Hungary (1982)	6.9	35.8
Portugal (1973–74)	5.2	49.1
former Yugoslavia (1978)	6.6	38.7
Panama (1973)	2.0	61.8
Argentina (1970)	4.4	50.3
South Korea (1976)	5.7	45.3
Venezuela (1970)	3.0	54.0
Trinidad & Tobago (1975–76)	4.2	50.0
Israel (1979–80)	6.0	39.9
Hong Kong (1980)	5.4	47.0
Spain (1980–81)	6.9	40.0
Ireland (1973)	7.2	39.4
New Zealand (1981–82)	5.1	44.7
Italy (1977)	6.2	43.9
UK (1979)	7.0	39.7
Belgium (1978–79)	7.9	36.0
NL (1981)	8.3	36.2
France (1975)	5.5	42.2
Australia (1975–76)	5.4	47.1
FRG (1978)	7.9	39.5
Finland (1981)	6.3	37.6
Denmark (1981)	5.4	38.6
Japan (1979)	8.7	37.5
Sweden (1981)	7.4	41.7
Canada (1981)	5.3	40.0
Norway (1982)	6.0	38.2
USA (1980)	5.3	39.9
Switzerland (1978)	6.6	38.0

Source: World Bank (1988) *World Development Report*: 310–11.

The more egalitarian Western developed and underdeveloped societies tended to discriminate even less against the poorest 20 per cent than 'real socialism'. Trehub (1988), Markos (1988), and Vinton (1988), could show in articles based on official documents and census materials, that poverty spread during the latter half of the 1980s in the former USSR, Hungary and in Poland. Single-parent families, households with many children and old-age pensioners particularly were poor by any standards, and also according to the official statistics. Contrary to state socialist thought, capitalist systems with an egalitarian rural asset distribution and relatively good access for females and the poor to higher education showed a considerable degree of equality, reaching its optimum in the political cultures of Western Europe and Japan. Certainly the equality success of liberal capitalism and the rapid growth experience of some capitalist countries, like Scandinavia or Japan, after the Second World War, provide the basis for many debates to come between the new, socio-liberal development theory and earlier models. In times of *Glasnost* we all of a sudden came to know that there are 57 million poor in the former USSR.

According to the World Bank figures for 1988 there were quite a number of progressive or 'socialist' countries which had severe problems with lowering or even keeping constant their infant mortality rate. It is instructive to compare their performance with some capitalist nations, which, back in 1965, had similar infant mortality rates (see Table 8.6).

Table 8.6   Infant mortality decline 1965–86 in capitalist and socialist nations with about equal infant mortality rates in 1965

Country	Infant mortality 1965	Infant mortality 1986
Ethiopia	165	155
Tanzania	138	108
Guinea	196	148
PD Yemen	194	142
Mongolia	88	47
former USSR	28	30
for comparison:		
India	151	86
Costa Rica	72	18
Spain	38	11
Italy	36	10

Source: World Bank, *World Development Report*, 1988, Table 33. Figures for South Yemen infant mortality rate in 1965: World Bank, *World Development Report*, 1987.

All the Eastern European countries except the former GDR (infant mortality per 1000 live births: 9) had a higher rate of infant mortality than Spain and New Zealand, the negative record-holders among the Western nations. Environmental pollution, alcoholism and poor health system performance made the socialist human development situation in many ways similar to that of middle-income LDCs (see Table 8.7).

Table 8.7   Infant mortality and life expectancy patterns in semi-periphery nations

Country	Infant mortality	Average life expectancy
Chile	20	71
Uruguay	28	71
Hungary	19	71
Portugal	18	73
Poland	18	72
Panama	24	72
Argentina	33	70
South Korea	25	69
Greece	12	76
Hong Kong	8	76
Singapore	9	73
Romania	26	71
Albania	41	71
Bulgaria	15	72
North Korea	25	68
Mongolia	47	64
former USSR	30	70
by contrast:		
OECD nations (pop. weighted)	9	76

Source: World Bank, *World Development Report*, 1988.

Mongolia's record was especially depressing, since that nation, from 1924 onwards, was ruled by a Communist Party and was, after the former USSR, the world's second nation to 'reach the historical stage of socialism'. Behind those historical figures are the mounting social problems of the East and the ascent of many periphery nations.

In that context, I cannot escape mentioning the – paradoxically enough – good record of the repressive regime in Chile in lowering infant mortality rates and in changing mortality patterns. This process has not only been reported by the World Bank, but also by social scientists working for the political opposition in Chile (Raczynski and Oyarzo, 1981). From their thorough analysis it follows that, in real terms, state sector health expenditures increased considerably per mothers and babies, although health expenditures per inhabitant remained constant over the years. There was an important shift away from subsidizing hospitals with public money, and the state concentrated its expenditures on mothers and infants. As a result, infant mortality rates could be reduced in Chile. This holds even in a regional and social perspective. The poorest regions of Chile (7th region to 11th region according to the official count; i.e., the area from Santiago to the south) experienced the most dramatic fall in infant mortality rates between 1974 and 1979; and babies, whose mothers had only basic education, survived much better in 1979 than they did in 1969 and 1973 (Raczynski and Oyarzo, 1981: 47–54). This is all the more paradoxical, since Chile's record on other indicators of development looks rather gloomy (Flechsig, 1985: esp. 217).

I estimate the real purchasing power of the poorest 20 per cent of the respective populations around 1980 on the basis of World Bank figures on household income shares of the poorest 20 per cent and on real purchasing power parity rates (see Table 8.8).

Table 8.8   Income distribution and purchasing power in capitalist and socialist semi-peripheries

(1) Share of the poorest 20% in total incomes
(2) Average purchasing power in % of US average purchasing power
(3) Average purchasing power in US$ equivalents
(4) Purchasing power of the poorest 20% in $

	(1)	*(2)*	*(3)*	*(4)*
India	7.0%	5.0%	572.5$	200$
Brazil	2.0%	29.3%	3355.0$	335$
Hungary	6.9%	40.4%	4626.0$	1596$
Portugal	5.2%	33.4%	3824.0$	994$
former Yugoslavia	6.6%	35.3%	4042.0$	1334$
Argentina	4.4%	33.5%	3836.0$	844$
South Korea	5.7%	22.5%	2576.0$	734$
Israel	6.0%	59.4%	6801.0$	2040$
Hong Kong	5.4%	62.4%	7145.0$	1929$
Spain	6.9%	55.5%	6355.0$	2192$
Ireland	7.2%	47.9%	5485.0$	1974$
Italy	6.2%	68.0%	7786.0$	2414$

(1) directly from Table 26, WDR, 1987
(2) directly from Table A.2, WDR, 1987
(3) calculated from Table A.2: entry for column (2)*11450 US$
(4) ((3) x (1))/20, WDR, 1987
Source: Calculated from World Bank, *World Development Report*, 1987.

On the basis of Polish microcensus data (1978), covering the whole population, including peasants, worker peasants, pensioners, we obtain a comparison of the living standards of the poorest 40 per cent in Poland with eleven other semi-periphery nations (see Table 8.9).

Table 8.9   Purchasing power in semi-periphery countries including Poland

Country	Income share of bottom 40% (%)	Average purchasing power per capita in $	Per capita purchasing power of poorest 40%
India	16.2	573	232
South Korea	16.9	2576	1088
Hungary	20.5	4626	2371
Poland	15.0	4317	1619
Portugal	15.2	3824	1453
former Yugoslavia	18.7	4042	1890
Argentina	14.1	3836	1352
Israel	18.0	6801	3060
Spain	19.4	6355	3082
Ireland	20.3	5485	2784
Italy	17.5	7786	3406

Data Sources: Polish Income Distribution Microcensus 1978, reported in Tausch, 1985, exclusively based on Polish Statistical Yearbook (G.U.S.); others: World Bank, *World Development Report*, 1987, including Polish average incomes in real purchasing power.
Note: Income Distribution in Poland at the end of the Gierek years was probably more unequal than in many other (former) socialist countries, with the plausible exception of the former USSR (see Trehub, 1988).

The graphic comparison of the real purchasing power of the poorest 40 per cent in semi-periphery countries is to be seen in Figure 8.5.

Since the World Bank mission to China gained access to the first-ever Chinese census results, inequality in China can reasonably be compared to that in other developing countries. Urban income distribution was more equal than in other Asian countries (Bangladesh, India, Pakistan, Sri Lanka, Indonesia, Malaysia, Philippines, Thailand), but through the effect of the great differences between the city and the countryside, and by the considerable rural income inequality, the overall share of the poorest 40 per cent in total incomes (18.4 per cent for the whole of China) did not differ much from other Asian developing countries (Tausch, 1984c). Thus the share of the poorest 40 per cent in total incomes and per capita average incomes in some Asian countries were comparable to the one in China (see Table 8.10).

Figure 8.5   Purchasing power of the poorest 40% in semi-periphery countries, ranked by per capita incomes

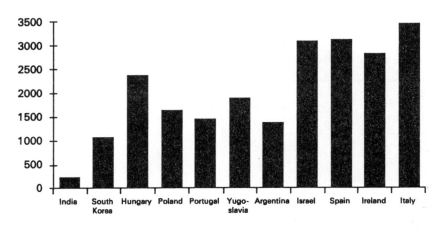

Table 8.10   Poverty in Asia

Country	Per capita income, 1986 ($)	Share of the poorest 40%	
Bangladesh	160	17.3%	(1981–82)
India	290	16.2%	(1975–76)
China	300	18.4%	(1979–80)
Sri Lanka	400	15.9%	(1980–81)
Indonesia	490	14.4%	(1976)
Philippines	560	14.1%	(1985)
Thailand	810	15.2%	(1975–76)
Malaysia	1830	11.2%	(1973)
South Korea	2370	16.9%	(1976)

Source: World Bank, *World Development Report*, 1988: 310–11 (German edition); World Bank (1981) *China: Socialist economic development*, vol. 1; see also *The Economist*, 20–26 June 1981; Tausch, 1984c.

Income distribution in China means that the poor receive only about half the average per capita income of society; in this respect, there are really no important differences as compared to other Asian countries; and life expectancies, too, are distributed unevenly according to the different provinces. Shanghai, Tianjin and Heilongjiang have an average life expectancy of more than 70 years, while Jilin and Guizhou each have a life expectancy of below 60 years. Jilin (56.8 years) has a life expectancy that was comparable to the Indian average. Thus, China was far from presenting what Griffin (1987) called a 'shining example' of regional development.

Not only real scarcity, but real poverty, high infant mortality and stagnating life expectancies belonged to the array of social problems of socialism. Also inflation, once thought to be the exclusive vice of a capitalist system, had crept into the workings of the socialist models before their dissolution (see Table 8.11).

Table 8.11   Average yearly inflation rates 1980–86 in per cent, in socialist and capitalist nations

	%
India	7.8
Pakistan	7.5
Egypt	12.4
South Korea	5.4
Spain	11.3
Italy	13.2
Hungary	5.4
Poland	31.2
former Yugoslavia	51.8

Source: World Bank, *World Development Report*, 1988.

In a comprehensive survey of basic human needs satisfaction in the world system, based on the World Bank data tape (1980), it was proposed to measure development efficiency by residuals from the following equations (see Table 8.12).

Table 8.12   Development efficiency/deficiency of socialist systems, considering their degree of environmental pollution/energy consumption

Development efficiency in	*Predicting equations based on*
Life expectancy	Plateau-curve of basic human needs
Life expectancy increases	1st derivate of Plateau-curve, Life expectancy level tn-1
All other basic human needs satisfaction increases	1st derivate of Plateau-curve, Basic human needs satisfaction tn-1

Measured concepts:

Reduction of infant mortalities, reduction of lack of doctors per population, reduction of lack of hospital beds per population, increases in literacy.

All calculations were performed on the basis of SPSS IX, listwise deletion of missing values and inclusion level < .05 to avoid redundant predictors. Thus, for example, decreases/increases in infant mortality rates 1960–77 were predicted by the Plateau-curve of basic human needs (1st derivate), presented in Chapter 6 of this book, and the level of infant mortality reached in 1960. The unadjusted variance explained, $R^{**}2$ of that equation, was 71.3 per cent; the calculation was possible for 51 countries of the world economy. The 'Matthew's effect', the Kuznets curve and the Plateau-curve of basic human needs all were calculated on the basis of energy consumption per capita rates in order to correct for undervalued socialist exchange rates with Western currencies. The results of such a comparison about the decreasing development efficiency of socialism are not surprising in terms of the overall message of this chapter (see Table 8.13).

Table 8.13   Subnormal development performance in socialist countries

Life expectancy reached in 1977:	CSFR, former GDR, Hungary, North Korea, Poland, Romania, former USSR (comparison with 121 other countries with complete data)
Life expectancy increases 1960–77:	former GDR, Hungary, Poland, Romania, Bulgaria, CSFR, former USSR (comparison with 112 other countries with complete data)
Reduction of infant mortality rates 1960–77:	Bulgaria, Cuba, CSFR, Hungary (comparison with 51 other countries with complete data)
Reduction of the lack of doctors per population, 1960–77:	Bulgaria, Cuba, CSFR, former GDR, Hungary, Poland, Romania, former USSR, former Yugoslavia (comparison with 110 other countries with complete data)
Reduction of the lack of hospital beds per population, 1970–77:	Cuba, CSFR, former GDR, Poland, former Yugoslavia (comparison with 101 other countries with complete data)
Expansion of secondary school enrolment ratios, 1970–77:	Bulgaria, CSFR, former GDR, Hungary, Mongolia, Poland, former USSR, former Yugoslavia (comparison with 116 other countries with complete data)
Expansion of literacy, 1970–77:	Hungary, Poland, former USSR, former Yugoslavia (comparison with 81 other countries with complete data)

Source: Tausch, 1986b, and Table 6.1 of this book, based on World Bank data tape. (CSFR before dissolution.)

Thus, socialist performance is not compared vaguely with other 'comparable countries'; it is compared to social performance in the world system, properly taking into account (i) the relatively good position of most socialist nations evident in early periods and due to the positive development efficiency of 'young socialism'; and (ii) the relatively high energy inputs, which socialism consumes in order to produce its results.

What emerges from this comparison is the relative stagnation of socialism at its later stages, of socialism as an ageing social system. The results for Cuba are nothing but a reflection of the fact that Cuba, soon after the revolution, had quite good basic human needs data, and therefore its performance was not at all extraordinary.

In the former Warsaw Pact, military expenditures amounted to one-third up to two-fifths of central government expenditures (US ACDA, 1988: 47). Such a drain on resources will have its effects for any type of economy. In the former USSR itself, available US intelligence community estimates (US ACDA, 1988: 77) put this figure at 49.5 per cent in 1985, and high military spending continued well into the Gorbachev era. Military expenditures not only consumed about half of the central government expenditures, they also amounted to 12.5 per cent of the Soviet 'national product' estimated in terms of Western national economic accounting: 4.5 million men in their most productive age served in the army, and arms exports were no less than 18.5 per cent of total exports. It is thus reasonable to centre this analysis of the development patterns of the now defunct socialism on the war economy, a perspective which was presented, amongst others, by M. Kaldor. The socialist war economy of the East had its repercussions, too, in the South. Arms imports in the LDCs amounted to $180 675 million during the period 1982–86, $78 740 million of which came from the former USSR alone. The former USSR thus outranked the US as the Third World's major arms supplier by almost 3:1 (see US ACDA, 1988: 127). The arms transfer business was the backbone of a number of quite enduring world political relationships that the former USSR built up over the years with some developing countries, such as the evolving Indian regional superpower (Banerjee, 1987; Das, 1987; Kumar, 1984; Mansingh, 1984; SIPRI, 1986), its most stable world political partner outside the former Warsaw Pact and the former COMECON. The former USSR was the main supplier of countries like Iraq and Libya (Figure 8.6 and Figure 8.7).

From the early 1970s, the former USSR and its allies tried hard to achieve military parity with the West. On a constant 1984 US dollar basis, military expenditures as well as levels of armed forces in thousands and arms transfers provide an insight into the global arms race between the two superpower blocs (see Table 8.14).

Figure 8.6   The arms suppliers: arms exporters, 1985

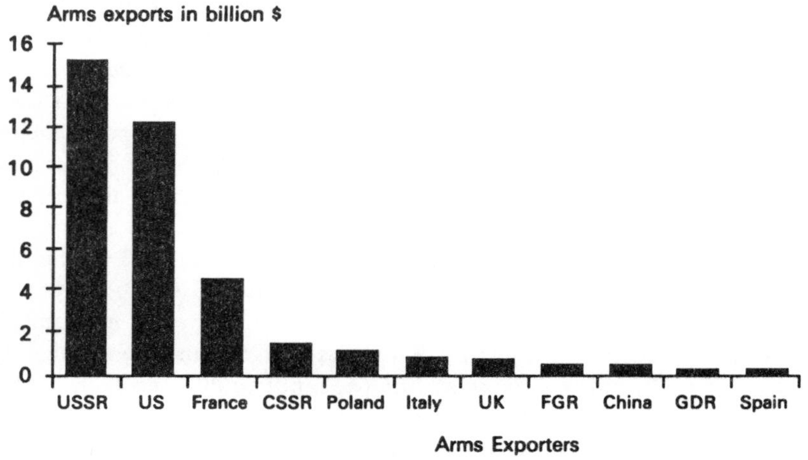

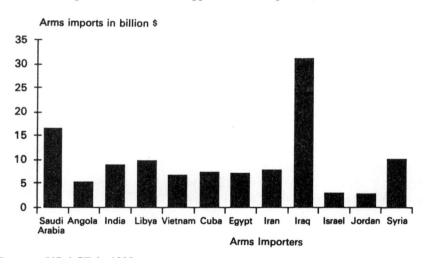

Source: US ACDA, 1988.

Figure 8.7   The arms suppliers: arms importers, 1982–86

Source: US ACDA, 1988.

Table 8.14   The global arms race

Year	MILEX $bns		Armed forces mns		Arms exports $bns	
	NATO	former WTO	NATO	former WTO	NATO	former WTO
1975	241.8	272.5	5.215	5.478	–	–
1976	234.0	275.2	5.251	5.580	–	–
1977	241.8	278.8	5.337	5.599	17.350	15.890
1978	245.3	282.9	5.271	5.562	17.690	18.930
1979	250.9	286.1	5.268	5.655	14.850	24.320
1980	266.8	292.7	5.358	5.760	17.080	22.980
1981	282.2	293.6	5.469	5.767	21.850	21.820
1982	301.6	299.3	5.539	5.898	19.440	22.590
1983	317.7	303.2	5.587	5.910	22.310	21.440
1984	331.0	308.7	5.621	5.909	21.160	21.410
1985	353.4	312.5	5.710	5.923	19.410	18.860
1986	–	–	–	–	12.480	19.940

Source: US ACDA, 1988.

In terms of military expenditures, the 'Reagan revision' (Bremer *et al.*, 1977) brought about a lead in Western power only after 1982; armed forces levels were always – throughout the time series – in favour of the Warsaw Pact, and military exports as the single most important indicator of the global power reach of a nation were in the West's favour before 1978, and for the years 1981, 1983 and 1985, with no clear pattern emerging ever since. I also present the essence of the statistical materials calculated on the basis of ACDA in the following Figures 8.8, 8.9 and 8.10. Each of these shows the strength of the military build-up under Brezhnev.

Considering the paradigmatic character of the Polish crisis (Hettne, 1989) it seems absurd that a country like Poland wasted its best human and material resources in the design and construction of arms which were also exported to Third World nations. Figures 8.6 and 8.7 clearly demonstrate the importance of the smaller Eastern European arms producers, ex-CSFR and Poland, in completing the former Warsaw Treaty supply line. Without arms transfers, paid for in hard currency, the Eastern European economies would have been in a still more precarious position, and it also remains to be seen how Poland and the ex-CSFR manage to get their hard currency from other sources, after the international arms market in the Third World contracted from $50.1 billion in 1984 to $36.9 billion in 1986, and after political democracy won in both countries in 1989. One important area, certainly, was Iraq, which turned to Eastern Europe after being temporarily let down by the former USSR (Cutler *et al.*, 1987: 284). But even the Iran–

Figure 8.8   The expansion path of Soviet military power under Brezhnev and beyond

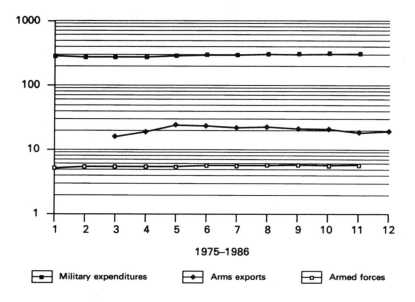

1975–1986

Military expenditures   Arms exports   Armed forces

Figure 8.9   Military spending in East and West

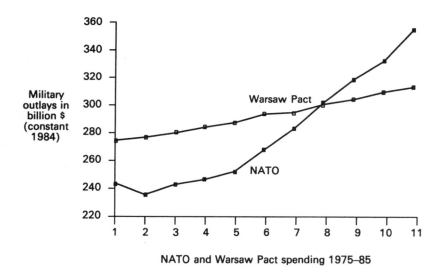

NATO and Warsaw Pact spending 1975–85

Figure 8.10   Global arms exports by Warsaw Pact and NATO, 1977–86

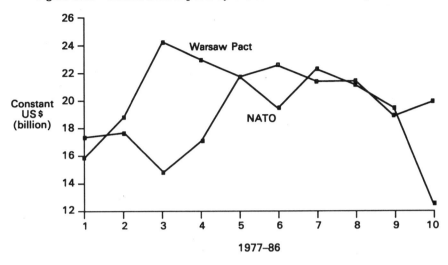

Iraq war could not help to solve the problem of how to earn hard cash, besides exporting fuels, including natural gas, and gold. In 1985, with similar tendencies detectable in previous years, CIA and Wharton Econometrics estimated the total hard currency gains of the former USSR to be at $29.7 billion, with a debt position of $13.7 billion. Net fuel sales amounted to $16 billion, gold sales $2 billion, and arms sales $4.3 billion (Cutler *et al.*, 1987: 279). The arms trade was more important to Eastern Europe's economies than other European countries' (see Table 8.15).

Compared to the vital economic mechanism of total export capacity of a country, the sale of arms in the former socialist countries of Europe with a tradition of arms manufactures (former USSR, ex-CSFR, Poland) exceeded any Western capitalist European nation with available data. Also I must here note the remarkable militarization of former Yugoslav foreign trade.

The former USSR, ex-CSFR and Poland account for 46.2 per cent of the mentioned Southern arms bill of $180 675 million, while the major Western suppliers, the USA, France, the UK and the Federal Republic of Germany, account for just about one-third: i.e., 32.8 per cent of the total. This state socialist arms export drive meant heavy inroads into market positions held formerly by the big Western suppliers, taking place in conjunction with an upsurge in arms sales by smaller LDC and OECD exporters.

A study, produced by the US Congressional Research Service in 1981, based upon US CIA estimates, testified to this military character of East–South relations. For each dollar of aid from the socialist Eastern European former WTO countries, there were 1.07 dollars of weaponry to Third World

Table 8.15   The weight of arms sales in total capitalist and socialist exports, 1986

Country	Arms sales per total exports (%)
Albania	0
Austria	1.5
Belgium	0.0
Bulgaria	2.6
ex-CSFR	5.0
Denmark	0.0
Finland	0.0
France	3.0
former GDR	0.8
FRG	0.2
Greece	0.1
Hungary	1.3
Ireland	0.0
Italy	0.3
Netherlands	0.2
Norway	0.1
Poland	5.1
Romania	1.4
former USSR	18.5
Spain	0.6
Sweden	0.5
Switzerland	0.1
Turkey	0.0
UK	0.7
former Yugoslavia	0.6

Source: My own compilation from US ACDA, 1988.

nations; for every academic civilian student there were 1.11 military officers trained in the East; and also, for every ten economic aid personnel, there were still 1.7 military advisers from former WTO nations in Eastern Europe. When Cuba is included, the militarization of overall East–South relations was even more pronounced, as a result of the massive amount of military personnel from Cuba stationed in other LDCs during the 1970s and 1980s. Cutler *et al.* remark on the long-term negative consequence of arms exports on planned, Soviet type economies:

If the Soviet Union seeks to sell the maximum quantity of arms in order to obtain the maximum amount of precious hard currency, then it must at the same time expend its own precious raw materials for this purpose and use production capacity and skilled labor that could be allocated to other production. Consequently, and in this sense, it is possible to pose the question of whether arms exports represent a significant burden on the Soviet economy (Cutler *et al.*, 1987: 280).

The economic power and even superior number of inhabitants of the advanced Western capitalist countries organized in NATO made the arms race for the East hopeless from the start. Yet, qualitative and quantitative expansion continued under Gorbachev (US Department of Defense, 1989). In current billion of US$, total NATO GNP amounted to $6 781 billion, while former Warsaw Pact economic potential in 1986 was only $3 022 billion. The OECD countries together, i.e., the whole capitalist bloc, had an economic potential of $8 840 billion out of a world economic potential of $14 510 billion. The NATO countries in 1986 comprised 599.6 million people, while the whole former Eastern alliance comprised a population of only 390.5 million. Military burden rates to the tune of around 11 per cent of total product severely hampered the accumulative capacity of the former socialist countries. In many ways, the armaments drive of the 1970s to achieve 'parity' at all costs with the West, was a common illusion of the late Brezhnev years, just as enlarging the 'socialist world system' temporarily to include Afghanistan, Angola, Ethiopia, Kampuchea, Laos, Mozambique proved very costly indeed. These new allies offered practically nothing in terms of imperial economic benefits. In contrast to the expanding economies of the newly industrializing countries, 'socialist latecomer' growth was slow and their poverty all too apparent:

Table 8.16   The socio-economic weakness of socialist 'latecomers'

Country	GNP per capita 1986	Growth 1965–85	Life expectancy 1985 (%)	Current resource balance per BIP
Ethiopia	120	+0.0	46	−7
Afghanistan	—	—	45	—
Vietnam	—	—	65	—
Angola	—	—	44	—
Lao PDR	—	—	50	—
Mozambique	210	—	48	−10

Source: Own compilations from *World Development Report*, 1988.

Third World socialism included not only what K. Griffin (1987) thought to be a 'considerable improvement in the well-being of the rural population' in the twelve countries of the world with communal land tenure systems (China, former USSR, Vietnam, Romania, North Korea, East Germany, ex-Czechoslovakia, Hungary, Cuba, Bulgaria, Albania and Mongolia), but also the development debacle of Kampuchea and Ethiopia (famines 1979 and 1984, see also Griffin, 1987). In Ethiopia alone, some 500 000 people died of starvation in the first half of 1985, while the state class spent £200 million on the tenth anniversary celebrations of the revolution in 1984. There were approximately 500 000 to 700 000 Ethiopian refugees in Sudan, and another 700 000 in Somalia (Griffin, 1987: 195–200). There are a number of estimates about the number of victims of the 'Great Leap Forward', among them Rummel, 1990. Griffin also documents what the 'Great Leap Forward' meant for China: disastrous famine 1959–61. The death rate rose from 11.98 to 25.43 per 1000 in 1960, and crude birth rates fell from 29.22 in 1958 to just 18.02 in 1961 (Griffin, 1987: 23). After the recovery began, birth rates climbed again to 37.01 per 1000 population, and death rates fell again to 10.02. Estimated roughly, there were 1.9 million victims of the 'Great Leap' in 1959, 2.5 million in 1961, and 9.5 million in 1960 (estimated from Griffin, 1987: 23, assuming 654.5 million inhabitants per 1960 and a nonlinear downward trend in death rates over time). Even if the true numbers might be 4 starvation deaths per 1000 inhabitants in 1959 and 1961 and 13 per 1000 in 1960, it does not alter the fact that altogether *at the very least 13–15 million Chinese fell victim to 'Great Leap Forward', deaths which would not have occurred under normal economic conditions before and after this 'utter failure'* (a term which I borrow from Griffin, 1987: 12). These figures bring the Chinese experience well into the vicinity of famine and terror under Stalin with an estimated 20 millions of victims (R. Medvedev, *Moscow News*, 3 February 1989; Radio Liberty Report on the USSR, 1, 7, 17 February 1989: 27). Some others, like Rummel and Kent, even estimate that *30 million people were killed by the catastrophe of the 'Great Leap'*.

Cross-national models on the crisis and global death of socialism are relatively rare. On the basis of the machine readable data set (Tausch, 1982c) it is possible to construct a causal path model of the share of arms exports per total exports in the Eastern European nations and their effects on accumulative capacity. To start with, I further extend the reasoning along the lines developed in Tausch (1991a) on extensive agriculture, rural backwardness and development. In the capitalist periphery countries it was intensive agriculture (measured, for example, by the ratios of inhabitants per agriculturally used square mile) which proved to be an institutionally determined major cause of faster economic growth.

In the socialist world – with and without the former USSR – there was a quite stable empirical relationship between rural backwardness, measured by low hectare yields of grain, a low economically active population proportion per hectare of land (extensiveness) and long-term accumulation bottlenecks, measured by the incapacity of the industrial consumption goods sector to have a higher share in total exports.

Socialist countries with a deficient agriculture used militarization to ameliorate the external and internal long-term repercussions of their developmental deficiencies. Where now are the links in my causally interpreted path model? Intensive agriculture and rural efficiency worked against high militarization, while extensive socialist land-use and low hectare yields caused a high military burden ratio. Ethnic and linguistic fractionalization in former state socialism, in turn, led in some notable way towards a migration from rural areas, basically because the economic rewards of agriculture were very low in heterogeneous socialist societies, and former state socialism did not entirely overcome this heterogeneity (see, in general terms, Elsenhans, 1983).

While an efficient agricultural system, measured in terms of hectare yields for wheat, worked in favour of an industrially more competitive development, manifesting itself in industrial consumer goods per total exports, militarization very negatively affected such industrial competitiveness. The 'way out' of this, in the 1960s and 1970s, clearly was an offensive programme of arms sales especially to Third World countries, in order: (i) to lower the per capita debt position; and (ii) to achieve a better overall convertible currency position in view of the deficient trade and payments balance with leading Western countries while trends in labour productivity showed no sign of becoming better.

This circuit could have been broken only by a radical attack on the basic problem of structural heterogeneity between rural and urban development politically, i.e. by creating mechanisms that ensure a higher yield ratio per hectare in agriculture and by not allowing a deterioration of the quality of life for the rural populations in ethnically heterogeneous socialist societies. Here, results from Chapter 7 must directly be compared with my path model. I had shown for global society that public investment (as a measure of state class influence) and ethnic heterogeneity as indicators of the existence of distribution coalitions must considerably hinder an improvement in the relationship: energy input → quantity of life both at given time points and over time in world society. In former state socialism, this mechanism worked via the crisis in agriculture, again a by-product of the low quality of life in the rural areas, which led, in the distribution coalition environment of socialism, to the 'answer', consisting of militarization, which again blocks technological civilian development, so vital for non-military exports. Bureaucratic former state socialism then looked for an answer in an increased arms trade with the South, for there was at least some cash to fill the balance of trade and other critical outward balances of the system and unfortunately could do so even in future due to the economic constraints of the *perestroika* strategy and the reforms after August 1991. By its low profile as an industrial consumption goods exporter, it could not and cannot obtain other hard currency earnings in a very competitive world market for manufactured civilian products.

The system reacted by stagnating or decreasing labour productivity. The fate of that restructuring depended to a great extent on internal militarization and external superpower competition, which could increase again due to renewed Russian arms sales to the Third World.

My path model shows that there was, by the way, one pressure group which definitively lost out from the original set-up, indeed the one which pushed the Gorbachev reform movement at first: state security and 'civilian' intelligence. Their share per total population (i.e., per 1000 inhabitants) suffered greatly from a highly inefficient agriculture – measured in hectare productivity of grain – in a very direct way. Of course, Western social science had at its disposal no reliable estimates about the KGB budget, but the rate of people engaged in internal security professions per population could be taken as a first and certainly not too reliable yardstick about the overall economic and political power of the internal security apparatus. The necessary grain imports of agriculturally inefficient societies cost a great deal of money, constraining especially the hard cash budget of police and intelligence forces, at given internally and externally determined military expenditure shares per total product. One of the most tragic aspects of the present situation is that, during the *perestroika* years, the shortages in food supplies had even worsened. In graphic representation, my model is to be found in Figure 8.11.

Except for the hectare yields→state security trade-off, and the ethnic fractionalization→EAP per hectare land trade-off, my relationships achieve quite good significance values which are nearly all below the 5 per cent error mark, and all of them below the 10 per cent error mark. In the following we will see that, especially countries with very entrenched distribution coalitions, like in the Arab world, were almost 'natural allies' of the Eastern economies, at the other end of the arms supply line. In future, discontented national elites, with very big and unresolved agrarian problems at home, could be tempted to 'play the China card', should the debt crisis become worse, thus ending the *perestroika* isolationism and perhaps opening a new era of confrontation in the periphery. Other candidates for Chinese future Third World influence could be Argentina, Peru, Indonesia, etc . . .

Among the peace researchers of our time, the Hungarian economist T. Szentes most clearly formulated hypotheses about the effects of militarization on different types of socio-economic systems. For Szentes, any arms race leads principally to lower economic and political development. By creating a real or assumed threat, the arms race may have induced socialist

Figure 8.11 Path model of state socialism and arms exports

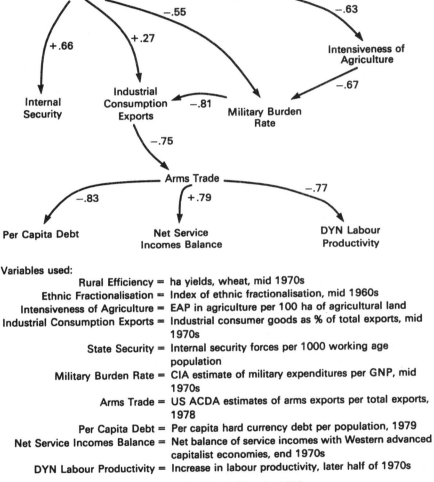

Variables used:

Rural Efficiency = ha yields, wheat, mid 1970s
Ethnic Fractionalisation = Index of ethnic fractionalisation, mid 1960s
Intensiveness of Agriculture = EAP in agriculture per 100 ha of agricultural land
Industrial Consumption Exports = Industrial consumer goods as % of total exports, mid 1970s
State Security = Internal security forces per 1000 working age population
Military Burden Rate = CIA estimate of military expenditures per GNP, mid 1970s
Arms Trade = US ACDA estimates of arms exports per total exports, 1978
Per Capita Debt = Per capita hard currency debt per population, 1979
Net Service Incomes Balance = Net balance of service incomes with Western advanced capitalist economies, end 1970s
DYN Labour Productivity = Increase in labour productivity, later half of 1970s

Original data sources: All reported in Codebook, Tausch, 1982c.

Source: Multiple regressions, based on SPSS-IX, on the Tausch, 1982, aggregate data set on Eastern Europe.

or socialist-oriented regimes to acquire or preserve a militarized government. These problems tended to degrade the image of socialism in the Third World (Szentes, 1984: 48). Szentes clearly expects a 'negative correlation between economic growth and military expenditures' (Szentes, 1984: 50) and maintains that economies with a low level of integration of their informal sectors, i.e., structurally heterogeneous societies (Elsenhans, 1983; Cordova, 1973) such as those in the Third World, reap the negative effects of militarization, while economies with a high rate of unemployment and idle capital reap positive effects (Szentes, 1984: 52).

While I agree with Szentes on the perspective that militarization in the East tended to hinder the development of democracies there (Szentes, 1984: 61), the crucial hypothesis of this very respected social scientist needs further testing:

> Rightist or reactionary civilian and military regimes, however, performed more poorly in these areas (i.e., rise of per capita GDP, manufacturing output, housing and food availability, infant mortality, and hospital beds per capita) than did progressive leftist or radical regimes, whether civilian or military. (Szentes, 1984: 61)

For Szentes, the supposed negative effects of militarization in the periphery were circumvented in 'countries which have either a people's militia or a revolutionary army, as well as extensive relations to permit a wide range of options' (i.e., trade relations with the former CMEA countries) (Szentes, 1984: 63). In view of my contradictory research results, it is worthwhile to reiterate that Szentes expects a stronger negative effect of militarization in the periphery than in the centre (Szentes, 1984: 64). According to my results, militarization will be connected positively with growth in the capitalist 'rimlands', and Soviet clients performed worse than other nations on the social and growth accounts. The nature of these results, though, again compels 'critical development research' in the tradition of the writings of Galtung and Senghaas (1972–77) to think more about the role that the market, the state classes, and the military sector play in the course of development. My research results do suggest that the liberal economy of the world capitalist 'kernel' was less prone to accept arms expenditures as an instrument of growth than protective countries on the 'rim' of that world capitalist system. And this, I think, is an important qualification. How do I arrive at such results?

Militarization was the 'missing link' in the chain of causation described in Equation 6.6 of this book. I would expect that the established relationship for the OECD countries between state sector size, political system's age and economic growth described in Equation 6.6 even inverts itself for state class societies under inclusion of the variable 'military expenditures per total government expenditures' (IMF data, reported in Bornschier, Heintz *et al.*). For those regimes, militarization had become an 'engine of growth', and their growth – relative to other state class dominated societies – was faster under the condition of militarism.

My quantitative model of world market discipline, state class influence and development rests on the assumption most clearly developed by Elsenhans (1983) that the 'normal case' of periphery social development was based on bureaucratic systems of domination with centralized state classes, called tributary modes of production. In such systems there was a contradiction between agrarian producers and the urban-based state class, which collectively appropriates the greater part of the surplus through the state apparatus. In the absence of market competition this state class either invested the surplus product or squanders it now on luxury/militarization (Elsenhans, 1983: 23; see also Tausch, 1991a: ch. VII). The absence of market competition especially in combination with large land-holdings contributed to the strengthening of the 'enclave economies', where additional incomes from raw material exports were not redistributed among the mass producers. Specialization in raw materials leads to a strengthening of reactionary incomes, namely land rents, which, unlike profits, do not have to be invested in order to maintain competitiveness (Elsenhans, 1983: 25). The resulting tendencies towards cementing inequality in the periphery made it difficult for resistance movements to prevail as mass movements, and if they did so at all, they did so through the mediation of state planning. A strengthening of state influence, bureaucracies and protectionist behaviour will be the consequence of the lack of mass demand, to be observed in periphery capitalism, even when under-privileged classes in conjunction with elements of the state classes try to realize an 'anticapitalist' development path (Elsenhans, 1983: 25–33). Military expenditures substitute for mass demand.

The qualitative indicator 'number of memberships in selected intergovernmental international capitalist organizations' in 1973 will serve as operationalization of the concept of world economic protective behaviour. These organizations, according to Ballmer-Cao and Scheidegger, were the: (i) IMF; (ii) International Finance Corporation; (iii) GATT; (iv) International Union for the Protection of Industrial Property; (v) International Centre for the Settlement of Investment Disputes; (vi) International Institute for the Unification of Private Law; and the (vii) Hague Conference on Private International Law.

In the following, I will present the results of my politometric investigation into the differentials of growth among the countries of the world economy, which show at least some degree of protective behaviour *vis-à-vis* the leading institutions of world capitalism and thus – according to my theory – allowed the state classes to opt for inappropriate long-term solutions, divert political conflict into scapegoat-finding in the international arena and refrain from effectively fostering labour mobilization in the long run (Elsenhans, 1985b: 16).

Government finance data are from IMF sources included in the Ballmer-Cao and Scheidegger Compendium; growth is from World Bank data files, on a per capita constant dollar yearly basis converted at exchange rates; and date of constitution, i.e. youth of the political system in terms of constitution is from Taylor and Hudson, *World Handbook II*. The data on agricultural density rates are from Taylor/Jodice, 1983 (DENSITY **.50) (see Table 8.17).

Table 8.17   Military Keynesianism as a growth factor in ageing political systems of the state class economies

Countries with an integration score of below or equal to 6.0

Growth Predictors	Beta weight	Significance
Agricultural density**.50	+ .44944	.0000
MILEX per GOVEX, 1965	+ .38092	.0001
GOVEX per GDP, 1965	+ .32160	.0017
Date of constitution	+ .14857	.1335

$n = 71$; adj. $R**2 = 37.7$ per cent; $F = 11.59$; $p = .0000$

Countries with an integration score of below or equal to 4.0

Growth Predictors	Beta weight	Significance
Agricultural density **.50	+ .50325	.0001
Military expenditures per GOVEX, 1965	+ .40962	.0013
GOVEX per GDP, 1965	+ .29952	.0182
Date of constitution	+ .07017	.5709

$n = 46$; adj. $R**2 = 40.0$ per cent; $p = .0000$; $F = 8.52$

Data: Ballmer-Cao and Scheidegger; Taylor and Jodice (1983); Taylor and Hudson, 1972/75; World Bank, *World Development Report* (1985).

Thus, in state class economies the role of mass demand was taken over by military outlays. The most disturbing aspect of my analysis in terms of its implications for world peace was that in the state class dominated systems of the periphery and the semi-periphery, arms expenditures are positively and significantly related to economic growth, in addition to the positive effect of the Keynesian variable 'government expenditures per GDP'. My result bodes ill for efforts to control arms expenditures in the former socialist countries of the East and in the world's South in the wake of the events of 1989 for the sake of growth, because observable experience in the 1965–83 period was indeed very different. Taking properly into account the freshness of the constitutional framework of a society and the negative effects on growth of extensive agriculture, we observe a dramatically positive influence of arms expenditures per total government expenditures (IMF data) on subsequent growth, 1965–83. This holds for the ample group of countries in the capitalist world economy professing a more protective capitalist integration policy. Institutional integration into the seven most important bodies of the world economy, mentioned above, becomes thus all the more important for both the new democracies in the East and in the South.

Thus I have to revise the Olson hypothesis in one important respect. In the state class dominated systems of the periphery and semi-periphery of the capitalist world economy there was an alarming positive effect of militarism and government expenditures on growth, which will make, I fear, measures of arms control obsolete in that part of the world, because governments find no immediate economic constraints against their booming military programmes. I maintain that a socio-liberal interpretation of development would expect that the deadly logic of arms accumulation leading to an illusion of growth was, in the last resort, highly relevant for those parts of the world where the institution of world capitalist competition has not enough weight to force state classes towards a more civilian, less military/state expenditure oriented development path. In 'real socialism' there developed a cycle of internal, mainly rural, crises, military expenditures, arms exports, short-term inflows of foreign cash and long-term stagnating labour productivity.

In this context, the military expenditures per GNP relationship for the countries of the world must be mentioned. Among the top 50 militarists out of 144 surveyed nations, spending more than 4.5 per cent of their GNP each on the military sector, there were only four Western democracies (including Israel and Greece) (see Table 8.18).

Thus, the scene was set for a massive militarization of the periphery, which we still witness today, aided by the positive trade-off between militarization and subsequent growth in countries with an institutional/juridical integration into the leading mechanisms of world capitalism of equal or less than 6.0 or 4.0. Here, then, was located enormous demand. How did suppliers interact with that demand and how did this affect socio-economic development? I venture the hypothesis that in the South, the former USSR and its former allies became attractive suppliers precisely for

Table 8.18   Military expenditures per GNP, 1985

> 25 per cent	> 15 per cent	> 10 per cent	> 4.5 per cent
Qatar, Iraq	Oman, Saudi Arabia, Syria, North Korea, Libya, N. Yemen, Jordan, Nicaragua	Egypt, Israel, USSR, Kampuchea, Mongolia, Cape Verde, S. Yemen	Laos, Ethiopia, Guyana, Lebanon, Bulgaria, Afghanistan, Taiwan, Mozambique, Angola, Iran, Greece, Peru, China, USA, Mauritania, Morocco, Lesotho, former GDR, Pakistan, Zimbabwe, Kuwait, Singapore, Zambia, Vietnam, Poland, CSFR, UAE, El Salvador, South Korea, Cuba, Albania, UK

Source: Own compilations from US ACDA, 1988.

those states with (i) a relatively low presence of the transnationals in the manufacturing sector; (ii) an excessive burden of government consumption as an indicator of existing distribution coalitions; (iii) significantly lower growth than in other Third World nations; and (iv) a considerable amount of political instability, measured by the frequency of illegal executive transfers from 1963 until 1977.

Thus, my hypothesis about a state class/distribution coalition environment, leading to a high share of arms imports from the former USSR and its allies per total arms imports of the South, receives at least some empirical confirmation. The dependent variable was measured by the cumulative share of weapons imports from the three major former WTO producers – former USSR, ex-CSFR, Poland – per total arms acquisitions for the period 1974–78, and was calculated from US ACDA annuals. The multiple stepwise SPSS regression gives the following, causally interpreted, results about the question, who imports from where and why (see Table 8.19).

Low capitalist penetration, high government consumption, slow growth and political instability (as in the Arab world) favour an East European client status in the periphery. Since I also report causal influences of arms imports from the East on socio-economic development, I should mention that the connection with growth and illegal executive transfer can be a reciprocal one, far beyond the reach of this simple OLS cross national regression model. Still, with the first two predictors, my results do not change very much, for the adjusted $R^{**}2$ was still at 22 per cent, the *F*-value

Table 8.19 Who gets arms from where and why? Towards explaining former USSR/WTO client status in the Third World

Predictor of USSR/WTO client	St. Regression Coefficient	Significance
MNC penetration by foreign direct investment from capitalist developed countries in the industrial sector	−.38307	.0005
Government consumption per GDP, 1965	+.34021	.0016
GNP per capita growth 1965–83	−.22032	.0394
Illegal executive transfers 1963–77	+.13010	.2214

$n = 70$ Third World + European Periphery Countries with complete US ACDA/ Ballmer-Cao and Scheidegger/World Bank, *World Development Report*/Taylor and Jodice data.
SPSS stepwise new regression procedure (SPSS IX)
adj $R^{**}2 = 27.3$ per cent; $F = 7.50$; $p = .0000$.

for the whole equation is 10.72, $p = .0001$ and both predictors influence former USSR/WTO client status significantly ($p < .003$ each). For 41 countries with data on former USSR/WTO client status at the end of the 1970s it is possible to roughly estimate the effect of that variable on growth (see Table 8.20).

Table 8.20 Eastern arms clientele status, military Keynesianism and economic growth in state class dominated countries of the capitalist world economy, 1965–83

Sample construction: Countries with an institutional integration score into the capitalist world economy (1973) (according to Ballmer-Cao and Scheidegger) of less than or equal to 4

Growth predictor	Beta-weight	Significance
Agricultural density **.50	+.46859	.0005
MILEX per GOVEX, 1965	+.46765	.0005
GOVEX per BIP, 1965	+.29514	.0217
Eastern arms clientele status, 1974–78	−.24393	.0557
Date of constitution	+.07577	.4858

$n = 41$ countries with complete Taylor and Jodice (density), World Bank and IMF0-Ballmer-Cao and Scheidegger (government finance), US ACDA (our own calculations for client status) and Taylor and Hudson (date of constitution) data. SPSS IX new regression procedure. Growth data: World Bank, *World Development Report*, 1985 adj $R^{**}2 = 44.7$ per cent; $F = 7.46$; $p = .0001$

Thus, the relationship between former USSR/WTO arms client status and economic growth was significantly negative. Now I turn to the dynamics of political violence. Certainly, the question of political violence – as already mentioned in Chapter 7 – is determined to some extent by sample choice and the corrections for all the outlying cases. The following analysis is based on LDCs and southern European peripheries, understood in the tradition of Seers.

In explaining the growth of political violence in the periphery, I emphasized the break-up of distribution coalitions in state class systems. Entrenched periphery socio-political interests, the continuation of present tax structures based on indirect taxes, favouring large state deficits and a high commodity concentration, will react violently against the break-up of the status quo and will increase the potential of overt political violence at the price of postponing necessary solutions, especially considering Westward world political orientation and its effects on state class political systems (see Table 8.21).

Table 8.21   The determinants of the growth of political violence considering the impact of former Soviet influence in the Third World

Predictor	Standardized regression coefficient	Significance
DYN indirect taxes per total gov. revenue	−.50938	.0001
World political identification with the West on some key issues (at UN General Assembly) as an indicator of political 'Westernness' in 1965	−.48991	.0004
DYN general government deficit per GDP	−.19944	.0818
Commodity concentration ('HIRSCHMANN-Index') of exports in 1965	−.27608	.0130
Arms imports from the former USSR/WTO per total arms imports around 1974–78 as an indicator of client status *vis-à-vis* the East	−.23468	.0535

$n = 39$ LDCs and European periphery nations with complete data;
adj. $R**2 = 64.6$ per cent; $F = 14.84$; $p = .0000$
SPSS IX stepwise regression
Data Sources: Taylor and Jodice (1983) on political violence; clientele status US ACDA (1980); other data from Ballmer-Cao and Scheidegger. Government deficits are provisionally calculated by subtracting for each time point, 1965, and 1973, GOVEX-GOVREV. The higher expenditures are in terms of revenue, the higher the deficits.

Precisely 'modernization' of the peripheral state, like a reduction in the relative weight of indirect taxes, a deficit reduction, and a less traditional export structure, works here in favour of increasing political violence. Originally Westward-oriented state classes were less prone to such a violence cycle. It is also certain that the former USSR clients at the end of the period (1977) favoured less violent internal policies than other Third World countries. This apparent contradiction should be explained. Westward UN voting behaviour in the mid-1960s did not necessarily coincide with actual arms import relationships with Western powers, as countries like Jordan demonstrated.

In terms of avoiding the growth of political violence, it simply pays to let the traditional distribution coalitions have their say in the running of a country. Deregulation will always have a very high immediate price in terms of increasing violence in the world periphery. But by postponing deregulation, one only postpones the outbreak of more intense and severe violence; as happens in many countries, such as Sri Lanka, where deregulation coincided with the onset of economic stagnation.

The correlation between Westward world political orientation (ranging from value 8, maximum to value 1 minimum) and later USSR–WTO client status was far from perfect, as my computer Figure shows on the basis of the Ballmer-Cao and ACDA data set (Figure 8.12).

Many countries were tempted to import Soviet arms, even when their original world political orientation was Western. The ensuing 'Eastern option' had to recognize that a pronounced Western political position in the international system, as a result of sharing basic ideological values of competitive, Western capitalism, worked originally against the outbreak of large-scale civil violence. Above I mentioned Sri Lanka. For many years it was also an unusual exception to my hypothesis about the public economy producing basic human needs stagnation, taking into account the separate, negative effect of ethnic fractionalization on human development. Now, the outlier in Figure 8.12 at the right hand is again Sri Lanka. In the mid-1960s its world political orientation under market-oriented rule was very pro-Western, followed by ethnic Singhalese 'socialism' in the 1970s. Government action until 1977 worked in favour of the Singhalese state class, while market success definitely continued to be on the side of the Tamil minority bourgeoisie and middle-income groups. The ethnic tensions, according to my hypothesis, grew worse, precisely when deregulation ended protection for Singhalese state class interests combined with the onset of social stagnation (for a more general debate on Sri Lanka see also Wulf, 1983a and Donner, 1983; for an analysis of subsequent developments see Boucher *et al.*, 1987).

Figure 8.12   Eastern bloc arms imports and world political orientation

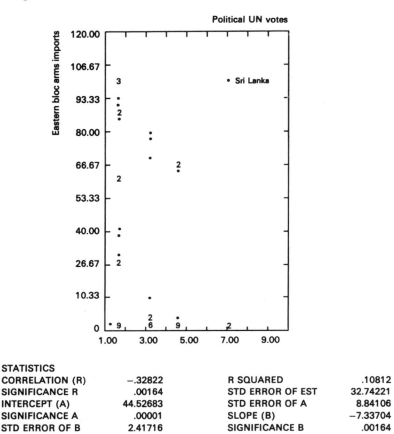

STATISTICS

CORRELATION (R)	−.32822	R SQUARED	.10812
SIGNIFICANCE R	.00164	STD ERROR OF EST	32.74221
INTERCEPT (A)	44.52683	STD ERROR OF A	8.84106
SIGNIFICANCE A	.00001	SLOPE (B)	−7.33704
STD ERROR OF B	2.41716	SIGNIFICANCE B	.00164

PLOTTED VALUES	78	EXCLUDED VAUES	0	MISSING VALUES	45

It was true, under certain conditions, that strategic dependence on the former USSR and its allies worked in some way against the open outbreak of large-scale civil violence. Precisely this, according to my analysis, was the case in Sri Lanka in the 1970s, but later on the positive contribution of former USSR–WTO strategic dependence towards avoiding manifest violence in Third World countries was offset by far by the negative effects of tax structure reforms, budget cuts and export modernization on the growth of political violence. No positive relationship between arms client status towards the East and the overall debt situation, especially in a dynamic way, could be found in the (semi)periphery. My model again is socio-liberal in the sense that it maintains that high government consumption and political systems stability in the preceding period were to be held responsible for the growing debt burden of the 1970s and 1980s. The debt burden was the product, according to this reasoning, of the inefficiency of distribution coalitions in stable institutional environments, aided in their detrimental consequences on economic development by high government consumption. Apart from these two variables and their causal influence, we notice that a long-term strategic client status *vis-à-vis* the East left some room for manoeuvre, somewhat ameliorating the growing debt burden, given the overall tendency to militarization in state class dominated societies:

Table 8.22   The causes of increasing indebtedness in LDCs, 1970–83

Predictor	Standardized regression coefficient	Significance
Political systems stability in the 60s	+ .26278	.0586
Strategic clientele status from the East (arms imports)	− .28770	.0397
Government consumption by GDP, 1970	+ .24957	.0745

$n = 51$ LDCs and European southern periphery nations with complete available data
adj. $R^{**}2 = 12$ per cent; $F = 3.28$; $p = .03$
SPSS IX, stepwise new regression, data: Ballmer-Cao and Scheidegger (Predictor 1 and 3), US ACDA (1983), World Bank, *World Development Report*, 1985, using the method described in the text above.

I have good reason to believe that the instability of the state class executive (in practice, military coups) in some part, at least, must be attributed to the effects of former USSR client status in the world's periphery. Why? Because this client status was not a solution, but an expression of the basic incapacity of a regime to solve the problems arising out of distributional coalitions at home. Clientele status *vis-à-vis* the former USSR allowed for some breathing space in the face of large-scale political violence, and it allowed state classes to get cheap weapons under already existing severe hard currency constraints. But some of the basic causes of executive instability, political violence and slow human development, such as excessive government consumption and inefficient public sectors, were part of the reason why a regime turned East and not West (or neutral, for that matter) for basic supplies to its armed forces (see Table 8.23).

What, then, remains of the claims voiced in the 1970s about an evolving 'socialist world system' to which increasingly also 'national democratic revolutionary' regimes in the Third World were to accede, in terms of social

Table 8.23 Executive instability, 1963–77, as a consequence of excessive state deficits and dependence on the former USSR–WTO for arms imports

Executive instability	Standardized regression coefficient	Predictor
Government saving per total saving, 1965	−.35060	
Long-term clientele status *vis-à-vis* the East in military matters, operationalized by: arms imports from the former USSR–WTO per total, 1974–78	+.32219	

$n = 58$ countries (LDCs and European Periphery) with complete data, p for all predictors and the whole equation $< .05$, F (equation) $= 6.754$, adj. $R**2 = 16.8$ per cent

development? When the share of Soviet/East European per total imported weapons was a tolerable indicator of such a national democratic revolutionary orientation (after all, that's what it boils down to), then at least I can make an estimate about the historical social consequences of Soviet client status of state classes in periphery and semi-periphery countries. First I turn to income distribution. On the level of the LDCs and European semi-periphery nations with complete data, it turns out that among the significant predictors influencing income inequality in the world system only two are significant here, i.e. long-term demographic dynamics and penetration by the multinational corporations. The significance of the third predictor, Soviet client status, was not good enough statistically (error probability 91.35 per cent), but considering the influence of the other two predictors, Soviet client status even led to a slightly higher income inequality in the periphery and the semi-periphery (see Table 8.24).

Table 8.24 Former Soviet clientele status and income inequality (GINI index)

Predictor	Beta weight	Significance
Crude birth rate, 1960	+.39807	.0038
MNC penetration 1967 **.50	+.34331	.0153
Soviet clientele status	+.01477	.9135

$n = 46$ LDCs and European semi-periphery countries with complete data (ACDA, 1980; World Tables, 1980 (birth rates) and Ballmer-Cao and Scheidegger (GINI index income inequality, around 1968–70; Stock of capital invested by MNCs in LDCs weighted by population and total energy consumption as a proxy for capital stock)
adj. $R**2 = 24.8$ per cent; $p = .0018$; $F = 5.95286$

I maintain as a general hypothesis that the state classes in the South, supported by Soviet and other East European weapons, were unable (from 1960 to 1982) to produce a reasonable, ecologically balanced human development. Again I use the methodology established in Equations 6.4 and 6.5. And again, it emerges that the interaction of ethnic heterogeneity with former state socialism or strategic dependence from such a former state socialism produced negative effects on the energy consumption–human development trade-off. These results are reported in Table 8.25.

Table 8.25   Strategic dependence on the East and human development in periphery and semi-periphery countries

Predictor	Beta-weight	Significance
ln Life expectancy,1960	−.85037	.0000
Energy cons. per cap. 1960 ** $(((1/(e^{**}2))-1)$	−.31104	.0038
Ethno-linguistic fractionalization	−.18699	.0582
Eastern European clientele status, 74–78	−.13096	.1395

$n = 77$ countries with complete data (ACDA, 1980, on arms transfers; Life expectancies from *World Tables/World Data Tape*, 1980; Energy cons. per cap. from Ballmer-Cao and Scheidegger, as well as ethno-linguistic fractionalization) from the LDC + European semi-periphery countries.
adj. $R^{**}2 = 42.7$ per cent; $p = .0000$; $F = 15.14$.

Thus, little remained in terms of the social, economic or political gains to be expected from being a Soviet or East European ally in the Third World and in the European periphery, even before the walls crumbled in 1989. Growth and human development were retarded, there was no redistribution to be expected, and executive instability was larger than usual by the workings of such a former USSR client development. Client status, however, did allow state classes in the South to import heavy arms, even when they had larger debts, and it did postpone the outbreak of large-scale political violence, at least for some time.

This rather sober assessment of the effects of the former USSR–WTO client status in the semi-periphery and periphery runs counter to Szentes' (1984) far more positive expectations. Meanwhile, the Third World competes with the East even in the field of weapons production and weapons exports (SIPRI, 1986; Thee, 1986). I maintain that the compelling mechanisms shaping, both internally and externally, former USSR behaviour in world society did not change as dramatically as was often expected in the age of *perestroika*. The continuing weight of militarism in the former USSR, in fact, was one of the main factors which finally led to its disintegration.

In Figure 8.13 I show Pentagon estimates (US Department of Defense, 1989) about arms production before and during the Gorbachev period in the former USSR: the military burden provided an enormous block against a more rational economic policy in the early reform years, valuable time which was lost *vis-à-vis* the rising tide of nationalism and all kinds of right-wing ideologies in the Soviet province in the late 1980s. And yet, the capacity of the economy to continue output in certain key military areas declined (see Figure 8.13).

Figure 8.13   Armament production before (black) and during the Gorbachev era (white) in the USSR according to Pentagon estimates

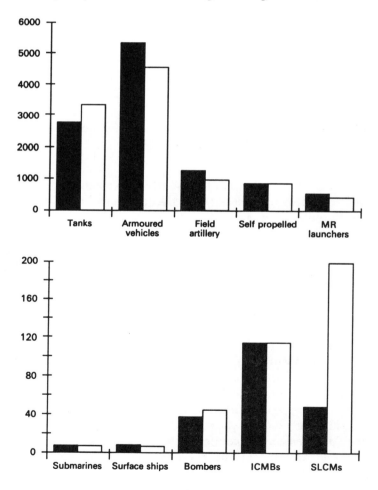

The weakness of socialist arms technologies in the South was the weakness of socialist models in the East and in the South. South Korea by far now outstrips North Korea in the production of major weapons systems. Soviet technology was on the retreat well before August 1991 and with the growth of Indian bourgeois and state class industrial power, it will export its own technologies to other countries and will adapt existing socialist arms technologies and market them accordingly. North Korea ruthlessly exports its arms to major crisis regions, regardless even of the few foreign policy constraints that the former USSR had (Cutler *et al.*, 1987: 295). But India's threat to CIS, ex-CSFR and Polish market shares was different in so far as India introduces advanced technological elements in its adaptations of existing Eastern military equipment. Egypt, another Soviet former stronghold, threw out the Soviets from its market and now depends on British and French technology. My macro-quantitative results about these processes pertain to the period of growth, apex and onset of decline of Soviet and East European influence in the Third World.

In short, I have shown that Soviet influence found its base in systems with distribution coalitions, but these, in the long run, block real development, while there might have been some short-run benefits in terms of lesser debts through lower prices of arms. Thus, former state socialism was not a viable development strategy either in the centre or the periphery.

It is now time to draw some inferences from the post-revolutionary experience in Eastern Europe for the future world order. World politics since the sixteenth century has produced a major system-wide war every 150 years (Goldstein, 1988), and there seems to be no reason to suppose that this fatal cycle of Kondratieff depressions and wars should not continue in the twenty-first century. Many authors, like Frank and Fuentes-Frank, speculate about the future constellations in the world system in the twenty-first century: Germany vs. rest again? A German–Russian-alliance against a North American Pacific block under the leadership of Japan and the US, including China? Three superpowers: Europe to the Urals, North America, Japan and China? Every multipolar system, up to now, has ended up in a sharp bi-polar conflict between a continental land mass, striving for a world empire, and the dominant nation in the capitalist world economy. *I am rather cautious about predicting conflict between the capitalist superpowers themselves: should Russian democracy fail and should there be no real peace in the Middle East, the formation of a Chinese–Russian world political and economic alliance, to be joined by radical powers in the Middle East and North Africa for the next decades and the end of democracy in the former USSR is a possibility during the next Kondratieff cycle.* The world would very much look like the pre-1914 international system: China in the role of Germany, quickly ascending industrially and increasing its sea power, and the former

USSR in the role of Austria (belated reforms and nationality conflicts). The system would still have some similarities to the immediate post-war period as well: two (post)communist powers with huge populations and territories against the Western capitalist powers.

What results, then, is a transformation not from socialism to capitalism, but the breakdown of the old social order in a semi-peripheral area of the world economy at the end of a world economic cycle, and the transition of that particular dictatorial order that was designed to be a strategy of ascent in the world economy to the mere standard-type underdevelopment profile. In contrast to the more optimistic assessment about economic reforms and the decline of poverty, which was evident in the literature from Flakierski's well-known essay, Hungary witnessed the spread of poverty and Latin American debt proportions both under communism and capitalism (see also Vienna Institute for Comparative Economic Studies, *Mitgliederinformationen*, 3, 1992). This was already present during the 1980s, and this tendency has increased even after the regime transformation (see Table 8.26).

Consumption and investment was stagnating before 1989 and does so today, the foreign debt is enormous, and Eastern Europe falls more and more behind Western Europe in terms of human development. Particularly revealing in this context are the data about the crude death rate (Hungary's is the largest in all the industrialized countries of the whole world), the extent of malnourishment of newly born babies (Hungary again surpasses all the industrialized world), the maternal death rate (just think about Romania) and the infant mortality rate. On such terms, I do in fact agree with Arrighi (1989) who maintains that the semi-periphery – to which countries like Hungary and Romania belong – is much more likely to repeat the stagnation and instability experience of Argentina than the democratization experience of Spain after the death of General Franco.

The reform communist project as a strategy to reverse the crisis has utterly failed, the USSR and the former Warsaw Pact have collapsed, civil wars rage in many parts of the former USSR, giving lie to the assumptions about the solution of the nationality conflict under socialism. The GDP of the whole region has declined by 3.9 per cent in 1990 and by 16.2 per cent in 1991, with an even larger decline in investments during the same period (The Vienna Institute for Comparative Economic Studies, *Mitgliederinformationen*, 3, 1992). The downward trend of Eastern Europe and the CIS with its unprecedented mixture of inflation, unemployment, shrinking foreign trade and declining agricultural production threatens the process of rebuilding or building democracies in Eastern Europe. Precisely the almost mindless application of the traditional IMF-type stabilization programmes to economies which are in such a deep historical transformation process has up to now produced almost no positive results in the region. Even in the case

Table 8.26 Crisis dimensions in selected East European countries, 1980–86

Crisis indicator	Hungary	Poland	Romania	USSR
(a) Economic stagnation				
Growth of private consumption 1980–86 per annum	+0.1%	−1.7%	—	—
Growth of gross domestic investment 1980–86 per annum	−3.2%	−0.8%	—	—
(b) Poverty and low living standards				
% of household expenditures spent				
on foodstuffs	25%	29%	—	—
on clothing and shoes	9%	9%	—	—
on rent, heating and electricity	10%	7%	—	—
% of household expenditures spent on basic necessities (3+4+5) together	44%	45%	—	—
(c) Accumulating foreign and domestic debts				
Foreign convertible currency reserves in months of import coverage	3.9	0.6	1.9	—
Total foreign debt 1986 in millions of US$	17218	36638	6639	—
Debt in % of GNP	59.6%	48.5%	—	—
State sector deficit in % of GNP	−3.3%	−0.3%	—	—
(d) Deficient human development and rising mortality rates				
Crude death rate	14	10	10	10
% of babies born with severe signs of underweight at birth	10	8	6	6
Maternal death rate per 100 000 live births	28	12	175	—
Infant mortality rate 1986	19	18	26	30

Source: Compiled from World Bank, *World Development Report*, 1988.

of the former GDR, there is an increasing political polarization in the old
Federal Republic about the burden of reunification, and in the seven new
Bundeslaender themselves rising unemployment and a marked political
swing to the authoritarian right and the old communist left (Butterwege,
1991; Dietz, 1991a; Rode, 1991; Wolf, 1991). In the other ethnically less
homogeneous societies of Eastern Europe, the situation is even worse, when
we take overall prospects for the nation-building process into account
(Andrejevich, 1991; Aslund, 1991 and 1992; Balibar, 1991; Bush, 1992;
Chase-Dunn, 1992; Furkes and Schlarp, 1991; Grosser, 1992; Hanson, 1991;
Juchler, 1992; Kurz, 1991; Nolte, 1991; Segbers, 1991; Tausch, 1989b,
1989c, 1991b; Tedstrom, 1991). In fact, Eastern Europe experiences the
worst slump since the days of the Great Depression (1929), and the chances
for a recovery in the framework of a democratic model are very slim indeed
(see Table 8.27).

Table 8.27   Economic performance in Eastern Europe and the former USSR since
the 1989 revolution (except for indebtedness, per cent changes over last
year)

Country	Real GDP	Agriculture	Investment
Bulgaria			
1990	−11.8	−8.7	−28.0
1991	−22.9	−5.0	—
Czechoslovakia			
1990	−0.4	−3.5	+7.7
1991	−15.9	−8.8	−30.9
Hungary			
1990	−3.3	−3.8	−9.8
1991	−9.0	−3.0	−10.0
Poland			
1990	−11.6	−2.2	−10.1
1991	−10.0	−2.0	−8.0
Romania			
1990	−7.4	−2.9	−38.3
1991	−13.5	−0.5	−26.8
former Yugoslavia			
1990	−8.5	−4.9	−18.3
1991	−20.0	+8.0	−30.0
former USSR/CIS			
1990	−2.3	−2.8	−8.7
1991	−17.0	−7.0	−15.0

Country	Wages	Prices	Gross debt in $bn
Bulgaria			
1990	+7.8	26.3	10.0
1991	−58.0	479.8	11.6
Czechoslovakia			
1990	−5.6	10.0	8.1
1991	−24.2	57.9	9.3
Hungary			
1990	−5.1	28.9	21.3
1991	−8.6	35.0	22.8
Poland			
1990	−27.6	585.8	48.5
1991	+3.6	70.3	46.5
Romania			
1990	+4.6	4.2	0.9
1991	−16.3	165.0	2.1
former Yugoslavia			
1990	−22.0	587.6	16.5
1991	−17.0	118.1	—
former USSR/CIS			
1990	+9.1	4.7	56.0
1991	−13.0	96.0	70.0

Output: output of industry, annual rate of change in %.
Agriculture: gross agricultural production, annual rate of change in %.
Investment: gross fixed investment at constant prices, annual rate of change in %.
Wages: real wages and salaries, annual rate of change in %.
Prices: consumer price increases, annual rate of change in %.
Gross Debt: gross indebtedness in convertible currencies US$bn
Source: The Vienna Institute for Comparative Economic Studies, *Mitglieder-informationen*, 3, 1992.

What can be learned from the countries of the Pacific in this context? A more supply-side oriented approach could quickly end the stagflation process in Eastern Europe. The centre of such a supply-side oriented way out of the crisis would have to be a thorough agricultural transformation, such as also formed the basis of the successful development strategies in the Far East in the recent decades. The whole canon of socio-liberal reforms, like (i) demographic transition measures; (ii) a policy of health and human capital formation; (iii) a foreign capital policy that avoids too high measures of dependency and would rather concentrate on creating employment via free production zones; (iv) new tax structures based on direct taxes; (v) a proper defence policy, based on conscription, conducive to nation-building would be of great relevance here. One of the most interesting problems in the light of the historical and empirical evidence presented in Chapter 10 and 11 is the relative downward inflexibility of wages in times of economic hardship, to be observed in Poland, 1991, and in the USSR in 1990. The less organized sectors of societies have to carry the main burden of the crisis, and unemployment skyrockets, while the monopolized sectors, already firmly entrenched in the previous socialist structures, also benefit from the distribution coalition environment existing in the new democracies.

9 Towards a Pacific Age of Capitalism?

It would be wrong to suggest that Third World industrialization escaped the attention of dependency and world systems theories. Early on, at a Polish–English symposium, which took place in October 1979 at Ojrzanow near Warsaw, G. Palma and M. Bienefeld were among the first writers from that tradition to have spelt out clearly hypotheses concerning the 'NIC' phenomenon. While Palma asserts that the 'stagnationists' (A. G. Frank, R. M. Marini, P. Baran) have thus developed schemas that are unable to explain the specificity of political development and political domination in the backward countries and that they 'have underdeveloped their contribution to the dependency school' (Palma, 1981: 64), Bienefeld has grasped even more fully what is at stake:

> The most prevalent explanation of the NIC phenomenon has placed very heavy emphasis on the internal policies pursued by the respective countries, with special stress on their efforts to get their prices right in relation to international opportunity costs and thereby to promote exports. For the dependency perspective these conclusions represent a considerable challenge in that they assert in a generalized way the prime importance of internal policy, the adequacy of market price signals as guides to resource allocation, and the effective insignificance of the potential problems which might be associated with the role of foreign capital. (Bienefeld, 1981: 88)

Such an analysis was, and remains, a minority position in the profession of dependency/world system oriented development research. Neoliberal economists and politicians, on the other hand, systematically integrated the 'Pacific' experience of newly industrializing countries into their thinking. In his now almost classic book on the Pacific century, Linder said:

> The successful Pacific countries are all market economies with private entrepreneurship and private property. They give considerable attention to efficient allocation by way of rational prices, and they have an outward-oriented development strategy focused on international trade. The success of the Pacific countries means that other regions are experiencing a relative decline as their share in world activity falls. This

decline will prove especially difficult for countries that rely on a different economic system from that of the successful Pacific countries. (Linder, 1986: 1–2)

The Pacific phenomenon, according to Linder, revitalizes the world and, in global terms, as he puts it, 'centre and periphery do not exist in some eternal arrangement.' (Linder, 1986: 4). For Linder, the Pacific 'phenomenon' is to be observed in the following countries as set out in Table 9.1.

Table 9.1   The Pacific age of capitalism

Japan, Australia, New Zealand Zealand, the US Pacific States (California, Oregon, Washington, Alaska, Hawaii)	S. Korea, Taiwan, Hong Kong, Singapore, Malaysia, Thailand, Indonesia, Brunei, Philippines, Papua New Guinea, China

which comprised in 1982:

33.2 per cent of the world population
18.1 per cent of the land surface of the earth
23.4 per cent of the world GDP

By contrast, Western Europe accounted for 30.6 per cent of the world's GDP, and the other LDCs not included in Linder's Pacific group barely 17.7 per cent (Linder, 1986: 8–9). Since 1960 there was a dramatic economic shift away from the Atlantic Basin area: in absolute GDP terms, Pacific economic potential in 1960 amounted to barely two-fifths of the economic potential of the Atlantic Basin; now this relationship is roughly three-fifths. As a share of world GDP, the most dynamic Pacific nations accounted, in 1960, for barely 16.2 per cent; now their share has increased to 23.3 per cent. Besides Western Europe, and the United States, the Pacific has become the third major capitalist power in the world (Linder, 1986: 10).

However, there are serious drawbacks to Linder's kind of analysis. The nature of future political and social development in the People's Republic of China is less clear than ever before; instability and the absence of a thorough land reform make the inclusion of the Philippines an illusion (Bello, 1989); there are severe doubts about the underlying political culture in Indonesia and Malaysia (Das, 1987), and the nature of events in China in June 1989 undermined the future of Hong Kong. Economic growth has slowed down during the 1980s in all the developing world, and it has even been slowing down in South and East Asia (Terhal, 1989; Preston, 1987). The existence of the NIC phenomenon and the rapid ascent of South East Asian countries in the capitalist world economy does not mean that all of South East Asia is ascending; neither does it mean that the ascent is free from the ups and down of the Kondratieff cycle, characterizing the whole of the world economy.

Quantitative investigations into the patterns of world-wide development would in principle be equipped to search for such peculiarities within the framework of general patterns, and in the literature there have been some attempts in such a direction, mostly based on network analysis techniques.

Recent macro-quantitative evidence suggests a growing homogenization in the world economy within the three basic categories that Wallerstein and his associates developed: the centre, the semi-periphery and the periphery. The basic empirical evidence for this hypothesis is to be found in the work by Peacock *et al.* (1988) which operationalizes the Hopkins, Wallerstein *et al.* categories to comprise the following national entities (see Table 9.2).

Table 9.2 The Peacock categories: centre, semi-periphery and periphery

Centre	*Semi-Periphery*	*Periphery*
	Strong:	
Japan, Belgium, France, FRG, Italy, NL, UK, CND, USA	Nigeria, India, Israel Philippines, Austria, Denmark, Finland, Greece, Ireland, Norway, Spain, Sweden, CH, Mexico, Argentina, Brazil, Venezuela, Australia	Ethiopia, Morocco, Uganda, Burma, Sri Lanka, Turkey, Costa Rica, El Salvador, Guatemala, Honduras, Nicaragua, Panama, Bolivia, Ecuador, Paraguay, Peru, Uruguay
	Weak:	
	Egypt, Kenya, Zaire, Pakistan, Thailand, Portugal, Chile, Colombia, New Zealand	

The network analysis technique, employed by Peacock *et al.*, is based on trade data and excludes, *a priori*, former socialist nations. My approach is quite different and tries to include indicators of economic structure that go far beyond trade patterns and thus will avoid the unacceptable hypothesis that core countries such as Sweden, Norway or Denmark are classified as 'semi-periphery' together with Nigeria or India. My approach uses the older and more classical technique of factor analysis, and the variables used will not consist of trade patterns alone.

Strictly speaking, Peacock's results are really meaningless and just reflect the choice of the sample. While in reality some semi-periphery countries historically moved up the ladder of international development, and some former socialist and capitalist and socialist centre or semi-periphery countries lost their positions – so there was quite an extensive mobility in the international system – Peacock and his associates suggest something very different: that the differences between the three blocs increased, and the intra-group differences decreased. But this is simply a statistical consequence of the inclusion of Israel, Austria, Denmark, Ireland, Australia, Norway, etc. in the same group of countries as the ascending semi-peripheries.

My results will by contrast lead towards new typologies of societies on the world systems rim, especially in South Asia. Factor analysis (see especially Kim and Mueller, 1978) can be used to classify the states of the world according to parsimonious criteria, representing a variety of variables on new, mathematically derived 'factors' which optimally reproduce the existing correlational relations between the variables in question. Thus it is possible to gain insights into processes and their relationship below the surface of measured variables. I should recall that in social science literature it is common to speak on the basis of factor analytical results about such complex phenomena as 'economic development', 'intensive agriculture', 'catholic culture', as, for example, in Russett (1967).

With the SPSS programme, it is possible to calculate factor analytical results which allow for a correlation among the new, mathematically derived dimensions ('factors'). I thus speak of 'oblique' solutions, in contrast to the more common, but less useful 'orthogonal' models which grouped the variables on the new factors in such a way that the correlation between them is minimal. The variables used in my first classification are set out in Table 9.3.

If not specified elsewhere, data about the underlying determinants of the growth patterns in world society 1965–83 refer to the starting point of the growth period; i.e., around 1965. The mathematical details of my model are shown in Table 9.4. The two factors correlate positively with each other ($+.14544$). The world capitalist rimlands are thus classified according to two, slightly positively related dimensions: state class influence and growth potential. Again I draw attention to the results about military Keynesian growth in periphery economies during the period under consideration (Chapter 8). State class influence deters MNC penetration, and MNC penetration influences growth slightly negatively, when we take other predictors into account. The new, mathematically derived dimensions of growth determinants on the 'rim' of the capitalist world system classify states in Asia as set out in Table 9.5.

Table 9.3 Key to variables for factor analytical model about the 'rim' of the capitalist world system

wi1	Weapons imports from former USSR + Poland + ex-CSFR per total arms imports 74–78
nu1	Economic growth per capita in constant $1965–83
DS2	Agricultural density **.50 around 1960
v44	Public investment per total investment
V257	Military expenditures per total government expenditures
v30	Government expenditures per GDP
v102	Galtung's trade structure index (+ 1.0 Industrial Exporting Country, −1 Classical Periphery)
v135	Economic voting at the UN with the bloc of Third World nations (0-pro Western, + 4-totally supporting Third World economic positions at the UN)
v266	Political voting at the UN with the Western bloc (1-pro Soviet, ranging up to 7, pro Western)
v166	Index of Natural Resources Potential
v603	Penetration by Capital, invested by transnationals, per total capital stock weighted by population (**.25)

Sample selection criterion: World Economic Integration Factor smaller or equal 4.0
Data Sources: With the exceptions mentioned in the text and tables above, Ballmer-Cao and Scheidegger.

Table 9.4 Factor analysis of growth patterns on the 'rim' of the capitalist world economy, 1965–83

DETERMINANT = .0145731 (.14573070E−01)
OBLIQUE FACTOR PATTERN MATRIX
AFTER ROTATION WITH KAISER NORMALIZATION

	FACTOR 1 State class influence	FACTOR 2 Growth potential 1965–83	
WI1	.74839	−.29148	Russian arms clients
NU1	.09093	.77901	Economic growth
DS2	−.04301	.53492	Rural density
V44	.53352	.04604	Public investment
V257	.33784	.19531	Military burden per gov. expenditures
V30	.12514	.01722	Government expenditures per GDP
V102	.30812	.75414	Galtung's Trade Elaborateness Index
V135	.47754	−.09226	Third World economic orientation
V266	−.71410	.05258	World political identification with West
V166	−.00750	.03254	Natural resources available for a nation
V603	−.46398	−.16706	Penetration by core capital

Table 9.5   State class influence and growth potential in Asia, 1965–83

Sequence number	State class influence	Growth potential 1965–83	Country
62	−.7494	−.3557	Iran
63	1.0024	−.2034	Iraq
65	.2907	1.5256	Israel
66	−.2259	.1758	Lebanon
67	−.1439	1.0934	Saudi Arabia
68	1.5476	.2630	Syria
72	.2298	−.3344	Afghanistan
73	.2959	−.0976	Burma
76	1.5522	.5506	India
81	.2929	2.5192	South Korea
83	−.5979	.6176	Malaysia
85	−.2580	−.2525	Nepal
87	−.7050	.3667	Philippines
88	.3089	2.2229	Singapore
90	−.6313	.1255	Thailand
121	−.7344	1.1196	Taiwan

Note: The Factor Model required oblique rotation and pairwise deletion of missing values according to the SPSS. My control cards required the SPSS to calculate factor scores only, when data were available for more than 8 variables of the model. Then, values still missing were calculated by the mean (control cards rotate = oblique, facscore = .33, options 2, 10, 13).

An important question must be raised here: will state class influence on the economy lead towards a more Eastward or a more Westward-oriented policy in the long run? State class control was very strong in Israel and in Egypt, but both countries turned, at different times, very decisively to the Western powers for support, while other Third World states very plausibly might start playing the 'Chinese card'. Certainly Argentina, Peru and Indonesia are candidates here, should the international recession and the debt crisis grow worse in the wake of yet another Kondratieff cycle low (1820–30; 1870–80; 1930s) in the early 1990s. The strength of the state class and a basic anti-Western world political attitude at the UN, combined with a low MNC-presence determines around 56 per cent of client status *vis-à-vis* the East. But the growth-intensive nations of Asia were not especially pro-Third World in their attitude at the UN, they bought practically no arms from the USSR, had higher military expenditures, sometimes quite a strong public economy, and were already higher 'above' on the ladders of the international division of labour.

The changes in the international economy also have their consequences in the relationships of world-wide military power(s). As some nations ascend and others decline relatively, what are the political and military consequences? Most of the client states of Russian arms transfers (and especially those in Asia) were countries whose growth potential in the past decades was lower than in the newly emergent South-East Asian 'dragons'. The internal and world political conditions unfavourable for the now defunct Russian 'Empire' could already be assessed from the results of the following factor analysis on the basis of the Taylor and Jodice data tape. An international comparison reveals that, in 1975, there was already an alarming weight of military expenditures per GNP in relation to education and health expenditures in the socialist orbit within the capitalist world economy, as is shown in Table 9.6.

Table 9.6   Military expenditures in comparison with education and health expenditures in the countries of the 'Socialist World System', 1975

Country	Military	Public education Expenditures per GNP (1975)	Health
Albania	10.0	—	—
Algeria	2.5	5.7	1.4
Bulgaria	8.9	3.6	2.8
China	11.0	—	—
Congo P.R.	4.3	8.2	—
Cuba	6.1	11.2	—
ex-CSFR	5.9	3.3	3.5
Ethiopia	3.8	3.0	.8
former GDR	6.4	4.7	2.8
Hungary	5.6	3.2	2.6
Kampuchea	11.0	—	—
North Korea	10.4	—	—
Laos	7.3	2.7	.4
Mongolia	8.5	—	—
Poland	6.0	3.8	3.3
Romania	4.8	2.3	1.8
former USSR	13.7	4.6	2.4
Vietnam	22.6	—	—
South Yemen	6.8	1.0	0.5
former Yugoslavia	4.5	4.9	—

Source: Taylor and Jodice Machine Readable Data Tape, 1983.

High military expenditures socially overburdened even the richer socialist countries, let alone poor nations such as Vietnam. Compared to the ever-present need for an expansive policy in education, health, and environmental protection, 'real socialism' in the centre and in the periphery of the 'socialist world economy' resembled much more a war-type economy than social priorities. The contrast between former world socialism and socio-liberal democracies in the world protestant regions and also with Japan was striking indeed (see Table 9.7).

Table 9.7   Military burden rates in advanced capitalist democracies

Country	Military burden (%)	Education (%)	Health expenditures per GNP (%)
Australia	3.2	9.3	4.0
Denmark	2.6	8.0	3.4
Finland	1.5	6.7	4.6
Japan	0.9	5.8	0.2
Netherlands	3.5	7.7	1.8
New Zealand	1.8	5.7	5.4
Norway	3.3	7.7	0.6
Sweden	3.2	7.2	4.7

Source: Own compilations from Taylor and Jodice (1983).

Periphery economies with a smaller integration profile into the juridical institutions of the capitalist world economy produced high growth by militarization. Socialist economies, I have said in Chapter 8, reacted differently in so far as their 'military-industrial-complex' assured some successes (lower debt ratios, better net service incomes balances) at the heavy long-term price of stagnating labour productivity and deficient industrial consumption exports. *Perestroika* above all should have meant a reversal of this trend: agrarian reform, increased labour productivity, increased industrial consumption exports (also to the capitalist world economy). Consumer goods industries favoured, in the beginning, the reversal, but the 'iron eaters' grew stronger again, when, as under the Gierek regime in Poland in the late 1970s, the external balances became weaker *vis-à-vis* the capitalist world economy. There are definite signs now of an alliance between heavy industry, nationalism, the top-level military establishment and the 'hard hats' among the working class, especially those losing jobs in the arms (exports) industries and living in separatist republics.

I believe that the patterns of government spending on defence, health and education cannot be separated from the underlying culture of a political system. M. Kaldor in her rightly famous book on the baroque arsenal (1981) has drawn attention to the devastating consequences which the 'military-industrial-complex' had on the social and political development of the former Soviet Union. In recent debates about Third World security issues, authors from neutral European countries maintained the high socio-political and even economic relevance of an alternative concept of security, based on a purely defensive approach to army strategy in contrast to a technocratic concept (Tuomi and Vaeyrynen, 1982; S. F. Hasnat and A. Pelinka, 1986). Quantitative development research efforts, such as the one by Weede, have shown that conscription and thus a higher military personnel ratio per population are very positively related to Third World economic growth. For Tuomi and Vaeyrynen the clear contrast between a technocratic and, ultimately, repressive army doctrine, such as in Pakistan or India, and a people's army concept, inherent in the defence policy ideas of especially European Social Democrats and Green Parties, emerges from Figure 9.1.

Figure 9.1   Defence strategies according to Tuomi and Vaeyrynen

Dimension	Technocratic army	People's army
Weapons and equipment	Capital-intensive modern carrier systems; tanks, aircraft, and fighting ships, mobile tank divisions; partly locally built and assembled	Simple: anti-aircraft and anti-tank missiles, light infantry weapons; mainly local production; diversified supply lines; marine equipment for coastal protection
Armed forces	Professional army: specialized troops in army, navy, air force	Militia system, personnel intensive, new organizational forms geared to serve also economic functions
Mobilization	Permanent mobilization of the professionals, limited reserves	In peacetime limited mobilization; in wartime total mobilization of the population
Command and structure	Hierarchical, centralized	Democratic, decentralized
Strategy	Defensive and offensive including potential for pre-emptive strikes	Defensive, reactive, territorial defence to prevent occupations

Elsewhere I have said that the most likely future world political constellation will be an alliance of China, the former USSR and some radical states in the Middle East and North Africa against the three capitalist centre blocks, North America, Western Europe and Japan. In 1988 these three capitalist centres controlled 15.1 per cent of world population, 20.5 per cent of world armed forces, 22.7 per cent of the world land mass, but 43.5 per cent of world military expenditures, 57.3 per cent of world GNP and 65.9 per cent of world exports. Each of these three centres slowly expands and brings other nations into its orbit: Japan expands towards Asia and the Pacific, the United States towards Mexico and Central America, and Western Europe towards Eastern Europe and towards neutral European countries. The countries of the former Warsaw Pact and the European neutrals would increase the share of the Western centres over world GNP by another 7.9 per cent and over world exports by another 11.4 per cent (our own calculations from US ACDA, 1988). Culturally, the three major capitalist blocks, even after German unity, will be very much united in sharing the values of liberal Western democracy, while the major confrontations will be along ideological, religious and economic lines.

Two major players in world politics in the twenty-first century – India and Brazil – have not yet been mentioned here. I dare the prediction that the values of Western democracy and religious tensions in India itself will finally decide India's place in the Western capitalist alliance, probably forming an economic triangle with Australia and Japan. In 1988, India accounted for 15.8 per cent of the world's population and 2.1 per cent of the world surface; while Brazil had 2.9 per cent of the world's population and 5.7 per cent of its surface. However, social and wealth disparities have up to now prevented both countries from playing a major role in the world economy. Both of them barely control 1.5 per cent of the world's GNP each. My empirical analysis will show that, by following the technocratic army concept, India could not manage even to become a major power – which is, after all, the aim of India's militarization. By international standards, India's power seems to be rather weak, and it is far from having the strong internal economic base which would enable it to support such a superpower policy, or make it, after the US, the former USSR, China, France, the UK, the sixth major force in world strategic affairs.

Figure 9.2 summarizes three important and very common indicators of international power: GNP, military expenditures and armed forces levels. When measured only by army strength, India's costly system of a large, professional army (incidentally, the fourth largest army in the world) produces a considerable lead over other nations. On the other hand, the economic basis to maintain such a large army is rather weak – the recurrent dilemma of India's expansionist policy (Figure 9.3).

Power, according to K. W. Deutsch (1978c), is the ability to prevail in conflict and to overcome obstacles (Deutsch, 1978c: 23). Indicators of the bases of power are, for example, military expenditures or military personnel; potential power is often measured by steel and energy production, number

Figure 9.2   Power in the world system: GNP, army size, military expenditures

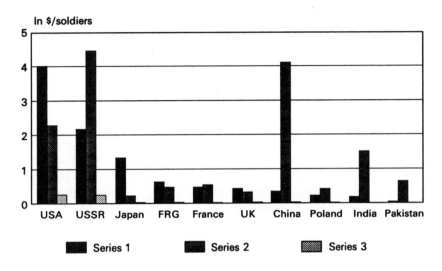

Source: US ACDA, US MILEX: 265800 Mill$.

Figure 9.3   Military build-up in Asia: arms transfers and military outlays

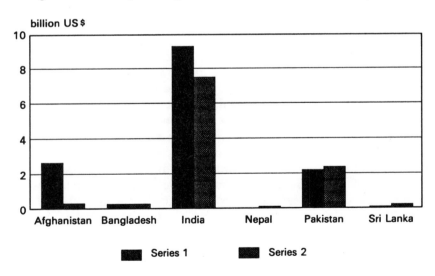

Source: US ACDA *Arms Transfers* 1982–86, MILEX 1986.

of inhabitants and the like. A power base for actor A is the amount of some value for actor B, which is under A's control. Actor A controls some possible increase or decrease in B's wealth, well-being or enjoyment of respect (Deutsch, 1978c: 24–7). Thus, vulnerabilities to international economic pressures must form part of any empirical research design (trade per GNP, concentration of export commodities, concentration of export recipient countries). Power also has a weight, a domain, a range and a scope, but those concepts are much more difficult to operationalize on the basis of the Taylor and Jodice data tape. Data on the weight of power of governments over their own populations could be measured, according to Deutsch's reasoning, by taxes, state investments, conscription patterns, law enforcement, and by the size of government in the respective nations. The domain of power is the collection of people subject and obedient to a political system, or, one might prefer to say, a geographic definition of the domain of government including even those who do not obey the governments' commands or passively comply with them. Especially important in this context are US political science data about separatism and the different forms of discrimination. A third power domain concept pertains not only to the persons subject or obedient to power, but also to the amounts of land, capital goods or resources controlled by it. Indicators again are population, area, GNP, but also scientific/technological human capital stocks (Deutsch, 1978c: 34–7). Thus I include in my analysis agricultural area, GNP and higher education.

I feel that the range of power – i.e., the difference between the highest rewards and the worst punishments which power holders can bestow (or inflict) – is not easily translated into an empirical measurement concept on the basis of existing cross-national data sets, such as the Taylor and Jodice data file. The possession of nuclear weapons, of course, determines to a great extent the range and also the scope of a nation's power in the world system. By scope of power, Deutsch defines the set of behaviour relations effectively subject to power. At the national level, this would mean government regulation of individual life, such as public health, old age pensions and other indicators of government sector influence. The scope of power of a given society in world society could differ, however, in so far as the bankers of nation X can command more behavioural relations of governments and individuals in nation Y than the bankers of nation Z. To further illustrate this case, Wall Street or City of London bankers have a greater scope of power over interest rates in, say, Ireland or Peru, than Finnish, Indian or Belgian bankers have in New York City. Such an analysis of power would have to be based on international economic dependence relations, which are actually overlooked in the Taylor and Jodice *World Handbook of Political and Social Indicators III* (1983).

My empirical analysis now focuses on three basic dimensions of power in the international system: military might; the absence of political/economic discrimination; and the absence of separatism in society (see Table 9.8).

Table 9.8 Factor analysis of international political, economic and military power, using US political science data

DETERMINANT = .0000070 (.69583299E-05)
OBLIQUE FACTOR PATTERN MATRIX
AFTER ROTATION WITH KAISER NORMALIZATION

	FACTOR 1	FACTOR 2	FACTOR 3	
B36	.92203	−.00895	.09726	Military manpower
B24	.88499	.06446	−.03943	Total defence expenditure
B102	.69812	−.05202	.12665	Working age population
B107	.79848	−.02192	−.00986	Agricultural area
B110	.76609	.02201	−.22843	Gross national product
B125	.37366	−.16034	−.16006	Coal production
B130	.33596	.03981	−.08959	Petroleum production
B225	.43031	−.05595	−.61679	Higher educational enrolment
B139	−.26113	−.09078	−.04975	Trade per GNP
B145	−.16109	.00633	.35748	Concentr. export commodities
B151	−.20208	.06519	−.07142	Concentr. export recipients
B56	.04868	.60374	.09390	Extension of political minority discrimination
B57	.06580	.65511	−.05560	Intensity of political minority discrimination
B64	.25137	−.03773	.75842	Extension separatism
B65	.11390	−.05373	.81698	Intensity of separatism
B60	−.07111	.70267	.03061	Extension of economic minority discrimination
B61	−.01527	.87936	−.16958	Intensity of economic minority discrimination

FACTOR PATTERN CORRELATIONS

	FACTOR 1	FACTOR 2
FACTOR 2	−.09745	
FACTOR 3	−.10806	−.04308

Source: Calculated from Taylor and Jodice (1983).

The three factors that result from this comparison of power of 155 nations in world society are not very closely related to each other. The factor pattern correlations are small. Classification results reflect, of course, the underlying data matrix, which, I must repeat, is the work of United States political scientists. These might raise some very serious doubts in other political science cultures, especially concerning the last two factors, discrimination and separatism (see Table 9.9).

Table 9.9   Power, discrimination and separatism in the world system

Results of a comparison of 155 nations

Country	Military might	Factor scores for factors Discrimination	Separatism
Argentina	.4952	−1.1283	−1.1898
Australia	1.1676	−1.2306	−1.0040
Brazil	.9174	.5767	−.5911
Bulgaria	−.0159	−.9186	−.3086
Canada	.6613	−.4931	−.8102
Cuba	−.0545	1.2404	−1.036
ex-CSFR	.2295	.2651	.0952
Egypt	.5178	.0658	−.4255
France	1.8322	1.1391	−.7226
former GDR	.0183	−1.1233	−1.1432
FRG	1.4577	1.1980	−.9269
Hungary	−.0254	−.6855	−.5582
India	.5716	−1.0542	.3729
Indonesia	−.2500	−.1937	1.1795
Iran	.5170	−.5545	1.3594
Italy	1.0837	−.7739	−.7597
Japan	.9685	−.9982	−1.2614
S. Korea	1.2080	−.5818	−.0966
Mexico	−.0213	−1.0114	−.8209
Pakistan	.4161	−1.0251	.6403
Poland	.7873	−.7789	−.7216
Romania	.1179	−.5798	.4497
South Africa	.0172	2.9209	.8578
USSR	7.4200	.2252	.6745
Spain	.9290	−.6178	.8745
Taiwan	.2611	.2316	−.1763
Turkey	.8243	−.6693	.3697
UK	.5834	.5084	−.1058
USA	5.6018	−.4091	−3.2251
former Yugoslavia	.4700	−.4265	.8556

Nobody would deny the fact that in 1975 the former USSR ranked very high in terms of military might, defined according to Deutsch above. But it is the economic and military strength of the US allies around the globe, which already, back in 1975, made the former USSR's quest for global parity a hopeless task. Within the former WTO alliance, practically only

Poland counted as a power, while India's ranking was still very low and was even lower than that of South Korea.

And in contrast to most NATO allies of the United States, the former USSR, according to these figures, had a more severe problem of minorities and regionalism with which to cope. Another analysis, this time on the basis of Ballmer-Cao and Scheidegger data file, further highlights the now historical problems of the relative power of the former USSR and its former allies by international comparison. The aim is to show the relative position of nations in the system of the international division of labour and secondly to assess the economic growth of countries.

I used the SPSS-IX programme to extract the two probably most closely related factors from the following variables: (i) economic growth 1965–83; (ii) growth of investment at the onset of the evolving new international division of labour 1965–75; (iii) commodity concentration of exports in the early 1970s; (iv) Galtung's foreign trade structure in the early 1970s; (v) MNC headquarter status; (vi) penetration by foreign patents as an indicator of technological dependence in the early 1970s; (vii) students of applied sciences per total higher educational enrolment (1970s); (viii) scientific and technical manpower per population (1970s); (ix) Weede's military personnel ratio around 1965 $(\ln(MPR + 1))$; (x) total GNP ** .33 (third root); (xi) DYN life expectancy 1977–83 as an indicator of social performance in the late 1970s and early 1980s; and (xii) world economic adjustment, 1975–83 (in the sense of maintaining the GDP growth rate in the second half of the Kondratieff cycle; see also Chapters 10 and 11).

In many ways, these concepts seem to be much more appropriate to Deutsch's theoretical positions on political power than the data available from the Taylor and Jodice data file. Although the determinant was again small (det = .00125), results still are interpretable. Again, my control cards should be mentioned, to make this result subject to possible further testing and critique. The number of factors was set at '2', rotation was again to be oblique, the upper boundary for the calculation of factor scores was 33 per cent missing data entries per case under consideration, missing values again were to be deleted pairwise and the mean was to be the substitute of missing values. Everything else was executed according to the preselected SPSS routines. The oblique factor pattern matrix then results as in Table 9.10.

The two factors, relative 'top-dog' and world economic adjustment and growth, reveal some very interesting classifications about medium Third World powers and Eastern Europe in contrast to the techno-scientific might of Western countries, now increasingly joined and even themselves challenged by the East Asian 'dragons' (see Table 9.11, which shows the end of the growth experience of some medium-sized industrialized countries).

Table 9.10   International power and international dependence

Variable	Oblique Factor Pattern Matrix	
	'Loadings' on Factor 1 Relative position as 'Top-dog' regarding scientific and technological capabilities in relation to size	Factor 2 World economic growth and adjustment, 1965–83
Economic growth	+.33288	+.89018
DYN investment 65–73	+.10048	+.55941
Commodity concentration	−.61069	−.22230
Galtung trade structure	+.75539	+.09134
MNC headquarter status	+.48058	−.33436
Patent penetration	−.53110	−.23752
Students in applied sciences rate	+.36740	+.08005
Scientific and technical manpower	+.83385	−.22905
Military manpower rate, log-transformed	+.67770	+.09544
GDP 1973 **.33	+.73110	−.03136
DYN life expect. 77–83	−.10545	+.16313
World economic adjustm.	+.20196	+.63172

Notes and sources: See text above; Factor Pattern Correlation +.11362.

In the past these medium-sized industrialized nations had a very privileged position in the world economy, and they are threatened now, as industrial exporters, by the newly emergent powers of South East Asia and other newly-industrializing countries. Prominent among the 'decliners', again, were some countries of the former socialist world as well. Both the former USSR and its former Warsaw Pact allies experienced sharp declines in their market shares in the Western industrialized countries in the 1980s, declines which brought about the severe socio-political crisis of these systems at the turn of the late 1980s and early 1990s (Figure 9.4).

So what message, then, have our debates for the countries of the South? Sen has recently pointed out – with justification – that Indian democracy with its unorthodox mix of policies under very extreme conditions has avoided the devastating mass famines so characteristic of the socialist development experience in China in the late 1950s and in the former USSR in the 1930s – famines that could repeat themselves all too probably in the former USSR. 'Socialist' famines must also be seen in the perspective of the many million political victims of Leninist regimes in the early post-revolutionary decades.

Table 9.11   Power, independence and world economic adjustment in European smaller nations, as compared to socialist countries and ascending nations in the world economy

Country	Top-dog position around 1975	Adjustment and growth performance 1965/75/83
(a) Typical 'ascenders'		
Tunisia	−.3122	+2.0969
Hong Kong	+.4337	+3.3365
South Korea	+.5684	+3.0121
Malaysia	−.1760	+1.3656
Thailand	−.1488	+1.2336
(b) European smaller nations		
Austria	+.1295	+1.1424
Belgium	+.9242	+.4282
Denmark	+.7200	−.7328
Finland	+.3570	+.8886
Greece	+.3151	+1.3767
Irish Republic	+.0172	−.4835
Netherlands	+1.3839	−.9798
Norway	+.8872	+.0559
Portugal	+.2498	+.7638
Sweden	+1.6648	−1.0974
Switzerland	+1.7151	−.9139
Hungary	+1.7350	+1.9124
(c) Larger European ex-socialist nations		
ex-CSFR	+2.8156	−2.1788
former Yugoslavia	+.5288	+1.2869
(d) Larger Western industrialized countries		
Canada	+.2786	+.1306
USA	+1.6358	−.4983
Japan	+1.8065	+1.1260
France	+1.2663	+.1810
FRG	+1.2604	+.2577
Italy	+.8138	+.5460
Spain	+.2834	+1.2549
UK	+.9089	+.4578
Australia	+.1361	−.5530

Source and notes: See text above.

Figure 9.4   Eastern Europe and the Soviet Union: shares in the Western market –
total market and market for manufactures

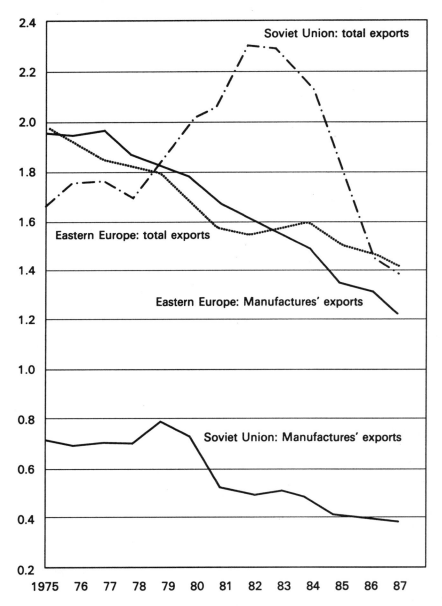

Source: ECE secretariat, as reported in UN ECE, 1988.

It would be wrong to assume that liberation theology as the most important thought pattern emerging from the periphery over the last decades did not take note of these developments so important for the future of democracy in the semi-periphery. A critical view of state socialist realities and a call for alternatives was voiced, *inter alia*, in the last article written by the late I. Ellacuria (1989), one of the six slain Jesuit priests and university professors in El Salvador, in what turned out to be his political testament. While Ellacuria both rejects the system of world-wide capitalism and state socialism and favoured a strong commitment to the 'social movements' that emerged in the capitalist world economy in the 1970s and 1980s, it is important to point out with him that there is also no ground for ideological complacency in countries like the United States ('*we have won the Cold War*'). There are indeed about 20 million people in the United States who are chronically malnourished; 20.6 per cent of all children under age 18 were poor in 1987, and the lowest 10 per cent in the US class structure experienced an absolute decrease in real incomes of 10.5 per cent between 1977 and 1988 (G. Kent, 1989). Particularly successful nations over the last forty years, like Hong Kong, Japan and Finland, by contrast, all have quite extensive basic social minimum nets that prevent the large-scale poverty that is so characteristic of United States society (N. Kent, 1990; Stauffer, 1990).

In his meticulous paper on the changes in the world system since 1950, Chase-Dunn (1984) maintains that the economic structure of the peripheral countries has indeed changed, but that they have not increased their share of world output as a whole. For Chase-Dunn, the difficulties of state socialism in the 'Second World' were too evident to be dismissed; and in contrast to Szymanski he early on disputed the contention of a separate world system of socialism as an alternative to capitalism. Rather, one should start, argues Chase-Dunn, integrating into theoretical and political experience the lessons of liberal corporatism on the European continent. Although I do not agree with Chase-Dunn's assessment of the changes in the capitalist world economy (the ascent of some semi-peripheral countries is more dramatic than expected), I do agree with him on the need to integrate the experience of liberal corporatism into world system research. Might not the future of Poland, the ex-CSFR and Hungary be the past experience of Sweden and Austria?

10 Corporatism, Development and the European Model

Europe is on the move. The EC – together with its new 'outer rim' – commands over 30 per cent of the world product and has a share of 43 per cent in world trade. Considering the severe economic and social crisis that 'real' (i.e. state) socialism and conservative capitalism (US-style) experience, it is no wonder that there has been a continuous world scholarly interest in those Western capitalist economies that combine a higher degree of state control over the economy with a powerful presence of both capital and labour organizations in the political systems of the countries concerned (Bornschier, 1992).

In Eastern Europe this interest is further increased by the fact that two countries, Finland and Austria, which, as a consequence of their participation in the Second World War on Hitler's side, were occupied by the Red Army, developed after 1945 in a capitalist pattern, but with a strong influence from social democracy and the trade unions. Both countries are neutral up to now, their bid to join the EC notwithstanding. Furthermore, Sweden and Switzerland, like Austria, are not only neutral, but strongly corporatist in their socio-political organization.

Interest in such 'neo-corporatist' models emerged from many quarters. For the long-cycle world system perspective, the 'neo-corporatist' model is at the basis of the world economic upsurge after the depression 1929–33 (Bornschier, 1988, 1992). For the long-cycle perspective, shared by Bornschier, three basic corporatisms exist within the broader range of 'Great Transformations' (see also Polanyi, 1944/57): (i) the socio-liberal New Deal in the USA; (ii) the social democratic Swedish 'folkhem' ('people's home') model since 1932, which is especially relevant as an object of study, since the political pact underlying the model lasted 44 years and Sweden's economic development was not interrupted by direct war involvement; and (iii) the fascist type of corporatism, most clearly present during the twelve years of Nazi terror in Germany.

For the older social transformation approach, elaborated by Polanyi in 1944, the contrast to the former market society model of the first and second long wave (1835–1883, 1883–1932) becomes permanent, while for the

Kondratieff cycle theory (Bornschier, 1988), the basic corporatist contract between capital and wage labour which arose at the time of the Great Depression (1929) draws to a close, thus ending the political and economic constellations which characterized the five decades after the 'Great Transformation' of capitalism in the 1930s. When we look at the even more divergent development experience at the end of 'third long wave', i.e. after the crisis 1973–74, insights from long-wave research into the career of socio-political models (Bornschier, 1988) will become relevant. Long-wave theories expect that growth rates at the end of each cycle will become more divergent than during recoveries and prosperities. Is corporatism really still the 'engine of growth'?

The question also has a very far-reaching importance for the social science debate in Latin America. For countries recovering from years of military dictatorship, there seems to be a considerable interest in the 'mixed economies' of Scandinavia, Austria and other democratic corporatist post-war reconstruction 'models' (Munoz, 1979; 1982; Valdes and Furtado, 1983). Especially in his 1982 paper on the mixed economy as a strategy to achieve full employment, Munoz revises the Keynesian 'model' in a way which will be quite familiar to the neo-corporatism debate in European and North American social science: 'the national agreement (*concertación nacional*)' on economic interests as a precondition of success for 'social Keynesianism'. The research design in this chapter is time-fitted with the periodization that long-wave research (Bornschier, 1988) has proposed: my socio-liberal explanations of OECD development are tested, roughly, for the period during and after the recession (from 1966 onwards) and the crisis of 1974–82. Of course, a full investigation into the phenomenon of corporatism would need a cross-national test for the recovery period 1932–45 and the (European and Japanese) recovery and prosperity cycle 1945–66. But long-wave research maintains that at the end of each long wave in world capitalism the future winners of the coming new wave have already become apparent. As a result of lack of data about the war and post-war recovery period I must concentrate on an investigation for the later phase, when social conflicts over the waning 'model' (i.e. after 1968) became sharper and the basic consensus broke down.

Neocorporatist theories of development (Hancock, 1983) generally maintain that a centralized and concentrated system of interest groups in industrial democracies provides the basis for stable capitalist growth. At the very heart of such a neo-corporatist set-up is the voluntary and informal coordination of policy-making between capital, labour and the state. Neo-dependency approaches to world development generally would question whether such a logic explains growth and stagnation in the OECD countries.

For capital and labour, the social partnership is not a deliberately created instrument for promoting capitalist growth at the centre: originally it was only a consequence of a past world economic constellation, which allowed for a rise in real wages at roughly the rate of productivity increases. Now, however, this constellation increasingly breaks down (Froebel, 1984; Esping-Andersen, 1987), and the breakdown is first felt in the industrially leading centre countries, but it slowly extends also to the less dominant smaller European nations, such as Scandinavia (Esping-Andersen, 1987). Thus, the maintenance of growth in the neo-corporatist smaller European nations in the time period of the late 1960s, 1970s and early 1980s would be a consequence of the fact that the world economic and political tide of change as yet had not fully hit those smaller and less dominant countries, while the United States, Japan, the Federal Republic of Germany and the United Kingdom were much earlier exposed to world economic changes.

A third pattern of explanation, a socio-liberal perspective, would not rule out the validity of hypotheses to be derived from the two approaches already outlined, but it would primarily emphasize the dialectics of institutional age and the activities of the state to account for the now highly divergent development patterns in Europe and in South Asia. In addition, it would hold – as I have already established in Chapters 5 and 7 – that the growth of government expenditure outside the field of education now retards economic growth in the stable institutional environment of ageing developed democracies. A socio-liberal perspective would not rule out the effects of the encompassing nature of interest groups on growth; it also cannot exclude the influence played by the industrial oligopolies at the centre in bringing about the transfer of jobs to the periphery, thus contributing to abrupt changes in established capitalist development patterns. A socio-liberal perspective would recognize the effects of institutional arrangements with the capitalist world economy on promoting capitalist growth. Contrary to neo-corporatism schools, however, my explanation will draw attention to the negative sides of the corporatist set-up, as predicted by Olson's hypothesis of the strongly anti-social behaviour of narrow distributional coalitions, leading especially towards fewer employment chances for the under-privileged groups, such as females or ethno-religious minorities.

A fourth and continuous thematic tradition must be mentioned as well. This tradition refers to the effects of economic size on the growth chances of a nation, and two competing hypotheses exist here. One small-state theory would hold, in the tradition of Rothschild, that smaller states find it more difficult than big ones to keep or to better their position in the world economy, while other small-state theories would expect just the opposite; i.e. an especially beneficial effect of small size on economic development and political patterns, leading to compromise, growth and reconciliation, at least at the level of industrialized Western democracies. This tradition is represented mainly by the writings of Katzenstein.

In that context, quite a number of scholarly efforts in the past have picked out the European smaller nations, and also those European nations in the 'grey' zone between the two power blocs dominant on the European continent (including the neutrals and former Yugoslavia). But such pre-theory, evident in the literature (Fabinc and Popovic, 1988; Hettne, 1988; Hoell and Kramer, 1986; Karlsson, 1988; McSweeny, 1987; Milanovic, 1987; Popovic, 1988; Senghaas, 1985b; Stajner, 1987 and Tausch, 1986d) does not reach a definite conclusion on the social and economic effects of the power status of a nation. A further complication is the breakdown of the former Warsaw Pact, which dominated six East European countries.

For reasons of conceptual clarity I opted to include, under the heading 'European small nations', only those countries whose population was smaller than 15 million people (see Table 10.1). Thus, the categories of 'smallness' and 'zero-block' nations do not completely overlap. Militarily and politically, by any standards, the former Yugoslavia was not a small country, while there are a number of small nations belonging to the two big military alliances. In these comparisons I face the severe problem of data limitations for some of these small or zero-block countries. My machine readable data files do not report much from Albania. By the exclusion of countries with less than 1 million inhabitants from most data files, Iceland and Luxembourg did not belong to the set of units to be analysed in the equations reported in Chapter 7. Thus, no residuals can be reported for those nations here in Chapter 10. In explaining the performance of smaller European countries the following social scientific theories will then be empirically especially relevant to us (Czada, 1987: 20–39): (i) the socio-liberal approach, already presented in Chapters 5 and 7. This approach will expect increasing developmental deficiencies in consequence of joint effects of state sector influence over the economy and distribution coalitions of special interest groups, thriving in ageing political democracies; (ii) Katzenstein's small state theory, which in a way is related to the neo-corporatist tradition and which explains growth and high world-economic adaptive capacities of a country by its small size and the strength of its interest groups participating in the economic policy-making process. Small domestic markets result in openness, creating a compelling need for national consensus, which achieves a sequence of political bargains and enhances the flexibility of sectorial organizations. Contrary to Olson, Katzenstein expects the promotion of industrial adjustment and economic growth by the effects of interest organizations.

Table 10.1   European small and zero-block countries

(a) European small countries population < 15.01 million inhabitants

European small country	World Political Status (1988)
Albania	Ex-WTO
Austria	Neutral
Belgium	NATO
Bulgaria	former WTO
Denmark	NATO
Finland	Neutral, Friendship Treaty with former USSR
Greece	NATO
Hungary	former WTO
Iceland	NATO
Irish Republic	Neutrality
Luxembourg	NATO
Netherlands	NATO
Norway	NATO
Portugal	NATO
Sweden	Neutral
Switzerland	Neutral

(b) European zero-block countries

Zero-block country	Small-country status
Albania	Yes
Austria	Yes
Finland	Yes
Irish Republic	Yes
Sweden	Yes
Switzerland	Yes
former Yugoslavia	No

Compiled from the literature, mentioned above.

Neocorporatism is generally understood to include: (i) the existence of an ideology of social partnership between capital and labour; (ii) a centralized and concentrated system of interest groups; (iii) a voluntary and informal coordination of policy-making between capital, labour and the state (Keman and Whiteley, 1987: 207)

Neocorporatists will expect that: (i) the higher the institutional integration of organized interest intermediation, the lower will be the extent of the distributive struggle; (ii) the higher the institutional integration of organized interest intermediation, the better will be the performance in terms of unemployment and inflation control; (iii) the higher the institutional integration of organized interest intermediation, the better will be the performance in terms of the Philips-curve-trade-off between unemployment and inflation; (iv) the higher the institutional integration of organized interest intermediation, the better will be overall economic performance and the lower will be the rate of fiscal expansion (Lehner, 1987: 54–60).

Critique of the neo-corporatist type of literature, so dominant in explaining OECD country economic growth in the late 1970s and early 1980s, has now accumulated in international social science (Therborn, 1986; Olson, 1986; Tausch, 1991a). For Olson, just to mention one critic, corporatism falls far short of the requirements for a scientific theory:

> But when one looks in the literature of neo-corporatism for a theory, or even a clear and logical if informal argument, of why it would work better (i.e. than 'pluralism'), the results could hardly be more disappointing. There is normally no theory or coherent explanation, if any argument at all, of why the more comprehensive neo-corporatist interest structures would be expected to work better. (Olson, 1986: 178)

Quite convincingly Olson warns: 'Science attempts to go beyond descriptions, histories, terminologies, and typologies to genuine hypothetico-deductive theory. Schools of scientific thought that fail to develop deductive theories resting on tested hypotheses never last' (Olson, 1986: 166). Representatives of the once so expanding ranks of 'corporatists' agree on the gloomy perspectives for their own model:

> Stagflation is detrimental to the success of corporatist modes of state intervention. This is because, on the one hand, there is a fading away of the 'symbolic' value of corporatism and, on the other, because positive sum-games are simply not feasible any more. It is therefore clear why most of the smaller European, corporatist countries show such a poor performance during the 1980s, after the second 'oil-shock'. These findings may oblige us to rethink much of the existing literature on corporatism, in particular the impact of institutional structures on the behaviour of interest groups. The declining efficacy of corporatism may for instance have to do with the increased independence of the actors within the corporatist structures. (Keman and Whiteley, 1987: 208)

Gerlich *et al.* (1988) are even more outspoken about the emerging paradigmatic crisis of neocorporatist approaches:

Notwithstanding a continuing high level of literary output, the academic growth industry of corporatism is now experiencing a crisis which coincides with the economic crisis of Western industrialized nations. Theoretical concepts which claimed the status of a new paradigm during the second half of the seventies and were claimed to be explanations of long-term trends have been confronted with the instability and change-ability of historical processes only a few years after their emergence. (Gerlich *et al.*, 1988: 209–10)

Such a rethinking of corporatism will be on my agenda, and although I will not claim to perform that task alone, I hope to furnish the debate with indications as to where a useful efficiency-analysis of corporatism should go in the future. The emphasis will be on corporatism's role in the stabilization of short-term growth at the end of a long-term Kondratieff cycle, and not just on the explanation in the cross-national variations of long-term growth rates since the prosperity recession during the mid-1960s (Chapter 11; see also Bornschier, 1988).

Most empirical investigations into the phenomenon of corporatism do agree on the rank order of the extent of corporatism in the stable democratic OECD nations concerned (see also Blaas, 1984; Lehner, 1987). Thus I am able to follow Lehner's definition (see Table 10.2).

Politometric tests of these complementary theories are not easy to carry out. Most tests for the socio-liberal proposition do not properly take into account the joint interaction of state sector influence and institutional rigidity or institutional age, which allow for distributional coalitions to emerge, while measures designed to cope with phenomena such as 'structural adjustment' or 'modernization' in the neo-corporatist literature cannot as yet fully satisfy methodological requirements.

For the politometrician who tries to orient her or his work to the standards of econometrics, some of the measurement techniques used by the neo-corporatist 'industry' fall within the lamentable and very common category of contradictory or unreliable measurement concepts. Factor analytical aggregations of variables or regression residuals yield far more reliable composite indicators than the mere unweighted aggregations of such concepts as

Overall economic performance according to the Neocorporatist School:

$$\text{Performance} = ((\text{Economic Growth}) + (\text{Unemployment Record})$$
$$+ (\text{Inflation Record}) + (\text{Balance of Payments}))/4 \quad (10.1)$$

Source: Keman and Van Dijk, 1987: 158

Table 10.2   Pluralism, corporatism and concordance in Western democracies
according to Lehner

Concept	Definition	Existing in:
Pluralism	Fragmented and segmented interest intermediation	USA Canada France
Weak corporatism	Institutionalized participation of organized labour in certain areas; narrow scope of collective bargaining	UK Italy
Medium corporatism	Sectorial participation, but broad scope of collective bargaining	Ireland Belgium FR Germany Denmark Finland Australia
Strong corporatism	Tripartite concertation with broad scope; encompassing co-ordination of income policies	Austria Sweden Norway Netherlands
Concordance	Encompassing co-ordination of the interactions of the private and the public sector	Japan Switzerland

Source: Taken from Lehner, 1987: 58.

For small exposed countries, the balance of payments will be more important than for big and economically dominant nations. That, according to Czada, economic growth correlates negatively with economic adjustment (1987: 25), certainly does not increase the reliability of adjustment's measurement.

Czada's adjustment scale strings together the employment gains of expanding and the employment losses of contracting sectors. The chosen sample of seven industrial key sectors (to mention them: textiles, leather, paper, glass, iron and steel, machinery, electric machinery) does not take into account the different weight that these sectors have for overall employment in the thirteen countries compared. In particular, the scale does not tell us how relevant the seven sectors are in terms of output and exports, neither does it tell us how competitive (non-competitive) these sectors have become in recent years in terms of the ascending semi-periphery international producers (US CIA, 1980). It is no surprise, then, that nations which adapted themselves fairly thoroughly to the evolving new structures, such as the US or the UK (US CIA, 1980), rank very low on Czada's scale, while there are no data about Japan at all (Czada, 1987: 48) and Ireland, Norway and Belgium are said to perform best on that 'adjustment scale'. Following other analyses, precisely those three countries have severe structural problems of adapting to the new industrial division of labour. Norway is nonetheless in a better position owing to its huge state sector revenues from North Sea oil (Esping-Andersen, 1987; Therborn, 1985). Thus Czada's results have to be treated with the utmost caution.

The success of the economic adjustment process (equivalent to the inverse rank order of the 'modernization' scale) can be measured with the rank correlations set out in Table 10.3.

Table 10.3   Rank correlations of the success of economic adjustment according to Czada

+ .49	Trade union centralization
+ .26	Unionization
+ .45	Real wage increases
− .33	Inflation
− .01	Real growth rate
+ .71	Foreign trade dependence (exports + imports per GDP)

Source: Czada, 1987: 24–5.

There is widespread agreement among the 'neo-corporatists' about their own ranking of the different nations of the OECD according to their basic concept. One of the most convincing econometric works published so far on the issue of neo-corporatism, Blaas (1984), developed the following rank scale of 'corporatism', which is based on the work of Crouch and which ranks OECD countries (see Table 10.4).

By introducing that well-established measurement scale for the neo-corporatist phenomenon into Equation 6.6, I attain a very high error probability for the influence of corporatism on growth (92 per cent; keeping in mind that the scale attributes the highest numerical value to the least neo-corporatist country and the lowest numerical value to the most neo-corporatist country). Thus, the influence of corporatism on growth within the framework of a socio-liberal explanation of OECD-country growth is rather small.

Weede is not alone in his contention that state economic influence leads to stagnation in ageing and stable market economy democracies. Bornschier (1988) too now concedes a reversal in the correlation between state sector influence over the economy and economic growth at the level of Western

Table 10.4   Corporatism rank-scale

Country	Blaas/Crouch Index of Corporatism
Australia	15
Belgium	9
Federal Republic of Germany	2
Denmark	7
Finland	8
France	13
UK	12
Italy	14
Japan	10
Canada	16
New Zealand	11
Netherlands	3
Norway	4.5
Austria	1
Sweden	4.5
Switzerland	6
USA	17

Source: Blaas, 1984: 168.

democracies during the period 1950–77. In the 1950s, the relationship was positive, reflecting the social force of the new basic societal contract between wage labour and capital in Western democracies under the auspices of Keynesian economic policies, neo-corporatist intermediation in the political system and United States predominance in the capitalist world economy. The consumption structure of the societal model was centred around the private car, and nearly one quarter of the total labour force in the industrialized Western world was directly or indirectly involved in the production and maintenance of that particular product (Bornschier, 1988, esp. chap. 4 and chap. 11).

Following the logic of long-wave analysis in the style of Kondratieff, during each prosperity recession at the middle of a sixty-year long wave, there emerged discontinuities of industrial processes, technologies and policies (Bornschier, 1988: 96–9) which were also reflected in the incipient breakdown of the corporatist/Keynesian consensus in the leading capitalist countries in 1968, which formed part of the cyclical continuity of revolutionary upheavals (1871, 1917, 1968). During the period 1960–75 the positive correlation between state expenditures and growth, still valid in the fifties, broke down and became indeterminate (−.07) (Bornschier, 1988: 309), and Keynesianism lost its effectiveness during the crisis years 1974–77 (correlation between state expenditure growth and economic growth $-.72$ in 21 Western democracies; see Bornschier, 1988: 309). The breakdown of the consensus around the political-economic 'contract' at the time, when new 'key projects' emerge, causes the clear 'W' shaped pattern of social conflict during each long-wave cycle. Internal conflict was high during crises, depressions and prosperity-recessions, and it was low during upswings and recoveries.

My own empirical evidence starts with the results achieved in Chapter 7. Introducing corporatism into my equations (Chapter 7) explaining world-wide development, I obtain the following results for the OECD nations, controlling for the openness of an economy as measured by the export rate in 1965 (exports per GDP). This control is necessary because Katzenstein expects a joint effect of economic small size and corporatism (see Table 10.5).

Table 10.5   Development and corporatism: introducing the 'Absence of Corporatism Scale' into development explanations

Effect of absence of corporatism on controlling for economic vulnerability as well	Beta-weight	Error prob %	n observations
Growth	$-.30423$	36.76	16
Income Concentration	$-.09415$	85.94	15
Life Expectancy	$+.40103$	37.09	16
Political Violence	$-.08530$	80.64	17
Female Violent Death Rates	$-.10664$	74.36	15
Male Violent Death Rates	$-.44574$	17.49	15

Source: Own calculations on the basis of the regressions in Chapter 7 in conjunction with Table 10.3, above.

Corporatism thus has: (i) a positive effect on growth but: (ii) blocks human development; (iii) leads to a higher destructive potential among the population; and (iv) only spuriously affects income concentration and political violence.

I should also mention here the effects of Katzenstein's control variable 'openness': it retards growth. My own measurement concept for adjustment is based on the logic of the Kondratieff cycle and thus on the comparison between the growth rates in two periods – 1965 to 1975 (Period 1) and 1965–83 (Period 2). In the mid-1960s the present Kondratieff cycle certainly reached its apex, and there is a decline in the capitalist world ever since (Bornschier, 1988). My concept predicts real per capita growth in constant

US$ in Period 2 by knowledge about real per capita growth in constant US$ in Period 1. The residuals from that regression (Y-^Y) are my measure of adjustment. Y-^Y will be the larger, the more rapid growth in the latter half of Period 2 was in comparison to Period 1. And Y-^Y will be smaller or will be negative, when the growth process was discontinued or came to slow down after 1975. Similar residual analyses could be performed for employment, human development and income distribution, but I will concentrate here on the adjustment process results for the growth performance.

Corporatism does have, on the one hand, a positive but not too strong influence on growth and the adjustment process, but it has very high costs in terms of 'social health'. While socio-liberal explanations of growth (Olson, 1982, 1986) accept that, by and large, encompassing interest groups affect growth less negatively than smaller groups, neo-corporatist theories quite overlook the other, affected variables. The above-mentioned regression results forcibly included predictors, which produce significant effects on development at the world level, but which might lose their significance in subsamples of the world system, such as the OECD democracies. Making the necessary corrections, therefore, I arrive at a statistically more satisfactory explanation of OECD country socio-economic development and adjustment than in Table 10.5. My hypotheses can be sketched in the following way:

A high institutional integration into the juridical mechanisms of the world economy contributes positively to the post-1975 adjustment record, while capitalist countries in the centre stagnate through the export of jobs to the periphery and semi-periphery by transnational capital, located in the centres. Corporatism insignificantly contributes to the overall growth rate 1965–83, but significantly stabilizes growth over a short time. Again, two predictors from Table 7.3 (government expenditure and public expenditure on education) are confirmed here. And finally, personal violence among males becomes lower through the disciplining effects of the market and world economic exposure on distributional coalitions, creating violence, to be measured by the share of exports in total GDP. Corporatism is quite strongly related to the occurrence of violent male death rates.

Corporatism interacts in determining adjustment success with private savings per total savings, which is an indicator of the predominance of private savings in the economy *vis-à-vis* government savings (or all too often, government debt) and the external position of the economy. Corporatism significantly supports the adjustment process, when the effect of private borrowing to the state and thus high private per total savings is taken into account. Short-term Keynesian stabilization policy without corporatism would not work (see also, Blaas, 1984); and the short-term Keynesian success needs, too, an appropriate world economic environment:

a liberal, institutionalized, foreign trade policy and the effective absence of many powerful, transnational oligolopolies which streamline, via their headquarter status, the home market and economic policies in the headquarter countries. The transnational character of their operations effectively forbids successful national crisis management (Bornschier, 1976, 1980). In Table 10.6, I present my final regression results for the OECD countries.

Table 10.6   The effects of corporatism on economic change reconsidered – results for the OECD countries

Predictor	Beta-weight	Error probability
(a) Explaining Economic Adjustment 1975–83		
Degree of institutional integration into the juridical mechanisms of the capitalist world economy 1970	+ .38886	.0665
Private saving per total savings, 1970	+ .37122	.0699
Absence of corporatism	− .42328	.0557
MNC headquarter status	− .35048	.0928

$n = 17$ OECD countries with complete data; $F = 4.53$; adj. $R^{**}2 = 46.9$ per cent; $p = .0184$

(b) Explaining economic growth 1965–83		
Growth of government expenditure	− .82310	.0005
Public expenditure on education	+ .61764	.0033
Absence of corporatism	− .17500	.2880

$n = 16$ OECD countries with complete data; $F = 10.27$; adj. $R^{**}2 = 65.0$ per cent; $p = .0012$

(c) Explaining violent male death rates		
Export share per GDP, 1965 (openness)	− .54261	.0597
Absence of corporatism	− .44000	.1183

$n = 16$ OECD countries with complete data; $F = 2.49$; adj. $R^{**}2 = 16.5$ per cent; $p = .1219$

Data Sources: Bornschier, Heintz *et al.* (explanatory variables except corporatism scale); World Bank (growth rates 1965–83, as reported in *World Development Report*, 1985); for my adjustment measure, see text above.

Specified properly, it can be shown that corporatism at the level of the industrialized Western nations has some stabilizing effect on short-term economic growth, but at a heavy social cost. My results thus again confirm Olson's reasoning in a fundamental way. The crisis of the neo-corporatist set-up will emerge when in the long run the relatively more encompassing parts of a neo-corporatist environment (like the majority of wage earners) will be economically discriminated against in comparison with the members of the units that are less encompassing (like members of very small trade unions in specialized branches or industries); i.e. the neo-corporatist set-up will break up into smaller and conflicting units:

> Organizations to cartelize markets or to lobby governments do not need a majority or even a plurality of the society to obtain their objectives, and thus are in a very different situation from the encompassing political party in an electoral system with some winner-take-all or other features favouring large parties. All a collusion or cartel needs is control over the supply in a single market. This means that the branch organizations of an encompassing neo-corporatist business or labor organization have an incentive to push for the interests of their own branch, even when this is not in the interests of the clients of the encompassing organization as a whole. (Olson, 1986: 184)

According to Olson, how could a society prevent subsets of members of the neo-corporatist organization with a legal monopoly of representation from becoming controlled in large part by internal lobbies working on behalf of internal subgroups that found the selective incentives needed to organize internal caucuses or lobbies? The neo-corporatist set-up will break up, especially under the pressure of the suboptimal employment record of the dynamics of the neo-corporatist system (Olson, 1986: 181), giving way to the 'strong antisocial behavior of narrow distributional coalitions, even in some contexts in which a look at only the top level of the interest group structure would have suggested that this was not something to fear' (Olson, 1986: 187).

This strong anti-social behaviour will have its immediate effects for indicators of social well-being. Thus, it is no coincidence that Austria, the leading neo-corporatist country in the world, had the lowest male life expectancy and the highest violent male death rate of all Western industrialized democracies (World Bank, *World Development Report*, 1988; UN Statistical Office, 1980). Let us remember here that Olson especially predicts a pronounced rising cleavage between the 'organized' and the 'unorganized' sectors in economies like Sweden or Austria:

> When the workers in any industry, craft, profession, or firm can organize to control the supply of labor in that category or market, they can set monopoly wages, salaries, or professional fees. At higher pay levels, less labor is purchased. The labor that would otherwise have been employed in markets in which there is organized control of the supply will have to

crowd into unorganized markets, thereby lowering the wages of those
unfortunate enough to be in these crowded areas. When most of the firms
in an economy have colluded and in effect cartelized their industries, or
when most of the labor markets are cartelized by professional associations
or labor unions, the scope for employment in unorganized sectors shrinks.
The process that has been described is not merely a theoretical possibility,
but rather one that has taken place in a great many economies, both
corporatist and non-corporatist. It mainly explains the increases in the
unemployment rates since the 1950s in a country such as West Germany,
for example, and is also part of the explanation of the reduction in rates of
economic growth. (Olson, 1986: 183)

The kind of world economic pressure that influences employment, growth
and adjustment in industrialized countries can be better understood by my
empirical results: rising employment opportunities are basically a function
of the evolving new international division of labour (Chapter 7), while
corporatism contributes *prima facie* only to the stability of advanced
capitalist adjustment, but has to face the necessity of a thorough institutional integration into the workings of the capitalist world economy, and
has to accept the predominance of private savings over accumulation.

An additional setback for the encompassing trade unions in OECD
countries is that MNC headquarter status additionally works against the
smoothness of the world economic adjustment process (see also F. Scharpf,
1987, for an extensive treatment of 'Volvoism' in Sweden and the relationship between transnational Swedish enterprise and the trade union
organization).

A crucial test for any social scientific theory is, of course, its predictive
capacity for instances and cases which are claimed to be well explained by
other theories. Neocorporatist approaches to development concentrated
their macro-quantitative evidence at the level of the OECD countries, while
dependency theories and other world societal interpretations of development were mainly tested at the level of the capitalist world economy or the
LDCs. For dependency theories, at least the more radical ones, like
Senghaas (1977), 'socialism' was a development alternative to capitalism,
and development is most precarious where the bonds of dependence are
strongest, such as in Latin America or the Philippines. For the 'corporatists'
the 'model' would be Austria, the OECD nation which most clearly fits the
neo-corporatist pattern. A development theory which claims to be valid for
the entire world economy, and which does not fail to explain such hotly
contested singular cases such as Japan, Austria, or even the now-defunct
European former state socialism at once, could claim to successfully

challenge the paradigmatic predominance of other, more established, macro-quantitative approaches to world development. Table 10.7 summarizes the results of my regression predictions presented in Chapter 7 of this book, and compares these predictions with real values in Asian growth economies; European zero-block nations; and (other) European small nations within the context of our debate on neo-corporatism.

The principle world economic challenge to the developed 'corporatist states' comes from the newly industrializing Asian growth economies; the principal theoretical challenge to neocorporatist theories is constituted precisely by the fact that socio-liberal theories quite successfully predict Asian and OECD country performance at the same time. Furthermore, hypotheses inherent in recent work about the possible special role of European 'zero-block' nations (Kiljunen, 1987) in world development receive little confirmation *vis-à-vis* my contending socio-liberal approach, since there is no emergent and clear pattern of different regression residuals for the group of European zero-block nations. Table 10.7 lists the predictive power of my models (Chapter 7) as they are presented there.

First of all, growth rates: Japan, South Korea and Austria are well within the reach of what is predicted by my model; here and in the following residual analyses, the chosen criterion to be considered as falling within the reach of the model was 1 standard deviation up or down in terms of * RESID. Only Malaysia and Finland present a residual value, which is > 1.36 per cent above or below the predicted growth rate. Thus, neither the Asian growth economies nor the European zero-block nations nor other European smaller countries present a problem for the new socio-liberal growth theory.

Next to attained human development levels, Malaysia, Singapore and Thailand have a very good performance in terms of my model, and in terms of the size of residuals for other countries. The standard deviation of residuals is 4.16 years: but these three countries are even considerably above the life expectancy prediction of Chapter 7. More detailed comparisons to account for these outliers are necessary in future, and it would be too easy to reduce the residuals to a question of diet or ethno-religious 'mentality'. Why is Malaysia 8.79 years above the predicted value, and Indonesia is 3.30 years below (when they share the same political culture)? It is also interesting to note that Japan is slightly below, but Singapore is very much above the predicted values.

The standard deviation of residuals for my model of the increases of life expectancy 1965–83 is 4.53 per cent. All Asian growth economies show again their dynamic with positive residual values while, among the European countries under consideration here, only Sweden, Greece and former Yugoslavia performed – at that time – better than expected. Yugoslavia's path into the present disaster, however, is to be explained by the fatal interaction between a state class control over the economy, ethnic fractionalization, and the trend towards distribution coalitions, which I have already discussed in Chapter 7. Denmark's residual is 4.54 per cent below expectation and especially bad. Again, my theory accounts quite well for the performance of Asian growth and European smaller/zero-block nations at the same time. Malaysia and Thailand are again above the expectations of this theory.

The results in Table 10.7.4 are calculated for the entire world economy and thus include former Yugoslavia, which is excluded from the world capitalist distribution model in Chapter 7 by definition. The reported results must be interpreted with care since most income distribution data, contained in classical machine readable data files are hardly comparable according to strict economic criteria. Another important qualification concerns the period in which most of the data used here were collected, i.e. around the year 1970. Thailand, Finland and the Netherlands presented a stronger positive residual of income inequality (GINI*100) (standard deviation of residuals = 5.36), while the former Yugoslavia and Taiwan around 1970 again were positive examples of redistribution. Yugoslav economic policy during the 1980s did everything to redress that positive redistribution, and its IMF-type stabilization programmes (at the time of their realization praised to be successful) did a lot to destabilize the country socially and politically. In a way, the former Yugoslavia's path to national disintegration could well be repeated by the other countries of Eastern Europe and the ex-USSR, if they continue their present strategies (Furkes and Schlarp, 1991).

Finland, however, has experienced a major improvement in its income distribution since the 1970s, as I have already noted in Chapter 8. Considering the level of political violence, all compared countries correspond to my expectations, except for Greece and Thailand, which had more illegal executive transfers than expected. Switzerland, together with France, leads the lamentable field of nations producing female auto- or hetero-destructive death rates. Austria's destructive death rate among males is almost 3 standard deviations up from my theoretical expectation. Finland's absolute value, although also high, is still easier to explain than Austria's. Austria's death rate exceeds the prediction by 31.34 per 1000 deaths, while Finland's value is 13.71 per 1000 higher than expected. Ireland has a very low violent male death rate. Higher negative residual values are to be observed in nations which share particular strong liberal common values (in my sample Norway and the Netherlands). Without exception, fascist movements were considerably stronger in the inter-war period in today's violent nations, and there could have been more widespread efforts after 1945 to overcome this past. According to this reasoning, these nations will become particularly vulnerable to the spread of hatred against 'foreigners', and to all kinds of nationalistic ideologies.

In Table 10.7, a positive residual will be interpreted as presenting positive development efficiency and, in the case of income concentration, violence and illegal executive transfers: a negative development efficiency.

Table 10.7   Long-term development in Asian growth economies, European smaller and zero-bloc nations: real values, predictions from socio-liberal theory and regression residuals

Country	Real value	Predicted value	Residual
(1) Economic growth 1965–83			

Predictors: Military personnel ratios, low increase in government expenditures, educational outlays of the state, increases in direct taxes *vis-à-vis* other revenue sources, low long-term transnational penetration, low institutional age, short-term growth in transnational capital investment

$n = 68$ countries; adj. $R^{**}2 = 48.3\%$; stand. dev. of * RESID 1.36

Among the 68 predictions, we find:

Country	Real value	Predicted value	Residual
(a) Asian growth economies			
Japan	+4.8	+4.0	+0.78
South Korea	+6.7	+6.4	+0.31
Malaysia*	+4.5	+2.9	+1.63
Thailand	+4.3	+3.0	+1.33
(b) European zero-block nations			
Austria	+3.7	+2.9	+0.83
Finland*	+3.3	+4.7	−1.39
Irish Republic	+2.3	+1.9	+0.38
Sweden	+1.9	+1.7	+0.25
(c) Smaller NATO nations			
Belgium	+3.1	+3.9	−0.84
Denmark	+1.9	+2.9	−0.99
Greece	+4.0	+4.0	−0.00
Netherlands	+2.3	+2.7	−0.45
Norway	+3.3	+3.1	+0.20
Portugal	+3.7	+2.7	+0.99

Table 10.7 *cont.*

Country	Real value	Predicted value	Residual
(2) Explaining attained human development level, 1977			

Predictors: Plateau curve of basic human needs, slow population dynamic, low ethno-linguistic fractionalization, low public investment

$n = 94$ countries; adj. $R**2 = 84.2\%$; stand. dev. of * RESID 4.16

Among the 94 predictions, we find:

(a) Asian growth economies

Country	Real value	Predicted value	Residual
Indonesia	48.0	51.3	−3.30
Japan	76.0	76.3	−0.32
Malaysia*	67.0	58.2	+8.79
Singapore*	69.5	61.2	+8.26
Thailand*	61.0	54.8	+6.23

(b) European zero-block nations

Country	Real value	Predicted value	Residual
Austria	72.0	75.0	−3.03
Finland	72.0	74.6	−2.63
Irish Republic	73.0	74.9	−1.93
Sweden	75.0	76.5	−1.52
former Yugoslavia	69.0	66.1	+2.94

(c) Smaller NATO nations

Country	Real value	Predicted value	Residual
Belgium	72.0	75.4	−3.36
Denmark	73.9	76.7	−2.84
Greece	73.0	73.9	−0.90
Netherlands	74.0	74.2	−0.15
Norway	74.5	76.2	−1.73
Portugal	68.7	70.9	−2.16

(d) Smaller former WTO nations

Country	Real value	Predicted value	Residual
Bulgaria	71.8	71.2	+0.55
Hungary	69.5	72.0	−2.46

(3) Explaining life expectancy increases 1965–83

Predictors: first derivate of Plateau curve of basic human needs satisfaction, catch-up effect of more rapid increases in life expectancy in nations with low attained level of life expectancy in 1960, low ethno-linguistic fractionalization, low public investment, slow increases in population dynamics

$n = 93$ countries; adj. $R**2 = 73.4\%$; stand. dev. of * RESID 4.53%

Among the 93 predictions, we find:

Country	Real value	Predicted value	Residual
(a) Asian growth economies			
Indonesia	+27.5	+25.7	+1.88
Japan	+12.4	+9.6	+2.87
Malaysia	+16.2	+12.7	+3.46
Singapore	+13.2	+11.7	+1.47
Thailand	+21.1	+17.2	+3.97
(b) European zero-block nations			
Austria	+7.1	+9.8	−2.74
Finland	+7.1	+8.6	−1.55
Irish Republic	+5.6	+7.7	−2.05
Sweden	+8.0	+5.6	+2.45
former Yugoslavia	+10.7	+7.8	+2.87
(c) Smaller NATO nations			
Belgium	+4.6	+6.2	−1.56
Denmark*	+2.6	+7.1	−4.54
Greece	+9.8	+9.4	+0.45
Netherlands	+3.9	+7.5	−3.58
Norway	+5.3	+6.8	−1.42
Portugal	+13.1	+13.9	−0.85
(d) Smaller former WTO nations			
Bulgaria	+4.5	+5.7	−1.18
Hungary	+4.2	+5.3	−1.01

(4) Explaining personal income inequality around 1970 in the capitalist world economy (GINI index*100)

Predictors: crude live birth rates, 1960, increases in birth rates, 1960–77, Kuznets Curve, low secondary school enrolment

$n = 63$ countries; adj. $R^{**}2 = 58.3\%$; stand. dev. of * RESID 5.36

Among the 63 predictions, we find

(a) Asian growth economies

Indonesia	44.4	47.5	−3.11
Japan	41.2	37.6	+3.44
South Korea	36.1	40.6	−4.53
Malaysia	50.6	46.5	+4.09
Thailand*	50.3	44.7	+5.57
Taiwan*	29.1	41.7	−12.65

Table 10.7 *cont.*

Country	Real value	Predicted value	Residual
(b) European zero-block nations			
Austria	37.1	32.5	+4.62
Finland*	46.3	39.8	+7.50
Sweden	34.9	37.2	−2.26
Yugoslavia*	34.8	42.0	−7.21
(c) Smaller NATO countries			
Denmark	36.4	38.5	−2.06
Greece	39.4	39.0	+0.42
Netherlands*	39.3	33.7	+5.58
Norway	36.1	37.7	−1.65

(5) Explaining political violence (deaths per pop. ratio) 1963–77

Predictors: low government savings, high military expenditures

$n = 79$ countries; adj. $R**2 = 24.3\%$; stand. dev. of * RESID .62

Among the 79 cases, we find the following predictions with a positive value for ^Y

(a) Asian growth economies			
Hong Kong	.02	.03	−.01
South Korea	.01	.39	−.38
Malaysia	.04	.13	−.09
(b) European zero-block nations			
Irish Republic	.02	.13	−.11
Switzerland	0	.11	−.11
(c) Smaller NATO nations			
Belgium	.01	.19	−.18
Greece	.00	.22	−.22
Netherlands	.00	.12	−.12
Norway	.00	.05	−.05
Portugal	.00	.40	−.39

(6) Explaining illegal executive transfers, 1963–77

Predictors: high income concentration among the rich, low earlier growth of domestic savings, low political party competition, low general government saving

$n = 53$ countries; adj. $R**2 = 40.1\%$; stand. dev. of * RESID 1.32

Among the 53 cases, we find the following predictions with a positive value for ^Y

Country	Real value	Predicted value	Residual
(a) Asian growth economies			
Malaysia	0	.78	−.78
Thailand*	4	1.39	+2.61
(b) European zero-block nations			
Austria	0	.41	−.41
Finland	0	.41	−.41
Switzerland	0	.53	−.53
(c) Smaller NATO nations			
Greece*	3	.88	+2.12
Netherlands	0	.51	−.51
Norway	0	.08	−.08

(7) Explaining female violent death rates

Predictors: logged level of industrialization, bureaucratization of the employment structure, government expenditures

$n = 28$ countries, adj. $R**2 = 62.8\%$; stand. dev. of * RESID 7.14

Among the 28 predictions, we find

(a) Asian growth economies			
Japan	40.6	46.2	−5.56
(b) European zero-block nations			
Austria*	59.4	51.5	+7.88
Finland	40.4	39.2	+1.15
Irish Republic	35.6	41.8	−6.17
Sweden	48.2	47.1	+1.14
Switzerland*	59.0	49.4	+9.58
(c) Smaller NATO nations			
Denmark	53.0	48.1	+4.89
Greece	35.5	30.5	+5.00
Netherlands	49.6	53.2	−3.63
Norway	42.2	44.4	−2.23

(8) Explaining male violent death rates

Predictors: export commodity concentration, public investment, logged industrialization level, low military personnel rates as 'ersatz' for male aggressive behaviour

Table 10.7 *cont.*

Country	Real value	Predicted value	Residual
$n = 26$ countries; adj. $R**2 = 39.0\%$; stand.dev. of * RESID 12.29			
Among the 26 predictions, we find			
(a) Asian growth economies			
Japan	71.4	76.5	−5.05
(b) European zero-block nations			
Austria*	105.7	74.4	+31.34
Finland*	96.2	82.5	+13.71
Irish Republic*	53.2	69.9	−16.68
Sweden	75.8	73.6	+2.16
(c) Smaller NATO nations			
Belgium	74.4	69.2	+5.22
Denmark	71.6	74.0	−2.41
Greece	52.2	56.0	−3.82
Netherlands	56.9	67.7	−10.83
Norway*	61.7	74.7	−13.00
(d) Smaller former WTO nations			
Hungary	93.9	81.9	+11.96

Note and Sources: SPSS-IX-output for the equations, as reported in Chapter 7. Column (2) rounded at first, column (3) rounded at second decimal point. Data sources as reported in Chapter 7.

Thus, corporatism as such cannot be qualified as an ideal strategy of development in the period under consideration, whatever positive impact may have initially resulted from social reforms which characterize the early stages in the installation of a corporatist social contract. What emerges in terms of a message to the 'Second' and 'Third' Worlds, however, is the short-term (i.e. limited and short-run) adjustment capability of liberal corporatism.

11 The Future of the Socio-Liberal Model

In this chapter I analyse long- and short-term implications of my theory and assess the feasibility of a socio-liberal development strategy. Where socio-liberals must further develop and sometimes contradict Olson's theory is in regard to the problem of stability (not the cross-national variation in the overall velocity) of economic growth. I have already established that, at the level of the OECD countries, a Keynesian strategy which avoids high government savings and risks a higher public debt ratio (and hence a larger share of private savings per total savings) leads to a short-term boost in the growth rate 1975–83. OECD countries will find it advantageous to have a high degree of institutional integration into the mechanisms of the capitalist world economy (which would certainly still tally with Olson's analysis of trade and integration), and will also find it advantageous to have encompassing interest organizations, behaving in a corporatist manner to stabilize economic growth. It would still be possible to find enough anti-monopolistic statements in Olson's analysis to explain the clear negative influence that transnational corporations headquarter status wields on the adaptive economic capacity of a developed capitalist society. Olson's explanation regarding the extent to which a given country fell victim to the Great Depression in the 1930s is startlingly simple and must be reconsidered in the light of my own empirical evidence about the adjustment crisis in the 1970s and 1980s: for Olson, involuntary unemployment is caused principally by the collusive pressure of those who have a more secure job and by the downward inflexibility of wages (Olson, 1982–85: 264). My evidence, to be sure, is limited in its temporal dimension, and it must be very clearly qualified as such. During other phases of a Kondratieff cycle, another logic might hold – as indeed Bornschier (1988) has shown in his analysis of state expenditures in developed capitalist democracies. But I know of no reason for rejecting the neo-Marxist consensus (for example, Senghaas, 1972) that a military expenditure boom increases growth in the short term, because in a 'late capitalist system' (to use Mandel's term) militarism is the most important form of Keynesianism. This argument clearly holds only for the short term, especially for the logic of the post-1974 world economy as a whole, but the trade-off between economic success *vis-à-vis* past performance and militarism on the world level is inescapable.

Compatible with my other analyses, the demographic dynamics also play a role in determining a country's performance downward after 1975 on my adjustment scale. Olson is right in so far as institutional predictability increases (post-1975) the capacity to overcome cyclical downswings (Olson, 1982–85: 283–4). But my other results raise the necessity of revising the implications of Olson's theory on a short-term and cycle-relevant basis: two other variables clearly connected with a 'Keynesian' approach, such as a high social security programme experience and a negative current account balance, are very positively related to the post-1975 recovery in growth rates. Countries with low military expenditures, low state-run social security programmes and a high and positive current account balance have tended to have lower economic growth rates in comparison to their past performance, although their overall growth still might be high in absolute terms after 1975. The implication of the following regression result (Table 11.1), would be a sort of vulgar Keynesianism, explaining short-term adjustment in 88 countries and explaining 41 per cent of adjustment (without outliers like Israel the adjusted $R^{**}2$ even increases to 58.6 per cent, including 79 countries with complete data).

In Figure 11.2, the standardized residual plots are casewise analysed for the adjustment equation in Table 11.1, above. Let me repeat, that my adjustment scale measures practically nothing other than the capacity of an economy to maintain, or even to increase, growth in a world characterized by turbulence in the years after 1975. For the presentation of the residual plots it is necessary to provide readers with a key to the country abbreviations (Figure 11.1). For reasons of brevity, the residuals are listed with their sequence numbers according the Bornschier, Heintz *et al.* data tape and the country abbreviations (Figure 11.2).

Socio-liberal explanations explain the longer-term tendencies of world development very well. In the short run the following strategies emerged to halt a decline in growth rates after 1975: the more social security oriented, more externally financed and more militarized socio-political models were, the better could they redress growth rates in their favour after 1975. This does not sound at all paradoxical when we consider, first, that overall differences in growth rates (Chapters 7 and 10) are something other than the maintenance of growth or its increase under very adverse world economic conditions; and, second, that there seems to be a mechanism at work during the very last years of an outgoing Kondratieff wave consisting in a conscious policy on the part of the governments and the social movements which support it to overcome the 'market principle' via state sector expenditures to increase the efforts in the field of social policy and to incur larger negative current account balances.

Table 11.1   The global dimension of adjustment

MULTIPLE R	.66893
R SQUARE	.44747
ADJUSTED R SQUARE	.41378
STANDARD ERROR	1.22937

$n = 88$ countries with complete data

$F = 13.28160$ SIGNIF F = .0000

——————————— VARIABLES IN THE EQUATION ———————————

VARIABLE	B	SE B	BETA	T	SIG T
	.03807	.00897	.40430	4.246	.0001
MILEX per GOVEX 73 Military expenditures per total gov. expenditures					
	.01007	.00292	.30705	3.445	.0009
SIPE-Index Social insurance programme experience index					
	−.02179	.00581	−.35938	−3.752	.0003
Current acc. bal. 70 Current account balance per GDP					
	−.05579	.02713	−.17357	−2.056	.0429
DYN CBR 1960–77 Differences in crude life birth rates 1960–77					
	−.12415	.08893	−.12065	−1.396	.1665
Ill. Exec. transfers Number of illegal executive transfers 1963–77					
(CONSTANT)	−2.05104	.37849		−5.419	.0000

Data Sources: Bornschier, Heintz *et al.* (Predictors (1)–(3)); World Bank, World Tables, 1980 (Predictor (2)); Taylor and Jodice (Predictor (3)) Dependent variable: see note on the adjustment measurement concept, Chapter 11, above SPSS IX, new regression (stepwise)
z-standardized residuals > 1.499 Israel(−); Nicaragua(−); Uganda(−); Jamaica(−); Paraguay(+); Malaysia(+); Ecuador(+); Chile(−); Somalia(−). Regression result without these outliers:
$n = 79$; adj. $R^{**}2 = 58.6$ per cent; $F = 23.10$; $p = .0000$.

All predictors are significant at least at the 2.6 per cent level. Such short-term policy will not be conducive to long-term growth on the level of the world economy as a whole. Only where the market is relatively protected by a low level of integration into the main institutions of the capitalist world economy will such an *ad hoc* adjustment strategy yield more permanent

Figure 11.1   Key to country numbers and abbreviations (around 1984)

Angola	ANG	1	El Salvador	ELS	43	Malaysia	MAL	83
Burundi	BDI	2	Guatemala	GUA	44	Mongolia	MON	84
Cameroon	CAM	3	Haiti	HAI	45	Nepal	NEP	85
Central Af. R.	CAR	4	Honduras	HON	46	Pakistan	PAK	86
Chad	CHD	5	Jamaica	JAM	47	Philippines	PHI	87
Benin	DAH	6	Mexico	MEX	48	Singapore	SIN	88
Ethiopia	ETH	7	Nicaragua	NIC	49	Sri Lanka	SRI	89
Ghana	GHA	8	Panama	PAN	50	Thailand	THA	90
Guinea	GUI	9	Puerto Rico	PRI	51	Vietnam	VND	91
Ivory Coast	IVC	10	Argentina	ARG	52	(South Viet)	VNR	92
Kenya	KEN	11	Bolivia	BOL	53	Austria	AUS	93
Liberia	LIB	12	Brazil	BRA	54	Belgium	BEL	94
Madagascar	MAD	13	Chile	CHI	55	Denmark	DEN	95
Malawi	MLW	14	Colombia	COL	56	Finland	FIN	96
Mali	MLI	15	Ecuador	ECU	57	France	FRA	97
Mauritania	MAU	16	Paraguay	PAR	58	Germany		
Mozambique	MOZ	17	Peru	PER	59	Fed.	GFR	98
Niger	NIR	18	Uruguay	URU	60	Greece	GRE	99
Nigeria	NIG	19	Venezuela	VEN	61	Ireland	IRE	100
Rwanda	RWA	20	Iran	IRN	62	Italy	ITA	101
Senegal	SEN	21	Iraq	IRQ	63	Netherlands	NET	102
Sierra Leone	SIE	22	Israel	ISR	64	Norway	NOR	103
Somalia	SOM	23	Jordan	JOR	65	Portugal	POR	104
South Africa	SAF	24	Lebanon	LEB	66	Spain	SPA	105
Zimbabwe	SRO	25	Saudi Arabia	SAU	67	Sweden	SWE	106
Tanzania	TAN	26	Syrian Arab			Switzerland	SWI	107
Togo	TOG	27	Rep.	SYR	68	UK	UKI	108
Uganda	UGA	28	Turkey	TUR	69	Albania	ALB	109
Burkina Faso	UPV	29	Yemen Arab			Bulgaria	BUL	110
Zaire	ZAI	30	Rep.	YEM	70	CSSR	CZE	111
Zambia	ZAM	31	Yemen Dem.			German DR	DDR	112
Algeria	ALG	32	Rep.	YDR	71	Hungary	HUN	113
Egypt	EGY	33	Afghanistan	AFG	72	Poland	POL	114
Libyan A. R.	LYB	34	Burma	BUR	73	Romania	ROM	115
Morocco	MOR	35	China	CHA	74	Yugoslavia	YUG	116
Sudan	SUD	36	Hong Kong	HKG	75	USSR	USR	117
Tunisia	TUN	37	India	IND	76	Australia	AUT	118
Canada	CAN	38	Indonesia	INS	77	Papua N. G.	PNG	119
USA	USA	39	Japan	JAP	78	New Zealand	NZE	120
Costa Rica	COS	40	Kampuchea	KMR	79	Taiwan	TAI	121
Cuba	CUB	41	Korea, North	KOD	80	Bangladesh	BAN	
Dominican			Korea, South	KOR	81	Trinidad	TRI	123
Republic	DOM	42	Laos	LAO	82			

Figure 11.2   Adjustment policy – results on the level of the world system

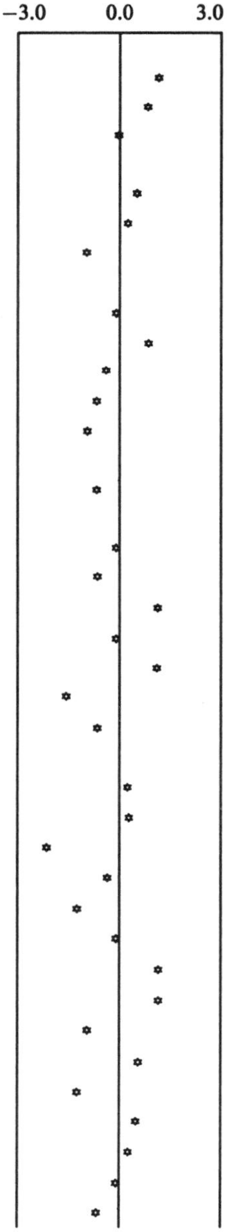

SEQNUM		−3.0 0.0 3.0	ADJ2 Adjustment	*PRED Prediction	*RESID Residual
1	ANG		−.1000E+07M	−9999.0000	−9999.0000
2	BDI		.9648	−.5568	1.5216
3	CAM		.2727	−.8233	1.0961
4	CAR		−.5953	−.3908	−.2405
5	CHD		−.1000E=07M	.5232	−9999.0000
6	DAH		.0607	−.8448	.9055
7	ETH		−.5430	−1.1185	.5755
8	GHA		−2.5314	−1.2270	−1.3044
9	GUI		.3425	−9999.0000	−9999.0000
10	IVC		−.7920	−.8976	.1056
11	KEN		−.2250	−1.2839	1.0588
12	LIB		−1.4951	−1.2756	−.2695
13	MAD		−1.6720	−.7970	−.8749
14	MLW		−1.2608	−.0837	−1.771
15	MLI		.1547	−9999.0000	−9999.0000
16	MAU		−1.3922	−.6930	−.6992
17	MOZ		−.1000E+07M	−9999.0000	−9999.0000
18	NIR		−.3094	−.3568	.0474
19	NIG		−.8010	.1099	−.9109
20	RWA		1.3754	−.3126	1.6880
21	SEN		−.8268	−.6628	−.1640
22	SIE		.2402	−1.3740	1.6142
23	SOM		−1.7189	.1529	−1.8717
24	SAF		−.4023	.4161	−.8185
25	SRO		−.1000E+07M	−9999.0000	−9999.0000
26	TAN		−.8060	−1.2681	.4621
27	TOG		−1.0130	−1.2718	.2588
28	UGA		−4.9218	−1.8683	−3.0536
29	UPV		1.1823	1.5308	−.3485
30	ZAI		−2.8382	−.9981	−1.8401
31	ZAM		−1.9269	−2.0479	.1210
32	ALG		1.7133	.1103	1.6030
33	EGY		3.2660	1.7638	1.5021
34	LYB		−3.5241	−2.3391	−1.1850
35	MOR		1.0258	.2557	.7701
36	SUD		−3.1774	−1.5539	−1.6235
37	TUN		1.2688	.4553	.8135
38	CAN		.2930	−.2226	.5156
39	USA		.1831	.2054	−.0223
40	COS		−.3469	.5628	−.9097

Fig 11.2 cont.

SEQNUM		ADJ2 Adjustment	*PRED Prediction	*RESID Residual
41	CUB	−.1000E+07M	−9999.0000	−9999.0000
42	DOM	−.6053E−03	.8070	−.8076
43	ELS	−1.5239	−.4586	−1.0652
44	GUA	−.7228	−.6192	−.1036
45	HAI	.2709	−9999.0000	−9999.0000
46	HON	−.2996	−.6679	.3684
47	JAM	−3.0143	−.2782	−2.7362
48	MEX	1.2016	.3715	.8301
49	NIC	−3.3415	−.2643	−3.0773
50	PAN	.8098	−.4504	1.2602
51	PRI	−.1000E+07M	−9999.0000	−9999.0000
52	ARG	−1.1650	−.4330	−.7320
53	BOL	−1.3283	−.6986	−.6297
54	BRA	.9416	.1752	.7664
55	CHI	−1.2313	.6700	−1.9013
56	COL	.8572	.4952	.3620
57	ECU	1.3426	.3435	1.9992
58	PAR	2.5339	.0932	2.4407
59	PER	−1.4292	−.4466	−.9826
60	URU	.9937	−.5081	1.5018
61	VEN	−.2790E−02	−.4964	.4937
62	IRN	−.1000E+07M	.8216	−9999.0000
63	IRQ	−.1000E+07M	−.8521	−9999.0000
64	ISR	.0455	3.2852	−3.2397
65	JOR	7.1285	5.7330	1.3955
66	LEB	−.1000E+07M	.0865	−9999.0000
67	SAU	−.3392	−1.4293	1.0901
68	SYR	1.6702	1.3560	.3142
69	TUR	−.4775	.1642	−.6417
70	YEM	−.1000E+07M	−9999.0000	−9999.0000
71	YDR	−.1000E+07M	−9999.0000	−9999.0000
72	AFG	−.1000E+07M	−9999.0000	−9999.0000
73	BUR	1.5485	.1921	1.3563
74	CHA	−.1000E+07M	−9999.0000	−9999.0000
75	HKG	2.8162	−9999.0000	−9999.0000
76	IND	.3699	.3806	−.0107
77	INS	2.4467	.6617	1.7850
78	JAP	−.6178	−.7793	.1615
79	KMR	−.1000E+07M	−9999.0000	−9999.0000
80	KOD	−.1000E+07M	−9999.0000	−9999.0000
81	KOR	−.0977	1.3321	−1.4297
82	LAU	−.1000E+07M	−9999.0000	−9999.0000

Plot scale: −3.0   0.0   3.0

SEQNUM		ADJ2 Adjustment	*PRED Prediction	*RESID Residual
	−3.0　　0.0　　3.0			
83	MAL	1.8197	−.4778	2.2975
84	MON	−.1000E+07M	−9999.0000	−9999.0000
85	NEP	−.6657	−9999.0000	−9999.0000
86	PAK	.7135	.5835	.1300
87	PHI	.7420	−.3403	1.0823
88	SIN	.5639	1.1642	−.6002
89	SRI	1.3035	−.4785	1.7820
90	THA	1.0446	−.0589	1.1036
91	VND	−.1000E+07M	−9999.0000	−9999.0000
92	VNR	−.1000E+07M	−9999.0000	−9999.0000
93	AUS	.6784	.0480	.6304
94	BEL	.3710	.0486	.3224
95	DEN	−.2647	.1779	−.4427
96	FIN	.2912	−.1388	.4300
97	FRA	.1935	.2521	−.0585
98	GFR	.7174	−.0754	.7928
99	GRE	−.0773	1.2259	−1.3032
100	IRE	.3815	.1580	.2234
101	ITA	.4146	.0788	.3357
102	NET	−.0693	.5041	−.5734
103	NOR	.5693	.2478	.3215
104	POR	1.2546	1.0416	.2129
105	SPA	−.4875	.6085	−1.0960
106	SWE	.0312	−.0129	.0441
107	SWI	−.1609	−.0800	−.0809
108	UKI	.2842	.1110	.1733
109	ALB	−.1000E+07M	−9999.0000	−9999.0000
110	BUL	−.1000E+07M	−9999.0000	−9999.0000
111	CZE	−.1000E+07M	−9999.0000	−9999.0000
112	DDR	−.1000E+07M	−9999.0000	−9999.0000
113	HUN	−.1000E+07M	−9999.0000	−9999.0000
114	POL	−.1000E+07M	−9999.0000	−9999.0000
115	ROM	−.1000E+07M	−9999.0000	−9999.0000
116	YUG	.9578	.8893	.0685
117	USR	−.1000E+07M	−9999.0000	−9999.0000
118	AUT	−.4216	.5716	−.99932
119	PNG	−.8237	−9999.0000	−9999.0000
120	NZE	−.0458	.4180	−.4638
121	TAI	−.1000E+07M	1.4534	−9999.0000
122	BAN	.4745	−9999.0000	−9999.0000
123	TRI	1.5020	−9999.0000	−9999.0000

results in terms of growth (Chapter 8). The military Keynesianism of such countries was already apparent during the latter half of the present Kondratieff cycle and was not just a strategy of adjustment.

From a long-term perspective, countries with a higher military personnel ratio and with a low increase in government expenditures per GDP, but with a larger effort in state-sponsored human capital formation, had higher growth rates during the period 1965–83 than other countries. Furthermore, as suggested in Chapter 7, a reliance on direct taxes was important, and constraints on growth resulted from the institutional framework: institutional age and the long-term negative consequences of heavy foreign capital penetration – the short-term positive effects of foreign capital inflows notwithstanding.

These results do not necessarily contradict each other, neither do they necessarily contradict the socio-liberal development paradigm. Any reader of Polanyi's 'Great Transformation' will be familiar with his account of the crisis years during the end of the last Kondratieff cycle when, in an authoritarian or democratic fashion, one country after the other abandoned the logic of the market.

What emerges from my results, however, is the necessity to formulate precisely the 'laws of motion' for different groups of countries with a different degree of exposure to the forces dominating the world economy on the one hand and different phases of Kondratieff cycles on the other hand. Bornschier (1988) is quite right in stressing the different effects that state sector expenditures have on growth in industrialized countries, depending on the phase that the world-wide Kondratieff cycle has reached. In a way, Sweden combined aspects of successful short-term adjustment (described in Table 11.1) on the level of the world economy with the long-term growth strategy emerging from Tables 7.1 and 7.3.

Uninterrupted by the Second World War, Sweden symbolizes the 'New Deal' social corporatism of the present outgoing Kondratieff cycle (Bornschier, 1988). In my view, the socio-liberal essence of Swedish development experience from 1932 onwards rests precisely on the fact, quite overlooked by Olson, that equality measures – briefly, a 'social wage' and the strong influence of working-class organizations on the bourgeois state – made possible wage restraint by labour and what Olson calls the 'flexibility of wages' in a democracy. Thus was assured the predictability and stability of policies and institutions. Olson hints at this possibility (Olson, 1982–85: 283), but he does not develop it further.

By all existing accounts, Sweden's 'Folkhem' policy model, which emerged in 1932 with the victory of the Social Democrats, by far surpasses any of the other Western nations in its combination of political stability, respect for human rights and economic performance during the Depression.

While in Austria fascism brutally crushed the labour movement in the 1934 civil war (Rabinbach) and real wages fell for years, and in Germany Hitler ensured that wages also declined, Swedish Social Democracy ensured a unique strategy against the crisis. It consisted of a build-up of welfare mechanisms on all levels (Bornschier, 1988) in return for state non-interference in wage policy. This was negotiated in the historic compromise between wage labour and private capital sealed at Saltsjoebaden in 1938 by labour and capital (Esping-Andersen, 1985; Korpi, 1978).

The tragic contrast between Sweden and Austria, where the clerico-fascists hanged workers in 1934, could not be more pronounced. In the latter, the regime tried to save its skin and find its way out of the crisis and applied a policy mix which has become all too familiar today in the developing world (Zimmermann and Saalfeld, 1988): tight money, extreme social cuts, high exchange rates, protectionism, and huge subsidies for the economically protected power base of the regime (in the Austrian case, catholic farmers and landowners); in a word, latter-day IMF theory being, even before its formulation, put to the test of the socio-political practice of a heterogeneous society. By 1932 the budget was slashed, wages and salaries were pushed down, democracy was abolished in 1933, and the country was thrown into civil war in 1934. At the same time, tariff increases and import restrictions multiplied, protecting the fascist power-base; public investment, on the other hand, was cut by 95 per cent and practically no measures were taken on the labour market. The ghastly record of the clerical regime did a lot to prepare the ground for the strength of the Nazis in Austria thereafter.

Sweden could provide no greater contrast to such an experience: peasants were to a large extent resilient against the fascist temptation and they entered into a coalition with Social Democracy, which protected Swedish agriculture. But the exchange rate was low, following the 1931 abandonment of the gold standard, which in turn was made politically feasible by the absence of the inflation experience of the 1920s (Esping-Andersen, 1985). The labour movement accepted the rights of private property in exchange for an assurance that conservative forces would remain loyal to democracy and accept social reforms (social wage), which must have been, in perspective, an important step in the direction of a historical compromise. The zero-sum game of capitalism thus was transformed into a positive-sum game at a time when other nations were plunged into fascism and civil war.

It should be also noted that Sweden – in contrast to Nazi Germany and fascist Austria – had a very low rate of public consumption. The highest value reached in Sweden before the war was 9.6 per cent of GDP in 1932, while in Nazi Germany this was 20.6 per cent and in clerico-fascist Austria 13.4 per cent. The demographic transition in Sweden had occurred fairly early and was well pronounced, but nevertheless Austrian and Swedish crude live birth rates did not differ much at the end of the 1920s. Sweden did not expand state consumption; it redistributed and changed the tax structure. Its policy mix – low state consumption, redistribution, a new tax structure – all compares with Austromarxist socio-liberal traditions, as discussed in Chapters 4 to 7 (see also Esping-Andersen, 1985; Korpi, 1978; Tilton, 1979). This seemed to change the lot of the poor in a rather inexpensive way, to increase employment by a very well-designed foreign exchange and trade policy, and to assure political stability in the Depression. Certainly Swedish success was helped by the fact that social and human development before the Social Democratic victory in 1932 was more rapid than in many other countries, including Austria. Austria reached the level of Swedish infant mortality of 1886 (112 per 1000 live births) only in 1929.

And yet, important questions emerge from the above arguments: the Netherlands also had a catastrophic employment record, but bourgeois parties and social democracy saved it from fascism, as in Belgium. Military expenditures played a major role in the Dutch, British, and of course also the Nazi recovery from the Depression (Zimmermann and Saalfeld, 1988). Ironically enough, Sweden could also benefit from the Nazi recovery by its large volume of exports to the German Reich, one of its main trading partners (Esping-Andersen, 1985). Britain's recovery coincided with rising wages (Zimmermann and Saalfeld, 1988: 316) and a programme realized by the Conservatives but in fact in many ways designed by Labour: unemployment benefits, education, health and road construction programmes, and departure from the gold standard. Cheap money, protectionism, industrial reconstruction, tax decreases and repeal of wage cuts ensured a rise of 24 per cent in British GNP from 1932 to 1938 (Zimmermann and Saalfeld, 1988: 316–17).

The Swedish experience of overcoming the depression must be seen in the context of the combination of internal and external conditions which made the 'Swedish model' possible (Lundberg, 1985). Sweden undervalued its currency in the 1920s relatively early, and devalued it again in September 1931. Monetary policy was quite passive and interest rates were rather low by international standards. There was only a minimum of protectionism in the Social Democratic international economic policy, mainly in the field of agriculture. During the first years of Social Democratic government, taxes on profits were even reduced, and a 'free write-off' system on capital investment was introduced. The overall socio-economic climate of the country during the 1930s was described by Lundberg, himself one of the architects of the 'model', in the following way: 'There seemed to be a good economic and social climate of tolerance and balance, of acceptance of high profits and dynamic change, as well as of the growing strength of the labor movement with its reform policies' (Lundberg, 1985: 11).

Flora *et al.* showed in their data series that in cross-national comparison, Sweden's state-sector size was fairly moderate throughout the crisis, and the state sector increased sharply only after the outbreak of the Second World War. Throughout the Great Depression (1929), Sweden's Government controlled only one-sixth to roughly one-fifth of its GDP while in other European nations, such as Nazi Germany, fascist Italy or in the UK, government began to control more than a quarter of GDP well before 1938 (Flora *et al.*, 1983–87: I, 355). Social service spending was lower than in the UK, but was of course much higher than in Austria. The class character of the Swedish state changed from 1932 onwards: redistribution began early, mainly by means of the wage policy of the trade unions in favour of poorer workers. The agricultural policy of the government assured stable incomes for the farmers. Sweden continued its march towards a considerable reduction in infant mortality (58.8 in 1928; 39.2 in 1940) and the government shifted its revenue base towards direct taxes. Social spending at both the national and the communal and provincial levels was not spectacular, but efficient enough to prevent any dramatic rise in infant mortality rates during the worst years of the Depression. Spending for the military, administration, justice and police amounted to just around 3–4 per cent of GDP throughout the depression years while, in a comparative perspective, of course, Nazi Germany and fascist Italy led the field with more than 10 per cent on that combined indicator. Neither the Nazi kind of perverted Keynesianism (government spending per GDP in 1938 amounted already to 36.9 per cent) nor its Italian variant (a record was reached during the Ethiopian war with 54.9 per cent government spending of GDP) drastically changed infant mortality rates. During the Weimar Republic, German infant mortality had already fallen from 96.4 per 1000 live births to 79.2 per 1000 in 1932 and 76.6 per 1000 in 1933, and after the Nazi takeover it decreased to 65.8, to remain fairly constant at that level. It would be very interesting to investigate the reasons for this decline in infant mortality during the Great Depression (1929) in Germany: was it due to health policy, was it due to birth control among the poor who knew that their babies would not survive, was it due to changed sexual habits or was it due to abortion among the poor? In Italy, the fascists never could decrease infant mortality below 95 per 1000 live births, and there was practically no change as compared to 1930. Unfortunately, Flora and his associates do not mention any data about the very probable social and religious split of infant mortality developing in fascist regimes. Jewish infant mortality rates must have increased very sharply in Nazi Germany already well before the horrors of the *Reichskristallnacht*; just as in Italy, the south carried the main burden of ongoing social stagnation.

By contrast, the UK experience is mixed (Flora, 1983–87): government increased its spending during the Depression, and again after 1937. In a social perspective, England and Wales could do much better in terms of infant mortality reduction than Scotland and Northern Ireland. Rates of economic growth were higher than ever in British twentieth-century history once the nadir in the Depression was reached (Zimmermann and Saalfeld, 1988: 316). Equally astonishing was the degree of socio-regional cleavage that developed in the country at that time. In 1929, England, Wales, Scotland and Northern Ireland had an infant mortality rate of 86 per 1000. A decade later, at the beginning of the Second World War, it was 50.8 in England and Wales, 71 in Northern Ireland and 68.5 in Scotland. There was 'Keynesianism', but the class character of the state did not change as dramatically as in Sweden, in terms of redistribution, direct taxation and infant mortality reduction.

What, then, is the point of the story? The corporatist model certainly contributed to world economic growth at the time of the Great Depression, and Polanyi was the first to foresee that such a depression leads to different kinds of social contracts. But Polanyi (1944) did not theorize about the possible trade-offs between social reform and growth. Dedicated humanist that he was, he simply saw them as necessary for the survival of humanity. Liberal corporatism did contribute to the stability of the growth path of Western capitalist societies after 1975, but the effects are not as big as expected by neo-corporatist theories. On the level of Western industrial societies and on the level of the capitalist world economy, the following strategies emerge as contributing to the stability of growth in times of world economic crisis at the end of a Kondratieff wave: (i) corporatism; (ii) institutional involvement of a country in the juridical structure of the capitalist world economy; (iii) absence of big transnational oligolopolies in the economic structure of a country; (iv) military expenditures; (v) social welfare policy; (vi) willingness to incur government deficits, hence high shares of private per total savings and a negative current account balance; (vii) adequate demographic transition; and (viii) political stability.

The error of Keynesian and neo-corporatist hypotheses lies in precisely the fact that such a strategy is only short-term. Such hypotheses overlook the long-term dynamics of development which, at least in the latter half of the present Kondratieff cycle, followed the socio-liberal logic. All these elements were present in the Swedish strategy in the 1930s. So I believe there are grounds for optimism concerning the positive trade-off between equality, reforms, democracy and economic growth. Polanyi once thought that the market principle interacts with the need of society to protect itself against the consequences of market rationality. Wide sectors of social democracy in the OECD countries believed just that after the war; and so they built up larger state sectors that brought about net transfers to the poor. But not only that: ageing democracies recognize that state sector outlays in such vital areas as education will enhance growth. But there is, at the close of the present Kondratieff cycle at least, some wisdom in the established liberal contentions about the age of democracy, state sector expenditures and economic growth, especially where non-educational state sector expenditures are concerned.

Polanyi's protection thesis must be further elaborated; indeed, there was a positive short-term adjustment success of strategies (all too often based on military Keynesianism) that corresponded not to the liberal market principle but to state-sector sponsored 'protectionist principle'. The validity of this could be shown both at the level of the OECD countries (where there is a closer connection between liberal corporatism and adjustment policy success in the short term) and at the level of the capitalist 'rim countries'. At the world level, however, and also at the level of former world socialism, the long-term preconditions that allowed for the ascent of countries like Sweden or Korea becomes clearer. Their policy success at two different times in history reveals the basic precondition that a capitalist economy needs in order to survive: socio-economic equality and a change in the class character of the state.

Polanyi, as the most esteemed theoretician of the Austro-Marxist tradition in the English-speaking world today, did not believe in such a basic precondition of capitalist economic growth. For him, the experiment of Red Vienna was but a continuation of Speenhamland (Polanyi, 1944: app. IX). Other social reformers of our century, like Mariategui, Wigforss, and above all Bauer, shared with him the critique of the mere substitution of private capitalism by state classes as an 'alternative' to capitalist society. But they were more optimistic in their belief about how much in terms of reforms and justice can be brought about even before the transition from capitalism to some distant form of self-administered socialism.

Marxists and Leninists of all denominations criticized the reformers for not breaking with the underlying logic of capitalist society. State socialism, what remains of it today, i.e. Leninist socialism – after a long period of what was termed 'extensive growth' – has reached an impasse too. By becoming an extractive economy in Bunker's sense, it needed more and more energy to pay back external debts and to maintain a heavy industrial/arms exporting economy at home. The state classes of the South, to be sure, benefited from this arms transfer machinery. But the extractive economy of the East became unable to satisfy basic human needs and is stagnant in terms of life expectancy and infant mortality reduction.

Seen in retrospect, reformers like Otto Bauer were correct in formulating the alternative: bolshevism or social democracy. And the reformers were right in avoiding a transition from capitalism to state socialism, which only leads back to periphery capitalism, nationalism and an extraction economy. What remains, then, of their socialist ideals, and what is the message in their reforms to us, today? In the words of a critic of government expenditures in advanced countries approaching two-thirds of GNP, Lundberg:

> An underlying egalitarian spirit, a 'passion for equality', lies behind the successful policies leading to the abolition of poverty and to reduced tensions among social classes. That the age-old fear of poverty has been replaced by a new-found social security is a fundamental achievement in Sweden as in the other Scandinavian countries. This achievement has lessened social and political strains, labor conflicts and resistance to technological change. Present crisis and bewilderment will not change the fundamental bases of the economic and social structure. (Lundberg, 1985: 34)

Or put in the words of Judaism, the first liberation theology:

> Wherefore have we fasted, say they, and thou seest not? Wherefore have we afflicted our soul, and thou takest no knowledge? Behold, in the day of your fast ye find pleasure, and exact all your labours. Behold, ye fast for strife and debate, and to smite with the fist of wickedness: ye shall not fast as ye do this day, to make your voice to be heard on high. Is it such a fast that I have chosen? A day for a man to afflict his soul? Is it to bow down his head as a bulrush, and to spread sackcloth and ashes under him? Wilt thou call this a fast, and an acceptable day to the Lord? Is not this the fast that I have chosen? To loose the bands of wickedness, to undo the heavy burdens, and to let the oppressed go free, and that ye break every yoke? Is it not to deal thy bread to the hungry, and that thou bring the poor that are cast out to thy house? When thou seest the naked, that thou cover; and that thou hide not thyself from thine own flesh? Then shall thy light break forth as the morning, and thine health shall spring forth speedily: and thy righteousness shall go before thee; the glory of the Lord shall be thy reward. Then shalt thou call, and the Lord shall answer (Isaiah, 58: 3–9)

Do democratic socialism and liberalism then represent a historical compromise and a coalition of reason, for the next cycle of the capitalist world economy? If my book stimulates debate on this vital issue of world development, it will have accomplished its task.

Bibliography

ABONYI, À. (1982), 'Eastern Europe's Reintegration' in C. K. Chase-Dunn (ed.), *Socialist States in the World System.* Beverly Hills, London, New Delhi: Sage Focus Edition, 181–202.

ACHEN, C. H. (1982), *Interpreting and Using Regression.* Beverly Hills: Sage University Paper, 29.

ACHEN, C. H. (1983), 'Toward Theories of Data: The State of Political Methodology' in A. W. Finifter (ed.), *Political Science: The State of the Discipline.* Washington D.C.: American Political Science Association, 69–93.

ADDICKS, G. and Buenning, H. H. (1979), *Strategien der Entwicklungspolitik.* Stuttgart, Berlin: Urban Taschenbuecher, W. Kohlhammer.

ADDO, H. (1981), 'Globale Oekonomie und eurozentrische Theorie: Eine Kritik traditioneller Imperialismustheorien' in Froebel, F. *et al.* (eds), *Krisen in der kapitalistischen Weltoekonomie.* Reinbek: rororo aktuell, 194–235.

ADDO, H. (1986), *Imperialism: The Permanent Stage of Capitalism.* Tokyo: United Nations University.

ADELMAN, I. and Taft-Morris, C. (1965), 'Factor Analysis of the Inter-Relationship between Social and Political Variables and Per Capita Gross National Product', *Quarterly Journal of Economics,* 79: 555–78.

ADELMAN, I. and Taft-Morris, C. (1973), 'An Anatomy of Income Distribution Patterns in Developing Nations – A Summary of Findings', *World Bank Staff Working Paper,* No. 116.

AFANASSJEW, J. *et al.* (eds) (1988a), *Der Kampf fuer Perestroika: Glasnost/ Demokratie/Sozialismus.* Moscow and Noerdlingen: Progress and Greno Publishing Co.

AFANASSJEW, J. *et al.* (eds) (1988b), *Es gibt keine Alternative zu Perestroika: Glasnost Demokratie Sozialismus.* Moscow and Noerdlingen: Progress and Greno Publishing Co.

AGANBEGJAN, A. (1988), 'Strategie der Beschleunigung der sozio-oekonomischen Entwicklung der UdSSR', *Europaeische Rundschau,* 16, 1: 93–110.

AHLUWALIA, I. J. (1985), *Industrial Growth in India. Stagnation since the Mid-Sixties.* Delhi, Bombay, Calcutta, Madras: Oxford University Press.

AHLUWALIA, M. S. (1974), 'Income Inequality: Some Dimensions of the Problem' in H. B. Chenery, *et al.* (eds), *Redistribution with Growth.* London, New York: Oxford University Press, 3–37.

AHLUWALIA, M. S. (1975), *Income Distribution and Development: Some Stylized Facts.* Washington D.C.: Development Research Center, International Bank for Reconstruction and Development.

AHLUWALIA, M. S., Carter, G. N. and Chenery, H. B. (1978), 'Growth and Poverty in Developing Countries', *World Bank Staff Working Paper* no. 309, July.

ALTIMIR, O. (1978), *La dimension de la pobreza en America Latina.* Santiago de Chile: CEPAL, L, 180/22–09.

ALMOND, G. (1987), 'The Development of Political Development' in M. Weiner, S. P. Huntington (eds), *Understanding Political Development.* Boston, Toronto: Little, Brown and Company: 437–90.

215

ALMOND, G. (1991), 'Capitalism and Democracy', *PS: Political Science & Politics*, 24, 3, Sep: 467–74.

AMIN, S. (1974), 'Zur Theorie von Akkumulation und Entwicklung in der gegenwaertigen Weltgesellschaft' in D. Senghaas (ed.), *Peripherer Kapitalismus. Analysen ueber Abhaengigkeit und Unterentwicklung*. Frankfurt, Edition Suhrkamp: 71–97.

AMIN, S. (1975), *Die ungleiche Entwicklung*. Hamburg: Hoffmann & Campe, Kritische Wissenschaft.

AMIN, S. (1979), '"Self-reliance" und die Neue internationale Wirtschaftsordnung' in D. Senghass (ed.), *Kapitalistische Weltoekonomie. Kontroversen ueber ihren Ursprung und ihre Entwicklungsdynamik*. Frankfurt, Edition Suhrkamp: 317–36.

AMIN, S. (1984), 'Was kommt nach der Neuen Internationalen Wirtschaftsordnung? Die Zukunft der Weltwirtschaft' in H. Fischjer and P. Jankowitsch (eds), *Rote Markierungen international*. Vienna: Europaverlag, 89–110.

AMIN, S. (1986), 'Krise, Sozialismus und Nationalismus' in S. Amin *et al.* (eds), *Dynamik der globalen Krise*. Opladen: Westdeutscher Verlag: 118–66.

AMIN, S. (1987), 'Democracy and national strategy in the periphery', *Third World Quarterly*, 9, 4: 1129–56.

ANDREAE, C. A. (1985), 'Fiskalisch bedingte Wachstumshemmungen. Prioritaeten einer angebotsorientierten Steuerpolitik', *Neue Zuercher Zeitung*, 82, Fernausgabe, 11, Apr: 15.

ANDREAE, C. A. (1986), *Taxes and Economic Growth*. Binghamton, N.Y.: Lecture Series, New York State University.

ANDREJEVICH, M. (1991), 'The Economy on the Verge of Collapse', *Report on Eastern Europe*, 2, 34, 23 August, 30–32.

ANKER, R. and Farooq, G. M. (1978), 'Population and Socio-Economic Development: The New Perspective', *International Labour Review*, 117, 2, Mar–Apr: 143–55.

ANTAL, L. (1988), 'Hungary's Economic Policy in the 1980s: Restrictive economic policy – uncertain, ill-assorted reforms', *WIIW Forschungsberichte*, Vienna Institute for Comparative Economic Studies, 148, August.

APTER, D. (1987) *Rethinking Development: Modernisation, Dependency and Post-Modern Politics*. Newbury Park, CA: Sage.

ARRIGHI, G. (1989), *The Developmentalist Illusion: A Reconceptualization of the Semi-Periphery*. Paper presented at the Thirteenth Annual Political Economy of the World System Conference, University of Illinois at Urbana-Champaign, 28–30 April.

ARRIGHI, G. (1990), *The Developmentalist Illusion: A Reconceptualization of the Semi-Periphery*. Binghamton, N.Y.: Fernand Braudel Center, State University of New York.

ARRIGHI, G. (1991), *World Income Inequalities and the Future of Socialism*. Binghamton, N.Y.: Fernand Braudel Center, State University of New York.

ASCHE, H. (1985), 'Ueber die jungen Industrielaender und Schwellenlaender in Ostasien', *Politische Vierteljahresschrift*, 26, Sonderheft 16: 97–112.

ASLUND, A. (1991), 'Gorbachev, Perestroika, and Economic Crisis', *Problems of Communism*, Jan–Apr: 18–41.

ASLUND, A. (1992), 'The Soviet Economy After the Coup', *Problems of Communism*, 40, Nov–Dec: 44–52.

BABLEWSKI, Z. (1989), 'Development Theory in Eastern Europe: Evolution and Critical Issues' in Z. Bablewski and B. Hettne (eds), *Crisis in Development*. Peace and Development Research Institute, Gothenburg University, papers: 112–30.

BALIBAR, E. (1991), 'Es gibt keinen Staat in Europa: Racism and Politics in Europe Today', *New Left Review*, Mar–Apr, 186: 5–19.

BALLMER-CAO and Scheidegger *see* Bornschier, Heintz *et al.*

BANNERJEE, J. (1987), 'Moscow's Indian Alliance', *Problems of Communism*, 36, 1: 1–12.

BARAN, P.A. (1966), *Politische Oekonomie des wirtschaftlichen Wachstums.* Neuwied and Berlin: Luchterhand.

BARNES, S.H., Kaase, M. *et al.* (1979), *Political Action. Mass Participation in Five Western Democracies.* Beverly Hills and London: Sage.

BAUER, O. (1980, posthumously) *Werkausgabe.* Herausgegeben von der Arbeitsgemeinschaft fuer die Geschichte der oesterreichischen Arbeiterbewegung, Vienna: Europaverlag.

BAUER, Lord P.T. (1984), 'Remembrance of Studies Past: Retracing First Steps' in G.M. Meier and D. Seers (eds), *Pioneers in Development.* New York and Oxford: Oxford University Press: 27–43.

BELLO, W. (1989), 'Confronting the Brave New World Economic Order: Toward a Southern Agenda for the 1990s', *Alternatives. Social Transformation and Humane Governance*, XIV, 2, Apr: 135–68.

BENARD, C. and Schlaffer, E. (1985), *Die Grenzen des Geschlechts. Anleitungen zum Sturz des Internationalen Patriarchats-Amnesty for Women.* Reinbek: rororo sachbuch.

BENNHOLDT-THOMSEN, V. (1980), 'Marginalitaet in Lateinamerika-Eine Theoriekritik', *Lateinamerika. Analysen und Berichte*, Berlin: Olle & Wolter, vol. 3: 45–85.

BERG-SCHLOSSER, D. (1985), 'Zu den Bedingungen von Demokratie in der Dritten Welt', *Politische Vierteljahresschrift*, 26, Sonderheft 16: 233–66.

BERG-SCHLOSSER, D. (1986), 'Vormarsch der Demokratie in der Dritten Welt?' in J. Betz and V. Matthies (eds), *Jahrbuch Dritte Welt. Daten. Uebersichten. Analysen.* Munich: C.H. Beck'sche Verlagsbuchhandlung, 63–74.

BERGSON, A. (1984), 'Income Inequality Under Soviet Socialism', *Journal of Economic Literature*, 22, 3: 1052–99.

BERRY, A. *et al.* (1981), 'The Level of World Inequality: How Much Can One Say?', *Ecole Normale Superieure*, Paris, Laboratoire d'Economie Politique, *Document* 38 (entire).

BERRY, W.D. and Feldman, S. (1985), *Multiple Regression in Practice.* Beverly Hills: Sage University Paper, 50.

BHAGWATI, J.N. (1989), 'Nation-States in an International Framework: An Economist's Perspective', *Alternatives. Social Transformation and Humane Governance*, XIV, 2, Apr: 231–44.

BIALER, S. (1988), 'Gorbachev's Program of Change: Sources, Significance, Prospects', *Political Science Quarterly*, 103, 3: 403–60.

BIENEFELD, M. (1981), 'Dependency and the Newly Industrializing Countries (NICs): Towards a Reappraisal' in D. Seers (ed.), *Dependency Theory: A Critical Reassessment.* London: Frances Pinter: 79–96.

BIRDSALL, N. (1980), 'Population and Poverty in the Developing World', *World Bank Staff Working Paper* no. 404, July.

BIRDSALL, N. *et. al.* (1984), *World Development Report 1984.* New York, Oxford, London: Oxford University Press.

BLAAS, W. (1984), 'Stabilisierungspolitik. Zur politischen Oekonomie marktwirtschaftlicher Instabilitaet', *Der oeffentliche Sektor*, 1–2 Mar (entire).

BOECKH, A. (1985), 'Dependencia und kapitalistisches Weltsystem, oder: Die Grenzen globaler Entwicklungstheorien', *Politische Vierteljahresschrift*, 26, Sonderheft 16: 56–74.

BOECKH, A. (1982), 'Abhaengigkeit, Unterentwicklung und Entwicklung: Zum Erklaerungswert der Dependencia-Ansaetze' in D. Bohlen and F. Nuscheler (eds), *Handbuch der Dritten Welt*, 2nd edn. Hamburg: Hoffmann & Campe, 133–51.

BOECKH, A. (1984), 'Dependencia-Theorien' in D. Nohlen (ed.), *Lexicon Dritte Welt*. Reinbek: rororo handbuch, 137–44.

BOEHM-BAWERK, E. von (1914) 'Macht oder oekonomisches Gesetz?', *Zeitschrift fuer Volkswirtschaft, Sozialpolitik und Verwaltung*, 23: 205–71.

BOHR, A. (1988), 'Infant Mortality in Central Asia', *Radio Liberty Research* (Munich), RL 352–88.

BOLI, J. (1983), 'The Contradictions of Welfare Capitalism in the Core: The Role of Sweden in the World System' in P. McGowan and C. W. Kegley Jr (eds), *Foreign Policy and the Modern World-System*. Beverly Hills, London, New Delhi: Sage: 187–221.

BOLLEN, K. A. (1979), 'Political Democracy and the Timing of Development', *American Sociological Review*, 44, Aug: 572–87.

BOLLEN, K. A. (1980), 'Issues in the Comparative Measurement of Political Democracy', *American Sociological Review*, 45, Jun: 370–90.

BOLLEN, K. A. (1983), 'World System Position, Dependency, and Democracy: The Cross-National Evidence', *American Sociological Review*, 48, Aug: 468–79.

BOLLEN, K. A. and Jackman, R. W. (1985), 'Political Democracy and the Size Distribution of Income', *American Sociological Review*, 50, Aug: 438–57.

BOOTH, D. (1985), 'Marxism and Development Sociology: Interpreting the Impasse', *World Development*, 13, 7: 761–87.

BORNSCHIER, V. (1976), *Wachstum, Konzentration und Multinationalisierung von Industrieunternehmen*. Frauenfeld and Stuttgart: Huber.

BORNSCHIER, V. (1982), 'World Economic Integration and Policy Responses: Some Developmental Impacts' in H. Makler, A. Martinelli and N. Smelser (eds), *The New International Economy*. Beverly Hills and London: Sage Studies in International Sociology, 26, 59–78.

BORNSCHIER, V. (1984), 'Weltsystem' in A. Boeckh (ed.), *Internationale Beziehungen. Theorien-Organisationen-Konflikte*. Munich, Zurich: Pipers Woerterbuch zur Politik, 5, herausgegeben von Dieter Nohlen, Piper, 535–541.

BORNSCHIER, V. (1985), *World Social Structure in the Long Economic Wave. A Research Note*. 7. Kongress der Schweizerischen Gesellschaft fuer Soziologie, 17. 10.–19.10., Arbeitsgruppe 'Weltgesellschaft', mimeo.

BORNSCHIER, V. (1988), *Westliche Gesellschaft im Wandel*. Frankfurt: Campus.

BORNSCHIER, V. (1992), *The Rise of the European Community. Grasping towards hegemony or therapy against national decline in the world political economy?* Paper presented at the First European Conference of Sociology, Vienna, 26–29 August 1992, Mimeo

BORNSCHIER, V., Heintz P. *et al.* (1979), *Compendium of Data for World Systems Analysis*. MRDF, Institut fuer Soziologie, University of Zurich.

BORNSCHIER, V. *et. al.* (1980), *Multinationale Konzerne, Wirtschaftspolitik und nationale Entwicklung im Weltsystem*. Frankfurt, New York: Campus.

BORNSCHIER, V. and Chase-Dunn, C. (1985), *Transnational Corporations and Underdevelopment*. New York: Praeger.

BOUCHER, J. *et al.* (1987), *Ethnic Conflict. International Perspectives.* Newbury Park, Beverly Hills, London, New Delhi: Sage.

BRAUN, A. and Day, R. B. (1990), 'Gorbachevian Contradictions', *Problems of Communism*, 39, 3: 36–50.

BRAUN, O. (1974), 'Wirtschaftliche Abhaengigkeit und imperialistische Ausbeutung' in D. Senghaas (ed.), *Peripherer Kapitalismus. Analysen ueber Abhaengigkeit und Unterentwicklung.* Frankfurt, Edition Suhrkamp: 137–55.

BREMER, S. A. *et al.* (1987), *The GLOBUS Model. Computer Simulation of Worldwide Political and Economic Developments.* Frankfurt and Boulder, CO.: Campus/Westview Press.

BRENNER, R. (1977), 'The Origins of Capitalist Development: A Critique of Neo-Smithian Marxism', *New Left Review*, 104: 25–92.

BRESSER PEREIRA, L. C. transl. M. Van Dyke (1984), 'Six Interpretations of the Brazilian Social Formation', *Latin American Perspectives*, 40, 11, 1: 35–72.

BRONSTEIN, I. N. and Semendjajew, K. A. (1972), *Taschenbuch der Mathematik*, 12th edn. Frankfurt and Zurich: Harri Deutsch.

BRUNDENIUS, C. (1979), 'Measuring Income Distribution in Pre-and Post-Revolutionary Cuba', *Cuban Studies*, 9, July: 29–44.

BRUNO, M. and Sachs, J. D. (1985), *Economics of Worldwide Stagflation.* Cambridge, Mass.: Harvard University Press.

BULATAO, R. A. (1984), 'Reducing Fertility in Developing Countries. A Review of Determinants and Policy Levers', *World Bank Staff Working Papers*, 680.

BUNKER, S. G. (1984), 'The Exploitation of Labor in the Appropriation of Nature: Toward an Energy Theory of Value' in C. Bergquist (ed.), *Labor in the Capitalist World Economy.* Beverly Hills, London, New Delhi: Sage: 49–73.

BUSH, K. (1991), 'The Economic Problems Remain', *Report on the USSR*, 3, 36, 6 Sep: 37–9.

BUSH, K. (1992), 'The Disastrous Last Year of the USSR', *RFE/RL Research Report*, 12, 20, Mar: 39–41.

BUTTERWEGE, C. (1991), 'Rechtsruck in Ostdeutschland? Neofaschismus, Rassismus und Auslaenderfeindlichkeit nach der Wiedervereinigung', *Zukunft*, Oct, 25–9.

CANAK, W. L. (1984), 'The Peripheral State Debate: State Capitalist and Bureaucratic-Authoritarian Regimes in Latin America', *Latin American Research Review*, XIX, 1: 3–36.

CARDOSO, F. H. (1972a), *O Modelo Politico Brasileiro, e outros ensaios.* São Paulo: CEBRAP.

CARDOSO, F. H. (1972b), 'Dependency and Development in Latin America', *New Left Review*, 74, Jul–Aug (German in Senghaas, 1974).

CARDOSO, F. H. (1972c), *Das brasilianische Entwicklungsmodell. Daten und Perspektiven.* Berlin: Deutsche Stiftung fuer Internationale Entwicklung, mimeo.

CARDOSO, F. H. (1973a), 'Associated-Dependent Development. Theoretical and Practical Implications' in A. Stepan (ed.) *Authoritarian Brazil. Origins, Policies and Future.* New Haven and London: Yale University Press.

CARDOSO, F. H. (1973b), 'Notas sobre o Estado Atual dos Estudos sobre Dependencia', *Cadernos Centro Brasileiro Rde Analise e Peanajemento*, 11.

CARDOSO, F. H. (1973c), *As contradicoes do desenvolvimento asociado.* Berlin: Deutsche Stiftung fuer Internationale Entwicklung, mimeo.

CARDOSO, F. H. (1973d), *As clases sociais e a crise politica da America Latina*. Berlin: Deutsche Stiftung fuer Internationale Entwicklung, mimeo.

CARDOSO, F.H. (1977), 'El Consumo de la Teoria de la Dependencia en los Estados Unidos', *El Trimestre Economico*, 173, 44, 1, Enero Marzo: 33–52.

CARDOSO, F. H.(1979), *Development under Fire*. Instituto Latinoamericano de Estudios Transnacionales, DEE/D/24 i, May (Mexico 20 D.F., Apartado 85–025). Reprinted in H. Makler *et al.* (eds) (1982), *The New International Economy*. Beverly Hills and London: Sage: 141–65.

CARDOSO, F. H. and Faletto E. (1971), *Dependencia y Desarrollo en America Latina*. Siglo XXI, Mexico City, Madrid, Buenos Aires.

CARUSO, I. (1972), *Soziale Aspekte der Psychoanalyse*. Reinbek: rororo studium.

CARVALHO, J. A. M. de and Wood, C. H. (1981), Crescimento Populacional e Distribuicao da Renda Familiar: O Caso Brasileiro', *Estudos Economicos*, 11, 3: 5–25.

CASSEN, R. (ed.) (1985), *Soviet Interests in the Third World*. London, Beverly Hills, New Delhi: Sage.

CHASE-DUNN, C. K. (1975), 'The Effects of International Economic Dependence on Development and Inequality: A Cross-national Study', *American Sociological Review*, 40, 6: 720–38.

CHASE-DUNN, C. K. (1982a), 'A World System Perspective on Dependency and Development in Latin America', *Latin American Research Review*, XVII, 1: 166–71.

CHASE-DUNN, C. K. (1982b), 'The Uses of Formal Comparative Research on Dependency Theory and the World-System Perspective' in H. Makler, A. Martinelli and N. Smelser (eds), *The New International Economy*. Beverly Hills and London: Sage Studies in International Sociology, 26, 117–137.

CHASE-DUNN, C. K. (1982c), 'Socialist States in the Capitalist World Economy' in C. K. Chase-Dunn (ed.), *Socialist States in the World-System*. Beverly Hills, London, New Delhi: Sage Focus Edition, 21–56.

CHASE-DUNN, C. K. (1984), 'The World-System Since 1950: What Has Really Changed?' in C. Bergquist (ed.), *Labor in the Capitalist World-Economy*. vol. 7, Political Economy of the World System Annuals, Beverly Hills, London, New Delhi: Sage, 75–104.

CHASE-DUNN, C. K. (1992), 'The National State as an Agent of Modernity', *Problems of Communism*, 41, 1–2: 29–37

CHENERY, H. B. (1983), 'Interaction between Theory and Observation in Development', *World Development*, 11, 10: 853–61.

CHENERY, H. B. *et al.* (1975), *Patterns of Development 1950–1970*. London, Glasgow, New York: Oxford University Press.

CHOMSKY, N. (1971), *Die Verantwortlichkeit der Intellektuellen*. Frankfurt, Edition Suhrkamp.

CHOMSKY, N. (1972), *Im Krieg mit Asien*. Frankfurt, Edition Suhrkamp.

CHOUCRI, N. (1974), *Population Dynamics and International Violence. Propositions, Insights and Evidence*. Lexington Mass., Toronto and London: Lexington Books, D.C. Heath.

CORDOVA, A. (1973), *Strukturelle Heterogenitaet und wirtschaftliches Wachstum*. Frankfurt, Edition Suhrkamp.

CORNIA, G. A. (1984), 'A Survey of Cross-sectional and Time-series Literature on Factors Affecting Child Welfare', *World Development*, 12, 3: 187–202.

CSIKOS-NAGY, B. (1988), 'Krisenerscheinungen in der ungarischen Wirtschaft und ihre Gruende', *Europaeische Rundschau*, 16, 2: 65–76.

CUTLER, R.M. *et al.* (1987), 'The Political Economy of East–South Military Transfers', *International Studies Quarterly*, 31, 3: 273–99.

CZADA, R. (1987), 'The impact of interest politics on flexible adjustment policies' in H. Keman *et al.* (eds), *Coping with the Economic Crisis*. London: Sage: 20–53.

DAS, P.K. (ed.) (1987), *The Troubled Region. Issues of Peace and Development in Southeast Asia*. New Delhi, Newbury Park, London: Sage.

DELACROIX, J. and Ragin, C.C. (1981), 'Structural Blockage: A Cross-national Study of Economic Dependency, State Efficacy, and Underdevelopment', *American Journal of Sociology*, 86, 6: 1311–47.

DEMOS-LEE, R. (1980), 'A Historical Perspective on Economic Aspects of the Population Explosion: The Case of Preindustrial England' in R.A. Easterlin (ed.), *Population and Economic Change in Developing Countries*. Chicago and London: University of Chicago Press, 517–66.

DENEMARK, R.A. and Thomas, K.P. (1988), 'The Brenner-Wallerstein, Debate', *International Studies Quarterly*, 32, 1: 47–66.

DENSLOW, D. Jr. and Tyler, W.G. (1983), 'Perspectivas sobre pobreza e desigualdade de renda no Brasil', *Pesquisa e Planejamento Economico*, 13, 3, Dec: 863–904.

DEUTSCH, K.W. (1960/66), 'Ansaetze zu einer Bestandsaufnahme von Tendenzen in der vergleichenden und internationalen Politik' in E. Krippendorff (ed.), *Political Science. Amerikanische Beitraege zur Politikwissenschaft*. Tuebingen: J.C.B. Mohr.

DEUTSCH, K.W. (1963/69), *Politische Kybernetik. Modelle und Perspektiven*. Freiburg: Dritte, unveraenderte Auflag, Rombach.

DEUTSCH, K.W. (1978a), 'On World Models and Political Science', *IIVG preprints*, Berlin: International Institute for Comparative Social Research, PV/78–15.

DEUTSCH, K.W. (1978b–1982) 'Major Changes in Political Science, 1952–1977', *IIVG preprints*, International Institute for Comparative Social Research, PV/78–2. Reprinted in W.G. Andrews (ed.), *International Handbook of Political Science*. Westport, Conn.: Greenwood Press, 9–33.

DEUTSCH, K.W. (1978c), *The Analysis of International Relations*, 2nd edn. Englewood Cliffs, N.J.: Prentice Hall.

DEUTSCH, K.W. (1979a), 'Limited Growth and Continuing Inequality: Some World Political Effects' in K.W. Deutsch, *Tides Among Nations*. New York: Free Press, Macmillan, 315–27.

DEUTSCH, K.W. (1979b), 'National Integration: A Summary of Some Concepts and Research Approaches' in *Tides Among Nations* (see Deutsch, 1979a), 269–94.

DEUTSCH, K.W. (1979c), 'Social Mobilization and Political Development' in *Tides Among Nations* (see 1979a), 90–132.

DEUTSCH, K.W. (1980), 'On the Utility of Indicator Systems' in C.L. Taylor (ed.), *Indicator Systems for Political, Economic and Social Analysis*. Oelgeschlager, Gunn und Hain, Anton Hain, Koenigstein/Ts.

DIETZ, R. (1991a), 'The Impact of the Unification on the East German Economy', *WIIW-Forschungsberichte*, 172, May 1991 (Vienna).

DIETZ, R. (1991b), 'The Reform of Soviet Socialism as a Search for Systemic Rationality: A Systems Theoretical View', *Communist Economies*, 2, 4: 419–39.

DITTMER, L. (1989), 'The Tiananmen Massacre', *Problems of Communism*, 38, 5: 2–16.

DIX, R. (1980), 'Democracy in Latin America', *Latin American Research Review*, xv, 3: 240–5.

DONNER, J. (1983), 'Sri Lanka' in D. Nohlen and F. Nuscheler (eds), *Handbuch der Dritten Welt*. Hamburg: Hoffmann & Campe, vol. 7, 226–48.

DOS SANTOS, T. (1970), 'The structure of dependence', *American Economic Review*, 60, 2: 231–6.

DUBIEL, I. (1984), *Der klassische Kern der lateinamerikanischen Entwicklungstheorie. Ein metatheoretischer Versuch*. Munich: Wilhelm Fink, vol. 24.

DUVALL, R. D. and Freeman, J. R. (1981), 'The State and Dependent Capitalism' in W. L. Hollist and J. N. Rosenau (eds), *World System Structure. Continuity and Change*. Beverly Hills and London: Sage Focus Edition, 223–42.

EFRAT, M. (1987), 'Disentangling the Economics of Soviet Arms Trade: Are Western Assessments Really Reliable?', *Osteuropa-Wirtschaft*, 32, 1: 38–59.

EHRKE, M. (1984), 'Spekulation und Auslandsverschuldung: Die Faelle Mexiko und Argentinien' in M. Ehrke *et al.* (eds), *Volkssouveraenitaet und Staatsschuld. Lateinamerika. Analysen und Berichte*, 8, Hamburg: Junius, 34–65.

EHRLICH, S. (1981), 'The Rationality of Pluralism', *The Polish Sociological Bulletin* (Warsaw), 54, 2: 27–38.

EISENSTADT, S. N. (1985), 'Civilizational Formations and Political Dynamics. The Stein Rokkan Lecture 1985', *Scandinavian Political Studies*, 8, 4: 231–51.

ELSENHANS, H. (1974), 'Aus der Oelkrise zu einer europaeischen Entwicklungspolitik', *Leviathan*, 1: 7ff.

ELSENHANS, H. (1979a), 'Grundlagen der Entwicklung der kapitalistischen Weltwirtschaft' in D. Senghaas (ed.), *Kapitalistische Weltoekonomie. Kontroversen ueber ihren Ursprung und ihre Entwicklungsdynamik*. Frankfurt: Edition Suhrkamp, 103–48.

ELSENHANS, H. (1979b), 'Das Gesetz des tendenziellen Falls der Profitrate. Einige Bemerkungen zu neoricardianischen und marxistischen Behauptungen', *Leviathan*, 7, 4: 584–97.

ELSENHANS, H. (1982), 'Die Ueberwindung von Unterentwicklung durch Massenproduktion fuer den Massenbedarf-Weiterentwicklung eines Ansatzes' in D. Nohlen and F. Nuscheler (eds), *Handbuch der Dritten Welt*, 2nd edn. Hamburg: Hoffmann & Campe, 152–82.

ELSENHANS, H. (1983), 'Rising mass incomes as a condition of capitalist growth: implications for the world economy', *International Organization*, 37, 1: 1–39.

ELSENHANS, H.(1984), *Nord–Sued-Beziehungen. Geschichte-Politik-Wirtschaft*. Stuttgart: Urban, W. Kohlhammer.

ELSENHANS, H. (1985a), 'Der periphere Staat: Zum Stand der entwicklungstheoretischen Diskussion', *Politische Vierteljahresschrift*, Sonderheft 16, 26: 135–56.

ELSENHANS, H. (1985b), *The Extension of State Functions and the Specific Requirements for a New International Economic Order Made by the Third World*. International Political Science Association World Congress, Paris, 15–20 July (mimeo, available on microfilm from IPSA Secretariat).

ELSENHANS, H. (1986a), 'Zu reich fuer alternative Entwicklungsstrategien-Das Dilemma der Dritten Welt', *Schweizerische Zeitschrift fuer Soziologie*, 12, 1: 155–72.

ELSENHANS, H. (1986b), 'Dependencia, Unterentwicklung und der Staat in der Dritten Welt', *Politische Vierteljahresschrift*, 27, 2, Jun: 133–58.

ELSENHANS, H. and Junne, G. (1974), 'Deformation und Wirtschaftswachstum', *Leviathan*, 4: 534ff.

ELLACURIA, I.S.J. (1989), 'Utopia y profetismo desde America Latina. Un ensayo concreto de soterologia historica', *Revista Latinoamericana de Teologia*, 6, 17: 141–84.

ENCYCLOPAEDIA JUDAICA (1972–) Jerusalem (17 volumes).

ESPING-ANDERSEN, G. (1987), 'Institutional accomodation to full employment: a comparison of policy regimes' in H. Keman *et al.* (eds), *Coping with the Economic Crisis*. London: Sage: 83–110.

ESPING-ANDERSEN, G. (1985), *Politics Against Markets. The Social Democratic Road to Power*. Princeton University Press.

EVANS, P. (1987), 'Foreign Capital and the Third World State' in M. Weiner and S.P. Huntington (eds), *Understanding Political Development*. Boston, Toronto: Little, Brown and Company: 319–52.

EVANS, P.B. and Timberlake, M. (1980), 'Dependence, Inequality, and the Growth of the Tertiary: A Comparative Analysis of Less Developed Countries', *American Sociological Review*, 45, 3: 531–52.

EVERS, T.T. and Wogau, P. von (1973), 'Dependencia: Lateinamerikanische Beitraege zur Theorie der Unterentwicklung', *Das Argument*, 79, Jul: 404ff.

FABINC, I. and Popovic, T. (1988), *Yugoslavia in the World Economy on the Threshold of the XXI Century*. Belgrade: Consortium of Economic Institutes.

FAJNZYLBER, F. (1987), 'Las economias neoindustriales en el Sistema Centro-Periferia de los ochenta', *Pensamiento Iberoamericano*, 11: 125–82.

FAY, M. *et. al.* (eds) (1980), *Strukturveraenderungen in der kapitalistischen Weltwirtschaft*. Frankfurt: Starnberger Studien 4, Edition Suhrkamp.

FEDER, E. (1972), *Violencia y despojo del campesino: el latifundismo en America Latina*. Siglo XXI, Mexico City, Madrid, Buenos Aires.

FELIX, D. (1983), 'Income Distribution and the Quality of Life in Latin America. Patterns, Trends and Policy Implications', *Latin American Research Review*, 28, 2: 3–33.

FERREIRA DE CAMARGO, C.P. *et. al.* (eds) (1975), *Sao Paulo 1975. Crescimento e Pobreza*, 4th edn. Sao Paulo: Loyola.

FILGUEIRA, C. (1984), 'El Estado y las clases: Tendencias en Argentina, Brasil y Uruguay', *Pensamiento Iberoamericano*, 6, 2: 35–62.

FLAKIERSKI, H. (1981), 'Economic Reform and Income Distribution in Poland. The Negative Evidence', *Cambridge Journal of Economics*, 1: 5ff.

FLECHSIG, S. (1985), 'Neokonservative Wirtschaftstheorie und-praxis im Suedke-gel Lateinamerikas', *Wirtschaftswissenschaft*, 33, 2: 204–21.

FLECHSIG, S. (1987), 'Raul Prebisch-ein bedeutender Oekonom Lateinamerikas und der Entwicklungslaender', *Wirtschaftswissenschaft*, 35, 5: 721–41.

FLECHSIG, S. (1989a), *The Contribution of ECLA to Development Theory*. Paper presented at the RIDC/EADI conference 'The trends towards the globalization of development theory', CSPS, RIDC, Warsaw, 22–23 June 1989.

FLECHSIG, S. *et al.* (1989b), *Oekonomische und gesellschaftliche Entwicklung in Lateinamerika: Krise und Suche nach einer Alternative*. Paper presented at the International Colloquium 'Gesellschaftliche Alternativen in Vergangenheit und Gegenwart', University of Rostock, 24–26 May 1989.

FLORA, P. *et al.* (1983–87), *State, Economy and Society in Western Europe 1815–1975. A Data Handbook.* 2 vols. Frankfurt: Campus; London and Basingstoke: Macmillan/Chicago: St. James Press.

FOYE, S. (1991), 'A Lesson of Ineptitude: Military-Backed Coup Crumbles', *Report on the USSR,* 3, 35, 30 Aug: 5–8.

FRANK, A. G.(1977a), 'Dependence is Dead. Long Live Dependence and the Class Struggle. An Answer to Critics', *World Development,* 5, 4: 355–70.

FRANK, A. G. (1977b), 'Long Live Transideological Enterprise!', *Economic and Political Weekly,* Bombay, XII, 6–8 Feb.

FRANK, A. G. (1983a), 'Global Crisis and Transformation', *Development and Change,* 14, 3: 323–46.

FRANK, A. G. (1983b), 'World System in Crisis' in W. R. Thompson (ed.), *Contending Approaches to World System Analysis.* Beverly Hills and London: Sage: 27–42.

FRANK, A. G. (1990), 'Revolution in Eastern Europe: Lessons for Democratic Social Movements (and Socialists?)', *Third World Quarterly,* 12, 2, Apr: 36–52.

FRANK, A. G. (1991), 'Politische Ökonomie des Golfkriegs', *Das Argument,* 186: 177–86.

FRANK, A. G. and Fuentes-Frank, M. (1990), *Widerstand im Weltsystem. Kapitalistische Akkumulation; Staatliche Politik; Soziale Bewegung.* Vienna: Promedia.

FRIEDEN, J. A. (1987), 'The Brazilian Borrowing Experience: From Miracle to Debacle and Back', *Latin American Research Review,* 22, 1: 95–131.

FROEBEL, F. (1980), 'Zur gegenwaertigen Entwicklung der Weltwirtschaft' in M. Fay *et al.* (eds), *Strukurveraenderungen in der kapitalistischen Weltwirtschaft.* Starnberger Studien, 4, Frankfurt: Edition Suhrkamp, 9–88.

FROEBEL, F. (1984), 'The Current Development of the World Economy: Reproduction of Labour and Accumulation of Capital on a World Scale' in H. Addo (ed.), *Transforming the World Economy? Nine Critical Essays on the New International Economic Order.* London, Sydney: Hodder & Stoughton: 51–118.

FROEBEL, F., Heinrichs, J. and Kreye, O. (1977a), *Die neue internationale Arbeitsteilung. Strukturelle Arbeitslosigkeit in den Industrielaendern und die Industrialisierung der Entwicklungslaender.* Reinbek: Rororo Aktuell.

FROEBEL, F., Heinrichs, J., Kreye, O. and Sunkel, O. (1977b), 'Internationalisierung von Kapital und Arbeitskraft' in JG in der SPOe Steiermark und Erklaerung von Graz fuer Solidarische Entwicklung (EV) (eds), *Armut in Oesterreich.* Graz: Leykam, 12–46.

FROEBEL, F., Heinrichs, J. and Kreye, O. (1974), *Die Armut des Volkes. Verelendung in den unterentwickelten Laendern. Auszuege aus Dokumenten der Vereinten Nationen.* Reinbek: Rororo Aktuell.

FROEBEL, F., Heinrichs, J. and Kreye, O. (1981), 'Einleitung. Ungleiche und ungleichmaessige Entwicklung in der kapitalistischen Weltwirtschaft heute' in F. Froebel, J. Heinrichs and O. Kreye (eds), *Krisen in der kapitalistischen Weltoekonomie.* Reinbek: Rororo Aktuell, 8–18.

FROEBEL, F., Heinrichs, J. and Kreye, O. (1986), *Umbruch in der Weltwirtschaft.* Reinbek: Rororo Aktuell.

FUKUYAMA, F. (1987), 'Patterns of Soviet Third World Policy', *Problems of Communism,* 36, 5: 1–13.

FURKES, J. and Schlarp, K. H. (eds)(1991), *Jugoslawiena: Ein Staat zerfaellt.* Reinbek: Rororo Aktuell.

GALTUNG, J. (1967), *Theory and Methods of Social Research.* Oslo: Universitets-forlaget.

GALTUNG, J. (1971), 'A Structural Theory of Imperialism', *Journal of Peace Research*, 8, 2: 81–118 (German transl. in Senghaas, 1972a).

GALTUNG, J. (1972), 'Intellektuelle und Entwicklung. Erziehungsmuster und Entwicklungsmuster', *Oesterreichische Zeitschrift fuer Politikwissenschaft*, 1, 3: 75–87.

GALTUNG, J. (1975), *Strukturelle Gewalt. Beitraege zur Friedens-und Konflikt-forschung*, 3rd edn. Reinbek: Rororo Aktuell.

GALTUNG, J. (1978), *Methodologie und Ideologie. Aufsaetze zur Methodologie*, 2nd edn. Frankfurt: Suhrkamp-Verlag.

GALTUNG, J. (1981), 'Global Processes and the World in the 1980s' in W. L. Hollist and J. N. Rosenau (eds), *World System Structure. Continuity and Change.* Beverly Hills and London: Sage: 110–38.

GEORGIOU, V. J. (1988), 'Greece and the Transnational Corporations: Dependent Economic Development and its Constraints on National Policy, 1965–1985', *Occasional Paper*, 15, *Transnational Corporations Research Project*, University of Sydney.

GERLICH, P., Grande, E. and Mueller, W. C. (1988), 'Corporatism in Crisis: Stability and Change of Social Partnership in Austria', *Political Studies*, 36: 209–23.

GOLDSCHEID, R. (1924/1983) 'Geburtenregelung und Menschenoekonomie in der kapitalistischen Gesellschaft', *Der Kampf*, 17: 314–21. Reprinted in G. Mozetic (ed.) (1983), *Austromarxistische Positionen.* Vienna, Cologne, Graz: Hermann Boehlaus Nachfolger, 455–465.

GOLDSTEIN, J. S. (1985a), 'Basic Human Needs: The Plateau Curve', *World Development*, 13, 5: 595–609.

GOLDSTEIN, J. S. (1985b), 'Kondratieff Waves as War Cycles', *International Studies Quarterly*, 29, 4: 411–44.

GOLDSTEIN, J. S. (1988), '*Long Waves. Prosperity and War in the Modern Age.* New Haven and London: Yale University Press.

GONZALES-CASANOVA, P. (1969/73), *Sociologia de la explotacion.* Siglo XXI, Mexico City, Madrid, Buenos Aires.

GORBATSCHOW, M. S. (1988), *Was ich wirklich will. Antworten auf die Fragen der Welt.* Berlin: Ullstein.

GORIN, Z. (1985), 'Socialist Societies and World System Theory: A Critical Survey', *Science and Society*, 49, 3: 332–66.

GRABENDORFF, W. (ed.) (1973), *Lateinamerika. Kontinent in der Krise.* Hamburg: Hoffmann & Campe.

GRANT, J. P. (1986), *Zur Situation der Kinder in der Welt 1986/87.* Wuppertal: P. Hammer.

GRIFFIN, K. (1981), 'Economic Development in a Changing World', *World Development*, 9, 3: 221–226.

GRIFFIN, K. (1987), *World Hunger and the World Economy. And Other Essays in Development Economics.* Basingstoke and London: Macmillan.

GRIFFIN, K. and Gurley J. (1985), 'Radical Analyses of Imperialism, the Third World, and the Transition To Socialism: A Survey Article', *Journal of Economic Literature*, 23, Sep: 1089–143.

GROSSER, I. (1992), *Szenarien des Ueberganges zur Marktwirtschaft in ehemaligen RGW-Laendern Europas.* Studie im Auftrag des Beirats fuer Wirtschafts-und Sozialfragen, Vienna Institute for Comparative Economic Studies.

GURR, T. R. (1974), 'The Neo-Alexandrians: A Review Essay on Data Handbooks in Political Science', *American Political Science Review*, 68, 1, Mar: 243–52.

GUS (eds) *Rocznik Statystyczny*. Warsaw: Ministerstwo Oswiaty y Wychowania (current issues).

GWATKIN, D. (1984), 'Mortality Reduction, Fertility Decline, and Population Growth. Toward a More Relevant Assessment of the Relationships among Them', *World Bank Staff Working Papers*, 686.

HABERLER, G. (1977), 'Less Developed Countries and the Liberal International Economic Order', *Zeitschrift fuer Nationaloekonomie*, 38, 1–2: 145–60.

HALBACH, U. (1988), 'Usbekistans Weg zur sowjetischen Skandalrepublik', *Aktuelle Analysen*, Bundesinstitut fuer ostwissenschaftliche und internationale Studien, Cologne, 23.

HALLER, M. *et al.* (1985), 'Patterns of careers: mobility and structural positions in advanced capitalist societies: a comparison of men in Austria, France, and the United States', *American Sociological Review*, 50, 5: 579–603.

HANCOCK, M. D. (1983), 'Comparative Public Policy: An Assessment' in A. W. Finifter (ed.), *Political Science. The State of the Discipline.* Washington D.C.: American Political Science Association: 283–308.

HANSON, P. (1991), 'Is There a "Third Way" between Capitalism and Socialism?', *Report on the USSR*, 3, 35, 30 Aug: 15–19.

HASEGAWA, T. and Pravda A. (eds) (1990), *Perestroika: Soviet Domestic and Foreign Policies.* London, Newbury Park, New Delhi: Sage.

HASNAT, S.F. and Pelinka, A. (eds) (1986), *Security For the Weak Nations. A Multiple Perspective. A Joint Project of Pakistani and Austrian Scholars.* Lahore: Izharsons.

HEIN, W. (1985), 'Konstitutionsbedingungen einer kritischen Entwicklungstheorie', *Politische Vierteljahresschrift*, 26, Sonderheft 16: 27–55.

HEINTZ, P. (ed.) (1972), *A Macrosociological Theory of Societal Systems, 1.* Bern, Stuttgart, Vienna: Huebner.

HEITGER, B. (1985), 'Bestimmungsfaktoren internationaler Wachstumsdifferenzen', *Die Weltwirtschaft*, 1: 49–69.

HELLEINER, G. K. (1986), 'Balance-of-Payments Experience and Growth Prospects of Developing Countries: A Synthesis', *World Development*, 14, 8: 877–908.

HETTNE, B. (1982), 'Development Theory and the Third World', Swedish Agency for Research Cooperation with Developing Countries, *SAREC Report*, 2 (entire).

HETTNE, B. (1983), 'The Development of Development Theory', *Acta Sociologica*, 26, 3/4: 247–66.

HETTNE, B. (ed.) (1988), *Development Options in Europe.* United Nations University: European Perspectives Project 1986–87, Peace and Development Research Institute, Gothenburg University, papers.

HETTNE, B. (1989), 'Three Worlds of Crisis for the Nation State' in Z. Bablewski and B. Hettne (eds), *Crisis in Development.* Peace and Development Research Institute, Gothenburg University, papers, 45–77.

HICKS, N. L. (1979), 'Growth vs. Basic Needs: Is There a Trade-Off?', *World Development*, 7: 985–94.

HICKS, N. L. (1982), 'Sector Priorities in Meeting Basic Needs: Some Statistical Evidence', *World Development*, 10, 6: 489–99.

HICKS, N. L. and Streeten P. (1979), 'Indicators of Development: The Search for a Basic Needs Yardstick', *World Development*, 7: 567–80.

HINDELS, J. (1986), *Das Linzer Programm. Ein Vermaechtnis Otto Bauers.* Bund sozialistischer Freiheitskaempfer und Opfer des Faschismus, Vienna: Vorwaerts-Verlag.

HIRSCHMAN, A. O. (1984), 'A Dissenter's Confession: The Strategy of Economic Development Revisited' in G. M. Meier and D. Seers (eds), *Pioneers in Development.* New York, Oxford: Oxford University Press: 87–111.

HOELL, O. and Kramer, H. (1986), 'Internationalization and the Position of Austria: Problems and Current Development Trends of a Small State' in S. F. Hasnat and A. Pelinka (eds), *Security for the Weak Nations.* Lahore, Pakistan: Izharsons: 201–30.

HOELL, O. and Tausch, A. (1980), 'Austria and the European Periphery' in J. de Bandt, P. Mandi and D. Seers (eds), *European Studies of Development.* London: Macmillan, 28–37.

HOLLOWAY, D. (1989), 'State, Society, and the Military under Gorbachev', *International Security,* 14, 3: 5–24.

HOLSTI, K. J. (1986), 'The Horsemen of the Apocalypse: At the Gate, Detoured, or Retreating?', *International Studies Quarterly,* 30, 4: 355–72.

HOLTHUS, M. (1987), *Die Auslandsverschuldung der Entwicklungslaender. Fakten, Probleme, Loesungen.* Entwicklungspolitik, Materialien 76, Bundesministerium fuer wirtschaftliche Zusammenarbeit, Bonn.

HOLY BIBLE (1958 edition), *Holy Bible. Containing the Old and New Testaments.* London and New York: Collins.

HOPKINS, T. K. (1982), 'The Study of the Capitalist World-Economy. Some Introductory Considerations' in T. K. Hopkins, I. Wallerstein *et al.* (eds), *World-Systems Analysis. Theory and Methodology.* Beverly Hills, London, New Delhi: Sage: 9–38.

HOPKINS, T. K., Wallerstein, I. *et al.* (1982), 'Patterns of Development of the Modern World System', in T. K. Hopkins, I. Wallerstein *et al.* (eds), *World-Systems Analysis. Theory and Methodology.* Beverly Hills, London, New Delhi: Sage: 41–82.

HUNTINGTON, S. P. (1987), 'The Goals of Development' in M. Weiner and S. P. Huntington (eds), *Understanding Political Development.* Boston, Toronto: Little, Brown and Company.

HUNTINGTON, S. P. and Nelson, J. M. (1976), *No Easy Choice. Political Participation in Developing Countries.* Cambridge, Mass.: Harvard University Press.

HYMER, S. (1973), 'Multinationale Konzerne und das Gesetz der ungleichen Entwicklung' in D. Senghaas (ed.), *Imperialismus und strukturelle Gewalt. Analysen ueber abhaengige Reproduktion.* Frankfurt: Edition Suhrkamp, 201–42.

HURTIENNE, T. (1974), 'Zur Ideologiekritik der lateinamerikanischen Theorien der Unterentwicklung und Abhaengigkeit', *Probleme des Klassenkampfes,* 14, 15, IV, 3.

INTERNATIONAL LABOUR OFFICE (ILO) (1984), *World Labour Report 1.* Geneva: ILO.

INTERNATIONAL LABOUR OFFICE (ILO)/UN Centre on Transnational Corporations (1988), *Economic and Social Effects of Multinational Enterprises in Export Processing Zones.* Geneva: ILO.

JACKMAN, R. W. (1979), 'Keynesian Government Intervention and Income Inequality. Comment on Stack...', *American Sociological Review,* 44, 1: 131–7.

JACKMAN, R. W. (1980), 'A Note on the Measurement of Growth Rates in Cross-national Research', *American Journal of Sociology*, 86, 3: 604–17.

JACKMAN, R. W. (1982), 'Dependence on Foreign Investment and Economic Growth in the Third World', *World Politics*, 2: 175–96.

JAGODZINSKI, W. and Weede, E. (1981), 'Testing Curvilinear Propositions by Polynomial Regression with Particular Reference to the Interpretation of Standardized Solutions', *Quality and Quantity*, 15: 447–63.

JAGODZINSKI, W. and Weede, E. (1980), 'Weltpolitische und oekonomische Determinanten einer ungleichen Einkommensverteilung. Eine international vergleichende Studie', *Zeitschrift fuer Soziologie*, 9, 2: 132–48.

JAGUARIBE, H. *et al.* (eds), *La dependencia politico-economica de America Latina.* Siglo XXI, Mexico City, Madrid, Buenos Aires.

JAIN, S. (1975), *Size Distribution of Income. A Compilation of Data.* Washington, D.C.: IBRD (World Bank).

JENKINS, R. (1987), *Transnational Corporations and Uneven Development: The Internationalization of Capital and the Third World.* London and New York: Methuen.

JODICE, D. H., Taylor, C. L. and Deutsch, K. W. (1980), *Cumulation in Social Science Data Archiving. A Study of the Impact of the two World Handbooks of Political and Social Indicators.* Koenigstein/Ts.: Anton Hain.

JOHNSON, T. H., Slater, R. O. and McGowan, P. (1984), 'Explaining African Military Coups d'Etat 1960–1982', *American Political Science Review*, 78, 3: 622–40.

JOHNSTON, J. (1972), *Econometric Methods.* New York: McGraw Hill.

JUCHLER, J. (1992), 'Zur Entwicklungsdynamik in den sozialistischen bzw. 'postsozialistischen' Laendern: Theoretischer Bezugsrahmen und empirische Tendenzen', *Diksussionspapiere des NFP 28*, Einsiedeln (CH).

KAASE, M. (1987), 'Vergleichende Politische Partizipationsforschung' in D. Berg-Schlosser and F. Mueller-Rommel (eds), *Vergleichende Politikwissenschaft. Ein einfuehrendes Handbuch.* Opladen: Leske & Budrich, 135–50.

KABASHIMA, I. (1984), 'Supportive Participation With Economic Growth: The Case of Japan', *World Politics*, 36, 3: 309–38.

KADAN, A. and Pelinka, A. (1979), *Die Grundsatzprogramme der oesterreichischen Parteien. Dokumentation und Analyse.* St. Poelten: Niederoesterreichisches Presse-haus.

KADT, E. de (1985), 'Of Markets, Might and Mullahs: A Case for Equity, Pluralism and Tolerance in Development', *World Development*, 13, 4: 549–56.

KALDOR, M. (1981), *Ruestungsbarock. Das Arsenal der Zerstoerung und das Ende der militaerischen Techno-Logik.* Westberlin: Rotbuch.

KALECKI, M. (1971a), 'Political Aspects of Full Employment' in M. Kalecki, *Selected Essays on the Dynamics of the Capitalist Economy, 1933–70.* Cambridge University Press.

KALECKI, M. (1971b), 'The Problem of Effective Demand with Tugan Baranovski and Rosa Luxemburg' in M. Kalecki, *Selected Essays on the Dynamics of the Capitalist Economy, 1933–70.* Cambridge University Press.

KALECKI, M. (1972), *The Last Phase in the Transformation of Capitalism.* New York: Monthly Review Press.

KALECKI, M. (1979a), 'Unemployment in Underdeveloped Countries' in M. Kalecki, *Essays on Developing Economies* (with an introduction by Professor Joan Robinson) Hassocks, Sussex: Harvester, 17–19.

KALECKI, M. (1979b), 'The Difference between Crucial Economic Problems of

Developed and Underdeveloped Non-Socialist Economies' in *Essays on Developing Economies* (*see* Kalecki, 1979a, above), 20–7.

KALECKI, M. (1979c), 'The Difference between Perspective Planning in Socialist and Mixed Economies' in *Essays on Developing Economies* (*see* Kalecki, 1979a, above), 28–9.

KALECKI, M. (1979d), 'Observations on Social and Economic Aspects of Intermediate Regimes' in *Essays on Developing Economies* (*see* Kalecki, 1979a, above), 30–40.

KALECKI, M. (1979e), 'The Problem of Financing Economic Development' in *Essays on Developing Economies* (*see* Kalecki, 1979a, above), 41–63.

KANE, R. H. T. O. (1981), 'A Probabilistic Approach to the Causes of Coups d'Etat', *British Journal of Political Science*, 2: 287–308.

KAPPEL, R. (1981), 'Grundbeduerfnisbefriedigung in Entwicklungslaendern: Illusion oder konkrete Utopie?' Berlin: International Institute for Comparative Social Research, Wissenschaftszentrum, *Discussion Papers, IIVG/dp* 81–110.

KARLSSON, S. (ed.) (1988), *Europe and the World*. United Nations University: European Perspectives Project 1986–87, Peace and Development Research Institute, Gothenburg University.

KATZ, C. J. *et al.* (1983), 'The Impact of Taxes on Growth and Distribution in Developed Capitalist Countries: A Cross-National Study', *The American Political Science Review*, 77, 4: 871–86.

KATZENSTEIN, P. J. (1984), *Corporatism and Change. Austria, Switzerland and the Politics of Industry*. Ithaca and London: Cornell University Press.

KAUTSKY, K. (1899/1971) *Die Agrarfrage. Eine Uebersicht ueber die Tendenzen der modernen Landwirtschaft und die Agrarpolitik der Sozialdemokratie*. Stuttgart, Verlag J. K. W. Dietz Nachf.; Graz: Photomechanischer Nachdruck der Ausgabe von 1899, Sozialistisches Verlagskollektiv.

KAY, C. (1991), 'Reflections on the Latin American Contribution to Development Theory', *Development and Change*, 22, 1: 31–68.

KEMAN, H. and Whiteley, P. F. (1987), 'Coping with crisis: divergent strategies and outcomes' in H. Keman *et al.* (eds), *Coping with the Economic Crisis*. London: Sage: 205–14.

KENNEDY, P. (1989), *The Rise and Fall of the Great Powers. Economic Change and Military Conflict from 1500 to 2000*. New York: Vintage Books, Random House (paperback edition).

KENT, G. (1989), *The Politics of Childrens Survival*. Honolulu: University of Hawaii, Department of Political Science (mimeo).

KENT, N. J. (1990), 'The End of the American Dream: A Break in Political Economy', *Occasional Papers in Political Science*, Manoa: University of Hawaii: Department of Political Science, 3, 3, Jan: 93–107.

KEYNES, J. M. (1936/1973) *The General Theory of Employment, Interest and Money* London and Basingstoke: Macmillan.

KEMAN, H. and Van Dijk, T. (1987), 'Political strategies to overcome the crisis: policy formation and economic performance in seventeen capitalist democracies' in H. Keman *et al.* (eds), *Coping with the Economic Crisis*. London: Sage: 127–62.

KHALATBARI, P. (1984), 'Demographische und demo-oekonomische Probleme der Entwicklungslaender', *Asien, Afrika, Lateinamerika*, 12, 5: 821–31.

KHOURY, A. (1980), *Toleranz im Islam*. Munich and Mainz: Kaiser und Grünewald.

KILJUNEN, K. (1979), 'Finland in the International Division of Labour' in D. Seers *et al.* (eds), *Underdeveloped Europe. Studies in Core-Periphery Relations.* Hassocks: Harvester: 279–302.

KILJUNEN, K. (1985), *Towards a Theory of International Division of Industrial Labour.* Helsinki: Helsingin Yliopiston Valtio-Opin Laitoksen Tutkimusia, Sarja A, 69.

KILJUNEN, K. (1987), *Draft Proposal for a Study Project on Adjustment Policies in Smaller European Countries.* Helsinki: Institute for Development Studies, Helsinki University (mimeo).

KIM, J. O. and Mueller, C. W. (1978), *Introduction to Factor Analysis. What It Is and How to Do It.* Beverly Hills and London: Sage University Paper, 13.

KNAKAL, J. (1987), 'El Bloque Socialista Europeo y sus Relaciones con el Sistema Centro-Periferia', *Pensamiento Iberoamericano,* 11: 185–227.

KONDRATIEFF, N. D. (1928) 'Die Preisdynamik der industriellen und landwirtschaftlichen Waren (Zum Problem der relativen Dynamik und Konjunktur)', *Archiv fuer Sozialwissenschaften und Sozialpolitik,* 60, 1: 1–85.

KORPI, W. (1985), 'Economic growth and the welfare state: leaky bucket or irrigation system?', *European Sociological Review,* 1, 2: 97–118.

KORPI, W. (1978), *The Working Class in Welfare Capitalism. Work, Unions and Politics in Sweden.* London: Routledge & Kegan Paul.

KOTHARI, R. (1986), 'Masses, Classes and the State', *Alternatives,* XI, 2: 167–83.

KRAMER, H. (ed.) (1983), *Oesterreich im Internationalen System.* Vienna: W. Braumueller.

KUHN, T. S. (1962/1976), *Die Struktur wissenschaftlicher Revolutionen.* Frankfurt: Suhrkamp Taschenbuch Wissenschaft.

KUMAR, S. (ed.) (1987), *Yearbook on India's Foreign Policy 1984–85.* New Delhi, Newbury Park, London: Sage.

KURUP, R. S. (1986), 'Demographic Transition in Kerala' in K. Mahadevan (ed.), *Fertility and Mortality. Theory, Methodology and Empirical Issues.* New Delhi, Beverly Hills, London: Sage, 184–96.

KURZ, R. (1991), 'Die Krise, die aus dem Osten kam. Wider die Illusion vom Sieg des Westens und seiner Marktwirtschaft. *Basler Magazin,* 44, 2. 11.: 6–7.

KUZNETS, S. (1955), 'Economic Growth and Income Inequality', *American Economic Review,* 45, 1: 1–28.

LAMB, G. (1981), 'Rapid Capitalist Development Models: A New Politics of Dependence?' in D. Seers (ed.), *Dependency Theory. A Critical Reassessment.* Frances Pinter, London: 97–108.

LANDAU, D. (1983), 'Government Expenditure and Economic Growth: A Cross-Country Study', *Southern Economic Journal,* 49, 3: 783–92.

LANDAU, D. (1986), 'Government and Economic Growth in the Less Developed Countries: An Empirical Study for 1960–1980', *Economic Development and Cultural Change,* 35, 1, Oct: 35–75.

LANDSBERGER, H. A. (1980), 'Die bourgeoise Modernisierungstheorie ist nicht tot; lang lebe die sozialistische Modernisierungstheorie!' in G. Hischier *et al.* (eds), *Weltgesellschaft und Sozialstruktur. Festschrift zum 60. Geburtstag von Peter Heintz.* Diessenhofen: Ruegger, 57–74.

LAL, D. (1985), 'Missverstaendnisse in der 'Entwicklungsoekonomie'. Die vielen Maengel des dirigistischen Dogmas', *Finanzierung und Entwicklung,* 22, 2, Jun: 10–13.

LANGE, O. (1964), *Entwicklungstendenzen der modernen Wirtschaft und Gesellschaft. Eine sozialistische Analyse*. Europa, Vienna Verlagsanstalt Frankfurt, Vienna: Europa-Verlag.

LEANTE, L. (1989), 'Perestroika at a Snail's Pace', *Telos*, 80, Summer: 79–92.

LEESON, P.F. (1978), 'The Lewis Model and Development Theory', *The Manchester School*, 47, 3: 196–210.

LEHNER, F. (1987), 'Interest intermediation, institutional structures and public policy' in H. Keman *et al.* (eds), *Coping with the Economic Crisis*. London: Sage: 54–82.

LENIN, V.I. (posthumously, 1973) *Werke*. Berlin: Dietz Verlag.

LEVITT-POLANYI, K. (1970), 'The Old Mercantilism and the New: A Canadian Perspective', *Social and Economic Studies*, 19, 4: 466–89.

LEVITT-POLANYI, K. and Mendell, M. (1986), 'Introduction' in K. Levitt-Polanyi and M. Mendell (eds), *Democracy, Fascism and Industrial Civilisation: Selected Essays of Karl Polanyi*. Budapest: Gondolat (in Hungarian); quoted here from the author's English language draft

LEWIS, Sir W.A. (1984), 'Development Economics in the 1950's' in G.M. Meier and D. Seers (eds), *Pioneers in Development. A World Bank Publication*. New York, Oxford: Oxford University Press, 121–37.

LEWIS, Sir W.A. (1978a), *The Evolution of the International Economic Order*. Princeton N.J.: Princeton University Press.

LEWIS, Sir W.A. (1978b), 'The Dual Economy Revisited', *The Manchester School*, 47, 3: 211–29.

LEWIS-BECK, M.S. (1980), *Applied Regression. An Introduction*. Beverly Hills and London: Sage University Paper, 22, Series: Quantitative Applications in the Social Sciences.

LEVY, W. (1989), *From Alms to Liberation. The Catholic Church, the Theologians, Poverty and Politics*. New York, Westport, London: Praeger.

LINDER, S.B. (1986), *The Pacific Century. Economic and Political Consequences of Asian-Pacific Dynamism*. Stanford, Calif.: Stanford University Press.

LINDERT, P.H. (1986), 'Unequal English Wealth since 1670', *Journal of Political Economy*, 94, 6: 1127–62.

LIPSET, S.M. (1959), 'Some Social Requisites of Democracy', *The American Political Science Review*, 53, 1: 69–105.

LIPTON, M. (1977), *Why Poor People Stay Poor. Urban Bias in World Development*. Cambridge, Mass.: Harvard University Press.

LIPTON, M. (1984), 'Comment on Bauer, P.T. Lord (1984), "Remembrance of Studies Past: Retracing First Steps"' in G.M. Meier and D. Seers (eds), *Pioneers in Development*. New York, Oxford: Oxford University Press, published for the World Bank, 44–50.

LUNDBERG, E. (1985), 'The Rise and Fall of the Swedish Model', *Journal of Economic Literature*, 23, 1: 1–36.

LUZA, R. (1984), *The Resistance in Austria, 1938–1945*. Minneapolis: University of Minnesota Press.

LYSKA, J. (1987), *Polityczny Atlas Swiata*. Warsaw: Wydawnictwo Wspolczesne.

McAULEY, A. (1979), *Economic Welfare in the Soviet Union: Poverty, Living Standards and Inequality*. Madison, Wis.: University of Wisconsin Press.

McAULEY, A. (1985), 'Soviet development policy in Central Asia' in R. Cassen (ed.), *Soviet interests in the Third World*. London, Beverly Hills, New Delhi: Sage: 299–318.

McCORMACK, T. (1981), 'Development with Equity for Women' in N. Black *et al.* (eds), *Women and World Change-Equity Issues in Development*. Beverly Hills, London: Sage: 15–30.

McGRANAHAN, D. *et al.* (1982), 'Methodologische Probleme bei Selektion und Analyse von Indikatoren fuer sozio-oekonomische Entwicklung' in D. Nohlen and F. Nuscheler (eds), *Handbuch der Dritten Welt*, 2nd edn. Hamburg: Hoffmann & Campe: 414–31.

McGRANAHAN, D. *et al.* (1981), 'Development Statistics and Correlations: A Comment on Hicks and Streeten', *World Development*, 9, 4: 389–97.

McGRANAHAN, D. and Hong, N. (1979), 'International Comparability of Statistics on Income Distribution', *United Nations Research Institute for Social Development, Report* 79.6, Geneva.

McNICOLL, (1984), 'Consequences of Rapid Population Growth. An Overview', *World Bank Staff Working Papers*, No. 691, 4 Dec.

McSWEENY, B. (1987), 'The Politics of Neutrality. Focus on Security for Smaller Nations', *Bulletin of Peace Proposals*, 18, 1: 33–46.

MAERZ, E. (1976), *Einfuehrung in die Marx'sche Theorie der wirtschaftlichen Entwicklung. Fruehkapitalismus und Kapitalismus der freien Konkurrenz. Mit einem Anhang von Kazimierz Laski.* Vienna: Europaverlag.

MAERZ, E. (1983a), 'Karl Marx und die Langlebigkeit des kapitalistischen Systems' in O. K. Flechtheim, *Marx heute. Pro und contra*. Hamburg: Hoffmann & Campe, 275–90.

MAERZ, E. (1983b), *Joseph Alois Schumpeter-Forscher, Lehrer und Politiker.* Vienna: Verlag fuer Geschichte und Politik.

MAERZ, E. and Szesci, M. (1984), 'Otto Bauer, als Wirtschaftspolitiker', *Wirtschaft und Gesellschaft*, 1: 61–77.

MAHADEVAN, K. (1986), 'Mortality, Biology, and Society: Analytical Framework and Conceptual Model' in K. Mahadevan (ed.), *Fertility and Mortality. Theory, Methodology, and Empirical Issues*. New Delhi: Sage, 239–301.

MAHAR, D. (1985), 'Preface' in D. Mahar (ed.), 'Rapid Population Growth and Human Carrying Capacity. Two Perspectives', *World Bank Staff Working Papers*, 690: VII–XI.

MALAN, P. S. and Bonelli, R. (1983), 'Crise Internacional, Crise Brasileira: Perspectivas e Opcoes', *Pensamiento Iberoamericano*, 4, Jul–Dec: 85–116.

MANDEL, E. (1973), 'Neokolonialismus und ungleicher Tausch,' in E. Mandel, *Der Spaetkapitalismus*. Frankfurt: Edition Suhrkamp, 318–43.

MANSINGH, S. (1984), *India's Search for Power. Indira Gandhi's Foreign Policy 1966–1982*. New Delhi, Beverly Hills, London: Sage.

MARIATEGUI, J. C. (posthumously, 1986) *Revolution und peruanische Wirklichkeit. Ausgewaehlte politische Schriften*, ed. E. von Oertzen, Frankfurt: isp-Verlag.

MARIN, B. (1983), 'Organizing Interests by Interest Organizations. Associational Prerequisites of Cooperation in Austria', *International Political Science Review*, 4, 2: 197–216.

MARINELL, G. (1986), *Multivariate Verfahren. Einfuehrung fuer Studierende und Praktiker*, 2nd edn. Munich: Oldenbourg.

MARINI, R. M. (1974), 'Die Dialektik der Abhaengigkeit' in D. Senghaas (ed.), *Peripherer Kapitalismus. Analysen ueber Abhaengigkeit und Unterentwicklung.* Frankfurt, Edition Suhrkamp: 98–136.

MARKOS, E. (1988), 'Poverty Spreading in Hungary', *Situation Report, Hungary*, 12, Radio Free Europe Research, Munich: 37–41.

MARSDEN, K. (1983), 'Links Between Taxes and Economic Growth. Some Empirical Evidence', *World Bank Staff Working Papers*, 605.

MARTINEZ-ALLIER, J. (1987), 'Economia y Ecologia: Cuestiones Fundamentales', *Pensamiento Iberoamericano*, 12, 2: 41–60.

MARX, K. and Engels, F. (posthumously, 1974) *Werke*. Berlin: Dietz Verlag.

MASON, T. D. and Krane, D. A. (1989), 'The Political Economy of Death Squads: Towards a Theory of the Impact of State-Sanctioned Terror', *International Studies Quarterly*, 33, 2: 175–98.

MENZEL, U. (1991), 'Das Ende der 'Dritten Welt', und das Scheitern der großen Theorie. Zur Soziologie einer Disziplin in auch selbstkritischer Absicht', *Politische Vierteljahresschrift*, 32, 1: 4–33.

MENZEL, U. and Senghaas, D. (1986), *Europas Entwicklung und die Dritte Welt. Eine Bestandsaufnahme*. Frankfurt, Edition Suhrkamp: Neue Folge.

MEYER, G. (1989), 'Die Nationalitaetenfrage in der UdSSR', *Blaetter fuer Feutsche und Internationale Politik*, 5: 597–604.

MEYER FEHR, P. (1978), 'Bestimmungsfaktoren des Wirtschaftswachstums von Nationen', *Bulletin des Soziologischen Instituts*, University of Zurich, 34: 1–105.

MICHELSEN, G. (ed.) (1984), *Der Fischer, Oeko-Almanach. Daten, Fakten, Trends der Umweltdiskussion*. Frankfurt: Fischer, Tachenbuch Verlag (and subsequent issues).

MIGDAL, J. S.(1983), 'Studying the Politics of Development and Change: The State of the Art' in A. W. Finifter (ed.), *Political Science: The State of the Discipline*. Washington D.C.: American Political Science Association, 309–38.

MIHALISKO, K. (1989), 'SOS for Native Peoples of Soviet North', *Report on the USSR*, 1, 5, 3 Feb: 3–7.

MILANOVIC, B. (1987), *Proposals for Introductory Country Surveys as Part of the Cross-Country Comparison Project*. Belgrade: Institute of International Politics and Economics.

MLYNAR, Z. (1983), *Krisen und Krisenbewaeltigung im Sowjetblock*. Cologne: Bund.

MUELLER, W. C. (1983), 'Economic Success without an Industrial Strategy: Austria in the 1970s', *Journal of Public Policy*, 3, 1: 119–30.

MUELLER, W. C. (1986), 'Mikrooekonomische Steuerung und Parteien-Konkurrenz in Oesterreich' in H. Abromeit *et al.* (eds), *Steuerungsinstrument oeffentliche Wirtschaft?* Berlin: Publication Series of the International Institute for Comparative Social Research, 160–208.

MUKERJEE, D. (1987), 'Indo-Soviet Economic Ties', *Problems of Communism*, 36, 1: 13–24.

MULLER, E. N. (1985a), 'Dependent Economic Development, Aid Dependence on the United States, and Democratic Breakdown in the Third World', *International Studies Quarterly*, 29, 4: 445–69.

MULLER, E. N. (1985b), 'Income Inequality, Regime Repressiveness, and Political Violence', *American Sociological Review*, 50, Feb: 47–61.

MULLER, E. N. (1986), 'Income Inequality and Political Violence: The Effect of Influential Cases', *American Sociological Review*, 51, Jun: 441–5.

MULLER, E. N. (1988), 'Democracy, Economic Development, and Income Inequality', *American Sociological Review*, 53, Feb: 50–68.

MULLER, E. N. and Seligson, M. A. (1987), 'Inequality and Insurgency', *American Political Science Review*, 81, 2, Jun: 425–52.

MUNOZ, O. (1982), 'La Economia Mixta Como Camino al Pleno Empleo. Lecciones de un Cuarto de Siglo', *Estudios CIEPLAN*, 9, Dec: 107–38.

MUNOZ, O. (1979), 'Desarrollo, Distribucion del Ingreso y Democratizacion', *Estudios CIEPLAN*, 32, Apr 1979.

MUSCAT, R. (1985), 'Carrying Capacity and Rapid Population Growth: Definition, Cases and Consequences' in D. Mahar (ed.), *Rapid Population Growth and Human Carrying Capacity. Two Perspectives*. World Bank Staff Working Papers, 690: 5–39.

MYRDAL, G. (1956/1974), *Oekonomische Theorie und unterentwickelte Regionen. Weltproblem Armut*. Frankfurt: Fischer, TB.

MYRDAL, G. (1972), *Politisches Manifest ueber die Armut in der Welt*. Frankfurt: Suhrkamp TB.

MYRDAL, G. (1984), 'International Inequality and Foreign Aid in Retrospect' in G. M. Meier and D. Seers (eds), *Pioneers in Development. A World Bank Publication*. New York and Oxford: Oxford University Press, 151–65.

NAYAR, P. K. B. (1986), 'Factors in Fertility Decline in Kerala' in K. Mahadevan (ed.), *Fertility and Mortality. Theory, Methodology and Empirical Issues*. New Delhi, Beverly Hills, London: Sage, 155–70.

NEHRU, J. (1946), *The Discovery of India*. J. Nehru Memorial Fund, New Delhi: Oxford University Press.

NIE, N. H. *et al.* (1975), *SPSS. Statistical Package for the Social Sciences*, 2nd edn. New York: McGraw-Hill.

NISSEN, H. P. (1982), 'Einkommensverteilung und Dritte Welt' in D. Nohlen and F. Nuscheler (eds), *Handbuch der Dritten Welt*. Hamburg: Hoffmann & Campe, vol. 1, 231–56.

NITSCH, M.(1979), 'Liegt die ordnungspolitische Zukunft Brasiliens im Staatskapitalismus?' in H. A. Steger and J. Schneider (eds), *Aktuelle Perspektiven Brasiliens*. Lateinamerika-Studien, Munich: Wilhelm Fink, vol. 4, 155–72.

NOHLEN, D. (1984), 'Entwicklung/Entwicklungstheorien' in D. Nohlen (ed.), *Lexicon Dritte Welt*. Reinbek: Rororo Handbuch, 171–3.

NOHLEN, D. (1985), 'Politikwissenschaftliche Lateinamerika-Forschung in der Bundesrepublik Deutschland', *Politische Vierteljahresschrift*, 26, Sonderheft 16: 436–50.

NOHLEN, D. and Mansilla, H. C. F. (1984), 'Modernisierungstheorien' in D. Nohlen (ed.), *Lexicon Dritte Welt*. Reinbek: Rororo Handbuch, 404–8.

NOHLEN, D. and Nuscheler, F. (1982), 'Indikatoren von Unterentwicklung und Entwicklung. Probleme der Messung und quantifizierenden Analyse' in their *Handbuch der Dritten Welt*. Hamburg: Hoffmann & Campe, 451–85.

NOLTE, H. H. (1982), *Die eine Welt. Abriss der Geschichte des internationalen Systems*. Hannover: Fackeltraeger.

NOLTE, H. H. (1988), 'Kontexte der Ost-West-Beziehungen', *Gegenwartskunde*, 2: 159–70.

NOLTE, H. H. (1990), 'Perestroika und Internationales System: Zur Rolle der Rüstung', *Das Argument*, 183, 32, 5: 759–68.

NOLTE, H. H. (1991), 'Traditionen des Rueckstandes: ein halbes Jahrtausend. Rußland und der Westen', *Vierteljahresschrift fuer Sozial-und Wirtschaftsgeschichte*, 78, 3: 344–64.

NUSCHELER, F. (1974), 'Bankrott der Modernisierungstheorien?' in D. Nohlen and F. Nuscheler (eds), *Handbuch der Dritten Welt*. Hamburg: Hoffmann & Campe, 195–207.

NUSCHELER, F. (1985a), 'Entwicklungslinien der politikwissenschaftlichen Dritte Welt-Forschung', *Politische Vierteljahresschrift*, 26, Sonderheft 16: 7–26.

NUSCHELER, F. (1985b), 'Dritte Welt: Welten von Reichtum, Armut und Massenelend' in I. Fetscher and H. Muenckler (eds), *Politikwissenschaft. Begriffe-Analysen-Theorien. Ein Grundkurs*. Reinbek: Rororo Enzyklopaedie, 361–98.

NUSCHELER, F. (1986), 'Zur Kritik von Entwicklungshilfe und zur Denunzierung von Entwicklungshilfekritik' in J. Betz and V. Matthies (eds), *Jahrbuch Dritte Welt 1986. Daten. Uebersichten. Analysen*. Munich: Beck'sche Verlagsbuchhandlung, 24–36.

OEKOINSTITUT FREIBURG I. BR. (eds) (1984), *Der Fischer, Oeko-Almanach. Daten, Fakten, Trends der Umweltdiskussion*. Frankfurt: Fischer, Taschenbuch-Verlag.

OFER, G. (1987), 'Soviet Economic Growth: 1928–1985', *Journal of Economic Literature*, 25, 4: 1767–833.

OERTZEN, E. von (1981), *Peru*. Munich: Aktuelle Laenderkunden, C. H. Beck.

OLIVA, K. (1985), *Teilnahme ohne Teilhabe. Kritik und Integration soziologischer Literatur zur Marginalitaet in der Weltgesellschaft*. Frankfurt and New York: Campus Forschung.

OLSON, M. (1963), 'Rapid Growth as a Destabilizing Force', *Journal of Economic History*, 23, 4: 529–52.

OLSON, M. (1982/85) '*Aufstieg und Niedergang von Nationen. Oekonomisches Wachstum, Stagflation und soziale Starrheit*. Uebersetzt von Gerd Fleischmann. Tuebingen: J. C .B. Mohr (Paul Siebeck).

OLSON, M. (1986), 'A Theory of the Incentives Facing Political Organizations. Neo-Corporatism and the Hegemonic State', *International Political Science Review*, 7, 2, Apr: 165–89.

OLSON, M. (1987), 'Ideology and Economic Growth' in C. R. Hulten and I. V. Sawill (eds), *The Legacy of Reaganomics. Prospects for Long-term Growth*. Washington D.C.: Urban Institute Press: 229–51.

OPP, K. D. and Schmidt, P. (1976), *Einfuehrung in die Mehrvariablenanalyse. Grundlagen der Formulierung und Pruefung komplexer sozialwissenschaftlicher Aussagen*. Reinbek: Rororo Studium Sozialwissenschaft.

ORTIZ, L. P. and Yazaki, L. M. (1985), 'As causas de morte e a diminuicao da mortalidade'. *Revista da Fundacao SEADE*, 1, 2: 14–22.

OSSADTSCHAJA, I. M. (1983), 'Die Krise des Keynesianismus und die Suche der buergerlichen Oekonomie nach neuen Konzepten', *IPW-Berichte*, 12, 12: 9–55.

OST, D. (1982), 'Socialist World Market as Strategy for Ascent?' in E. Friedman (ed.), *Ascent and Decline in the World System*. Beverly Hills, London, New Delhi: Sage, 229–54.

PALMA, G. (1981), 'Dependency and Development: A Critical Overview' in D. Seers (ed.), *Dependency Theory. A Critical Reassessment*. London, Frances Pinter: 20–78.

PALOHEIMO, H. (1987), 'Explanations of the economic crisis and divergent policy responses: an overview' in H. Keman *et al.* (eds), *Coping with the Economic Crisis*. London: Sage: 1–19.

PAPANEK, G. F. and Kyn, O. (1986), 'The Effect on Income Distribution of Development, the Growth Rate and Economic Strategy', *Journal of Development Economics*, 23, 1: 55–65.

PAUKERT, F. (1973), 'Income Distribution at Different Levels of Development: A Survey of Evidence', *International Labour Review*, 108: 97–125.

PEACOCK, W. G. *et al.* (1988), 'Divergence and Convergence in International Development: A Decomposition Analysis of Inequality in the World System', *American Sociological Review*, 53, Dec: 838–52.

PILLAI, V. (1982), 'Approaches to Development: A Critique', *Alternatives. A Journal of World Policy*, 8, 3: 351–68.

PINTO, A. and Knakal, J. (1973), 'The Centre-Periphery System Twenty Years Later', *Social and Economic Studies* (Mona, Jamaica), 22, 1: 34ff.

PFEFFERMANN, G. P. and Webb, R. (1979), 'The Distribution of Income in Brazil', *World Bank Staff Working Paper* 356, Sep.

POLANYI, K. (1922), 'Sozialistische Rechnungslegung', *Archiv fuer Sozialwissenschaft und Sozialpolitik*, 49, 2: 377–420.

POLANYI, K. (1924/1979), 'Die funktionelle Theorie der Gesellschaft und das Problem der sozialistischen Rechnungslegung. Eine Erwiderung an Professor Mises und Dr. Felix Weil', *Archiv fuer Sozialwissenschaft und Sozialpolitik*, 52: 218–27; also reprinted in Polanyi, K. (1979) 81–90.

POLANYI, K. (1925/1983), 'Neue Erwaegungen zu unserer Theorie und Praxis', *Der Kampf*, 18: 18–24; also reprinted in G. Mozetic (ed.) (1983), *Austromarxistische Positionen*. Vienna, Cologne, Graz: Hermann Boehlaus Nachfolger, 439–49.

POLANYI, K. (1944/1957), *The Great Transformation. The political and economic origins of our time*. Boston: Beacon Press.

POLANYI, K. (1944/1977), *The Great Transformation. Politische und oekonomische Urspruenge von Gesellschaften und Wirtschaftssystemen*. Vienna: Europa-Verlag.

POLANYI, K. (1979), *Oekonomie und Gesellschaft*. Frankfurt: Edition Suhrkamp, Suhrkamp Taschenbuch Wissenschaft.

POZNANSKI, K. (1986), 'Economic adjustment and political forces: Poland since 1970', *International Organization*, 40, 2: 455–88.

POWELL, G. B. Jr. (1981), 'Party Systems and Political System Performance: Voting Participation, Government Stability and Mass Violence in Contemporary Democracy', *American Political Science Review*, 75, 4: 861–79.

POPOVIC, T. (1988), *Structural Adjustment Policies and Position of Smaller European Countries in the International Division of Labour*. Conference Proposal, Belgrade: Institute of International Politics and Economics.

PRADETTO, A. (1991a), 'Internationale Politik osteuropaeischer Staaten. Grundlegende Bedingungen und Tendenzen', *Oesterreichische Osthefte*, 33, 4: 663–78.

PRADETTO, A. (1991b), 'Politik und Oekonomie im postkommunistischen Polen', *Osteuropa*, 41, 10: 941–52.

PREBISCH, R. (1984), 'Five Stages in My Thinking on Development' in G. M. Meier and D. Seers (eds), *Pioneers in Development. A World Bank Publication*. New York and Oxford: Oxford University Press, 175–91.

PREBISCH, R. (1983), 'The Crisis of Capitalism and International Trade', *CEPAL-Review*, 20, Aug: 51–74.

PRECHEL, H. (1985), 'The Effects of Exports, Public Debt, and Development on Income Inequality', *The Sociological Quarterly*, 26, 2: 213–34.

PRESTON, P. W. (1987), *Rethinking Development: Essays on Development and Southeast Asia*. London and New York: Routledge & Kegan Paul.

QUIJANO-OBREGON, A. (1974), 'Marginaler Pol der Wirtschaft und marginalisierte Arbeitskraft' in D. Senghaas (ed.), *Peripherer Kapitalismus. Analysen ueber Abhaengigkeit und Unterentwicklung*. Frankfurt, Edition Suhrkamp: 298–341.

QUR'AN (undated edition) *The meaning of the Glorious Qur'an*. Text, Translation and Commentary by Abdullah Yusuf Ali', Cairo and Beirut: Dar al Kitab al Masri and Dar al Kitab Allubnani.

RABINBACH, A. (1983), *The Crisis of Austrian Socialism. From Red Vienna to Civil War 1927–34*. Chicago and London: University of Chicago Press.

RABKINA, N. E. and Rimashevskaia, N. M. (1979), 'Distributive Relations and Social Development', *Problems of Economics*, Jul, 23, 3: 40–58.

RACZYNSKI, D. and Oyarzo, C. (1981), 'Por que cae la tasa de mortalidad infantil en Chile?', *Estudios CIEPLAN*, 6: 45–84.

RAFFER, K. (1979), 'Die Dependencia-Theorie: Die alte Welt-wirtschaftsordnung aus der Sicht der Dritten Welt' in K. Raffer (ed.), *Probleme des Nord-Sued-Verhaeltnisses*, edition OeH, Vienna (A 1090 Liechtensteinstrasse 13): 24–56.

RAFFER, K. (1981), 'Die Neue Weltwirtschaftsordnung-ein Verteilungskampf der Privilegierten', *Oesterreichische Zeitschrift fuer Politikwissenschaft*, 2: 165–83.

RAFFER, K. (1986), 'Die Verschuldung Lateinamerikas als Mechanismus des ungleichen Tausches', *Zeitschrift fuer Lateinamerika*, Vienna, 30/31: 67–84.

RAFFER, K. (1987), *Unequal Exchange and the Evolution of the World System Reconsidering the Impact of Trade on North-South Relations*. Basingstoke and London: Macmillan.

RAFFER, K. (1989), *Sovereign Debts, Unilateral Adjustment and Multilateral Control: The New Way to Serfdom*. New Delhi: Ashish Publishing House, New World Order Series.

RAFFER, K. (1990), 'Applying Chapter 9 Insolvency to International Debts: An Economically Efficient Solution with a Human Face', *World Development*, 18, 2: 301–11.

RAGIN, C. C. (1985), 'Knowledge and Interests in the Study of the Modern World-System', *Review*, VIII, 4, Spring: 451–76.

RAM, R. (1985), 'The Role of Real Income Level and Income Distribution in Fulfillment of Basic Needs', *World Development*, 13, 5: 589–94.

RAMIREZ, F. O. and Thomas, G. M. (1981), 'Structural Antecedents and Consequences of Statism' in R. Rubinson (ed.), *Dynamics of World Development*. vol. 4, Political Economy of the World-System Annuals. Beverly Hills and London: Sage, 139–64.

REMNER, K. L. and Merkx, G. W. (1982), 'Bureaucratic-Authoritarianism Revisited', *Latin American Research Review*, 17, 2: 3–40.

REYNOLDS, L. G. (1985), *Economic Growth in the Third World, 1850–1980*. New Haven and London: Yale University Press.

RIVERA Y DAMAS, Mons. A. *et al.* (1984), *El Salvador: Der Aufschrei eines Volkes. Ein Bericht der Zentralamerikanischen Universitaet in San Salvador. Mit einem Vorwort von Arturo Rivera y Damas, Erzbischof von San Salvador*. Mainz/ Munich: Gruenewald und Kaiser.

RODE, R. (1991), 'Deutschland: Weltwirtschaftsmach oder ueberforderter Euro-Hegemon?', *Leviathan*, 2: 229–46.

RODGERS, G. B. (1978a), 'Demography and Distribution', Population and Employment Working Paper, 49, *World Employment Programme Research Working Papers*. Geneva: ILO.

RODGERS, G. B. (1978b), 'Demographic Determinants of the Distribution of Income', *World Development*, 6, 3, Mar: 305–18.

RODGERS, G. B. (1979), 'Income and Inequality as Determinants of Mortality: An International Cross-Section Analysis', *Population Studies*, 33, 2: 343–51.

RODGERS, G. B. and Standing, G. (1981), *Child Work, Poverty, and Underdevelopment*. Geneva: ILO.

ROETT, R. (1986), 'The Transition to Democratic Government in Brazil', *World Politics*, 38, 2, Jan: 371–82.

ROEHRICH, W. (1978), *Politik als Wissenschaft. Eine Einfuehrung*, Munich: dtv Wissenschaftliche Reihe.

ROEHRICH, W. (1981), *Die repraesentative Demokratie. Ideen und Interessen*. Opladen: Westdeutscher Verlag, Studienbuecher zur Sozialwissenschaft, Band 40.

ROEHRICH, W. (ed.) (1986), *Gesellschaftssysteme der Gegenwart. Politoekonomische Systemanalysen im internationalen Kontext*. Opladen: Westdeutscher Verlag, WV Studium, 140.

ROEHRICH, W. and Zinn, K. G. (1983), *Politik und Oekonomie der Welt-Gesellschaft. Das internationale System*. Opladen: Westdeutscher Verlag.

ROEHRICH, W. and Narr, W. D. (1986), *Politik als Wissenschaft. Ein Ueberblick*. Opladen: Westdeutscher Verlag, WV Studium, 141.

ROÍ, Y. (1990), 'The Islamic Influence on Nationalism in Soviet Central Asia', *Problems of Communism*, 39, 4: 49–64.

ROSECRANCE, (1987), 'Long Cycle Theory and International Relations', *International Organization*, 41, 2: 283–301.

ROSENSTEIN-RODAN, P. N. (1984), 'Natura Facit Saltum: Analysis of the Disequilibrium Growth Process' in G. M. Meier and D. Seers (eds), *Pioneers in Development*. New York, Oxford: Oxford University Press, 207–c1.

ROSTWOROWSKI, E. (1979), 'Czasy Saskie: Oswiecenie' in J. Tazbir (ed.), *Zarys Historii Polski*. Warsaw: Panstwowy Instytut Wydawniczy: 295–370.

ROTHGEB, J. M. Jr. (1986), 'Compensation or Opportunity? The Effects of International Recessions upon Direct Foreign Investment and Growth in Third World States, 1970–1978', *International Studies Quarterly*, 30, 2: 123–52.

ROTHSCHILD, K. W. (1944), 'The Small Nation and World Trade', *Economic Journal*, Apr: 26–40.

ROTHSCHILD, K. W. (1958), (anonymous) 'Die weltwirtschaftliche Verflechtung Oesterreichs', *Monatsberichte des Oesterreichischen Instituts fuer Wirtschaftsforschung*, 5: 224–33.

ROTHSCHILD, K. W. (1959a), 'The Limitations of Economic Growth Models', *Kyklos*, 12, 4: 567ff.

ROTHSCHILD, K. W. (1959b), (anonymous) 'Die Auswirkungen des am 1. Jaenner 1959 wirksam gewordenen EWG-Vertrages auf Oesterreich', *Monatsberichte des Oesterreichischen Instituts fuer Wirtschaftsforschung*, 1: 23–7.

ROTHSCHILD, K. W. (1963), 'Kleinstaat und Integration', *Weltwirtschaftliches Archiv*, 90, 2: 239–75.

ROTHSCHILD, K. W. (1966), *Marktform, Loehne, Aussenhandel*. Vienna: Europa.

ROTHSCHILD, K. W. (1985), 'Felix Austria? Zur Evaluierung der Oekonomie und Politik in der Wirtschaftskrise', *Oesterreichische Zeitschrift fuer Politikwissenschaft*, 3: 261–74.

RUBINSON, R. (1976), 'The World Economy and the Distribution of Income Within States: A Cross-National Study', *American Sociological Review*, 41, 4, 638–59.

RUELAND, J. and Werz, N. (1985), 'Von der 'Entwicklungsdiktatur' zu den Diktaturen ohne Entwicklung-Staat und Herrschaft in der politikwissenschaftlichen Dritte Welt-Forschung', *Politische Vierteljahresschrift*, 26, Sonderheft 16: 211–32.

RUMMEL, R. J. (1990), '35,236,000 Victims: Chinese Communist Democide 1949–1987', *Occasional Papers in Political Science,* Department of Political Science, Manoa: University of Hawaii, 3, 4, Jan: 83–91.

RUSSETT, B. (1967), *International Regions and the International System. A Study in Political Ecology.* Westport, Conn.: Greenwood Press.

RUSSETT, B. (1978), 'The marginal utility of income transfers to the Third World', *International Organization*, 32, 4: 913–28.

RUSSETT, B. (1983a), 'International Interactions and Processes: The Internal versus External Debate Revisited' in A. Finifter (ed.), *Political Science: The State of the Discipline.* Washington D.C.: American Political Science Association, 541–68.

RUSSETT, B. *et. al.* (1983b), 'The Peripheral Economies. Penetration and Economic Distortion, 1970–75' in W. R. Thompson (ed.), *Contending Approaches to World System Analysis.* Beverly Hills, New Delhi, London: Sage Focus Edition, 79–114.

RUSSETT, B. *et al.* (1964), *World Handbook of Political and Social Indicators.* New Haven and London: Yale University Press.

RUSSETT, B. *et al.* (1981), 'Health and Population Patterns as Indicators of Income Inequality', *Economic Development and Cultural Change*, 29, 4: 759–79.

RUSSETT, B. and Starr, H. (1985), *World Politics. The Menu for Choice.* New York and Oxford: W. H. Freeman and Company.

SAAGE, R. (1983), *Rueckkehr zum starken Staat?.* Frankfurt, Edition Suhrkamp.

SAFFIOTI, H. B. (1978), *Women in Class Society.* New York and London: Monthly Review Press.

SANDNER, G. and Steger, H. A. (1973), *Lateinamerika.* Frankfurt: Fischer, Laenderkunde, vol. 7.

SANGMEISTER, H. (1985), 'Brasiliens Suche nach einem Ausweg aus der Krise', *Zeitschrift fuer Lateinamerika*, Vienna, 27: 46–62.

SASLAVSKAJA, T. (1988), 'Zur Strategie der sozialen Steuerung der Perestrojka' in J. Afanasjew (ed.)', *Es gibt keine Alternative zu Perestrojka: Glasnost', Demokratie Sozialismus.* Moscow und Nördlingen: Progress Verlag und Greno Verlagsgesellschaft, 21–72.

SASLAVSKAJA, T. (1990), 'Perestrojka und öffentliche Meinung' in K. Segbers (ed.), *Perestrojka: Zwischenbilanz.* Frankfurt und Moscow: Edition Suhrkamp und Progress-Verlag, 106–23.

SCHARPF, F. W. (1987), *Sozialdemokratische Krisenpolitik in Europa.* Frankfurt and New York: Campus.

SCHATTAT, B. (1976), 'Demo-oekonomische Modelle. Bevoelkerungswachstum und wirtschaftliche Entwicklung' in J. Schmid (ed.), *Einfuehrung in die Bevoelkerungssoziologie.* Reinbek: Rororo Studium Sozialwissenschaft, 204–55.

SCHLOSSER, O. (1976), *Einfuehrung in die sozialwissenschaftliche Zusammenhangsanalyse. Mit einem Vorwort von Helmut Klages.* Reinbek: Rororo Studium Sozialwissenschaft.

SCHLUPP, F., Nour, S. and Junne, G. (1973), 'Zur Theorie und Ideologie internationaler Interdependenz' in K. J. Gantzel (ed.), *Internationale Beziehungen als System.* Sonderheft 5 der Politischen Vierteljahresschrift, Opladen: Westdeutscher Verlag, 245–308.

SCHMID, J. (1976a), 'Zur Geschichte des bevoelkerungswissenschaftlichen Denkens. Dokumentation und Interpretation' in J. Shmid (ed.), *Einfuehrung in die Bevoelkerungssoziologie.* Reibek: Rororo Studium Sozialwissenschaft, 15–107.

SCHMID, J. (1976b), 'Bevoelkerungsgeschichte und Sterblichkeit (Mortalitaet)' in J. Schmid (ed.), *Einfuehrung in die Bevoelkerungssoziologie.* Reinbek: Rororo Studium Sozialwissenschaft, 108–60.

SCHMID, J. (1984), 'Bevoelkerungsprobleme' in P. J. Opitz (ed.), *Die Dritte Welt in der Krise. Grundprobleme der Entwicklungslaender*. Munich: C. H. Beck, 45–63.

SCHMIDT, A. (1982), 'Ungleicher Tausch' in D. Nohlen and F. Nuscheler (eds), *Handbuch der Dritten Welt*. Hamburg: Hoffmann & Campe, vol. 1, 117–32.

SCHMIDT, M. G. (1986), 'Politische Bedingungen erfolgreicher Wirtschaftspolitik. Eine vergleichende Analyse westlicher Industrielaender (1960–1985)', *Journal fuer Sozialforschung*, 26, 3: 251–73.

SCHMITTER, P. C. (1971a), 'Desarrollo retrasado, dependencia externa y cambio politico en America Latina', *Foro Internacional*, 12, 2: 135ff.

SCHMITTER, P. C. (1971b), 'Military Intervention, Political Competitiveness and Public Policy in Latin America: 1950–1967' in M. Janowitz and J. van Doorn (eds), *On Military Intervention*. Rotterdam University Press, Contributions to *Military Sociology*, vol. 2, 425–506.

SCHOEPFER, H. (1979), *Lateinamerikanische Befreiungstheologie*. Stuttgart: W. Kohlhammer.

SCHUETT, K. P. (1986), 'Bolivien. Bruechige Demokratie im Strudel wirtschaftlicher Strukturkrisen' in *Jahrbuch Dritte Welt. Daten. Uebersichten. Analysen*. Munich: Verlag C. H. Beck, 164–77.

SCHULTZ, T. P. (1982), 'Family Composition and Income Inequality', *Population and Development Review*, 8, Supplement: 137–50.

SEAGER, J. and Olson, A. (1986), *Der Frauenatlas. Daten, Fakten und Informationen zur Lage der Frauen auf unserer Erde*. Frankfurt: Fischer.

SEERS, D. (1981a), 'Introduction' in D. Seers (ed.), *Dependency Theory. A Critical Reassessment*. London: Frances Pinter, 13–19.

SEERS, D. (1981b), 'Development Options: The Strengths and Weaknesses of Dependency Theories in Explaining a Government's Room to Manouvre' in D. Seers (ed.), *Dependency Theory. A Critical Reassessment*. London: Frances Pinter, 135–49.

SEERS, D. (1978a), 'Patterns of Dependence' in J. J. Villamil (ed.), *Transnational Capitalism and National Development. New Perspectives on Dependence*. Hassocks, Sussex: Harvester, 95–114.

SEERS, D. (ed.) (1978b), *Underdeveloped Europe*. Hassocks: Harvester.

SEGBERS, K. (1991), 'Migration and Refugee Movements from the USSR: Causes and Prospects', *Report on the USSR*, 3, 46: 6–14.

SEN, A. (1990), 'Indian Development: Lessons and Non-Lessons', *India*, Jan: 18–25.

SENGHAAS, D. (1965), 'Horizonte einer Disziplin. Anmerkungen zur Theorie der Internationalen Politik', *Politische Vierteljahresschrift*, 6, 3: 375–410.

SENGHAAS, D. (ed.) (1971), *Kritische Friedensforschung*. Frankfurt, Edition Suhrkamp.

SENGHAAS, D. (ed.) (1972a), *Imperialismus und strukturelle Gewalt*. Frankfurt, Edition Suhrkamp.

SENGHAAS, D. (1972b), 'Zur Analyse internationaler Politik' in G. Kress and D. Senghaas (eds), *Politikwissenschaft. Eine Einfuehrung in ihre Probleme*. Frankfurt: Fischer, TB, 347–82.

SENGHAAS, D. (1972c), *Ruestung und Militarismus*. Frankfurt, Edition Suhrkamp.

SENGHAAS, D. (ed.) (1974), *Peripherer Kapitalismus*. Frankfurt, Edition Suhrkamp.

SENGHAAS, D. (1977), *Weltwirtschaftsordnung und Entwicklungspolitik*. Frankfurt, Edition Suhrkamp.

SENGHAAS, D. (1979), 'Vorwort' in D. Senghaas (ed.), *Kapitalistische Weltoekonomie. Kontroversen ueber ihren Ursprung und ihre Entwicklungsdynamik*, Frankfurt, Edition Suhrkamp: 7–30.

SENGHAAS, D. (1981), 'Socialism in Historical and Developmental Perspective', *Bulletin of Peace Proposals*, 12, 3: 287–301.

SENGHAAS, D. (1982a), 'Sozialismus-eine Interpretation aus entwicklungsgeschichtlicher und entwicklungstheoretischer Perspektive' in D. Senghaas, *Von Europa lernen. Entwicklungsgeschichtliche Betrachtungen*, Frankfurt, Edition Suhrkamp: Neue Folge, vol. 134, 277–320.

SENGHAAS, D. (1982b), 'Vorwort' in *Von Europa lernen. (see 1982a)*, 7–22.

SENGHAAS, D. (1982c), 'Autozentrierte Entwicklung trotz internationalem Kompetenzgefaelle. Problemstellung und allgemeiner Befund' in *Von Europa lernen. (see 1982a)*, 25–109.

SENGHAAS, D. (1982d), 'Elemente eines exportorientierten und autozentrierten Entwicklungsweges' in *Von Europa lernen. (see 1982a)*, 244–57.

SENGHAAS, D. (1982e), 'In der Nachfolge Europas? Ueber ostasiatische Entwicklungswege' in *Von Europa lernen. (see 1982a)*, 258–73.

SENGHAAS, D. (1982f), 'Wachstum und Verteilungsgerechtigkeit. Der skandinavische Entwicklungsweg' in *Von Europa lernen. (see 1982a)*, 113–46.

SENGHAAS, D. (1982g), 'Autozentrierte Entwicklung' in D. Nohlen and F. Nuscheler (eds), *Handbuch der Dritten Welt*. Hamburg: Hoffmann & Campe, 1: 359–79.

SENGHAAS, D. (1985a), *Europas Entwicklung und die Dritte Welt. Rueckblick und Ausblick auf die Entwicklungsproblematik*. University of Bremen, mimeo, Sep. Printed in Menzel and Senghaas, 1986.

SENGHAAS, D. (1985b), *The European Experience: A Historical Critique of Development Theory*. Shakopee, Minnesota: Berg Publishers (transl. Senghaas, 1982).

SHEARMAN, P. (1987), 'Gorbachev and the Third World: An Era of Reform?', *Third World Quarterly*, 9, 4: 1083–117.

SIEBER, M. (1985), 'Zur Verletzung von Modellannahmen in der Regressionsanalyse', *Schweizerische Zeitschrift fuer Soziologie*, 11, 3: 515–29.

SIGELMAN, L. and Simpson, M. (1977), 'A Cross-National Test of the Linkage Between Economic Inequality and Political Violence', *Journal of Conflict Resolution*, 21, 1: 105–28.

SIMATUPANG, B. (1987), 'Poland: External Economic Relationships and Economic Crisis (1970–1982)', *Research Memorandum* 8715, Department of Economics, University of Amsterdam, NL.

SIMATUPANG, B. (1991), *The Polish Economic Crisis of 1979–1982. Background, Circumstances and Causes*. Universiteit van Amsterdam, Academisch Proefschrift, Faculteit: Economische Wetenschappen en Econometrie: Offsetdrukkerij Kanters.

SIMON, J. L. (1981), *The Ultimate Resource*. Princeton, N.J.: Princeton University Press.

SINGER, P. I. (1971), *Dinamica de la poblacion y desarrollo*, editorial siglo XXI, Mexico City, Madrid, Buenos Aires.

SINGER, P. I. (1980), 'Beschaeftigung, Produktion und Reproduktion der Arbeitskraft' in V. Bennholdt-Thomsen *et al.* (eds), *Lateinamerika. Analysen und Berichte*, 2nd edn. Berlin: Olle & Wolter, 53–69.

SINGER, P. I. (1981a), 'Was heute Sozialismus ist' in V. Bennholdt-Thomsen *et al.* (eds), *Lateinamerika. Analysen und Berichte*, 2nd edn, vol. 5, Berlin: Olle & Wolter, 15–40.

SINGER, P. I. (1981b), 'O feminino e o feminismo' in P. I. Singer and Caldeira Brant (eds), *Sao Paulo: O Povo em Movimento*, 2nd edn, R. J./São Paulo: Editora Vozes/ CEBRAP Petropolis, 109–42.

SIPRI (eds) (1986), *Ruestungsjahrbuch 6*. Reinbek: Rororo Aktuell.

SLAY, B. (1992), 'Poland: The Rise and Fall of the Balcerowicz Plan', *RFE/RL Research Report*, 31 Jan: 40–7.

SNIDAL, D. *et al.* (1980), 'Eine Ueberpruefung der 'Dependencia'-Theorie: Das Yale Projekt ueber die Abhaengigkeit' in G. Hischier *et al.* (eds), *Weltgesellschaft und Sozialstruktur. Festschrift zum 60. Geburtstag von Peter Heintz.* Diessenhofen: Ruegger, 39–56.

SPENGLER, J. J. (1976), 'Adam Smith on Population Growth and Economic Development', *Population and Development Review*, 2, 2: 167–80.

SRINIVASAN, K. (1986), 'Modernisation and Fertility Change: A Review of Theoretical Developments' in K. Mahadevan (ed.), *Fertility and Mortality. Theory, Methodology and Empirical Issues*. New Delhi: Sage, 171–83.

STACK, S. (1978), 'The Effect of Direct Government Involvement in the Economy on the Degree of Income Inequality: A Cross-National Study', *American Sociological Review*, 43, 4: 880–8.

STACK, S. (1979), 'Direct Government Involvement in the Economy: Theoretical and and Empirical Extensions. Reply to Jackman, and Firebaugh', *American Sociological Review*, 44, 1: 146–54.

STAJNER, R. (1987), *Yugoslavia and Changes in the System of International Economic Relations*. Belgrade: Medjunarodna Politika.

STANDING, G. (1978), 'Labour Commitment, Sexual Dualism and Industrialization in Jamaica', *World Employment Programme Research Working Papers* (Geneva: ILO).

STANFIELD, J. R. (1989), 'Karl Polanyi, and Contemporary Economic Thought' in K. Polanyi-Levitt and M. Mendell (eds), *The Life and Work of Karl Polanyi.* Montreal: Black Rose (quoted here from the author's typescript, 1986)

STAUFFER, R. B. (1985), 'The Marcos Regime: Failure of Transnational Developmentalism and Hegemony-Building from Above and Outside', *Transnational Corporations Research Project*, Faculty of Economics, The University of Sydney, *Research Monograph* no. 23.

STAUFFER, R. B. (1990), 'Capitalism, 'Development', The Decline of the Socialist Option, and the Search For Critical Alternatives', *Occasional Papers in Political Science*, Department of Political Science, Manoa: University of Hawaii, 3, 3, Jan: 29–53.

STREETEN, P. (1985), 'Loesungen schaffen neue Probleme. Die Entwicklungsoekonomie hat nicht versagt', *Finanzierung und Entwicklung*, 22, 2, Jun: 14–16.

SUNKEL, O. (1978), 'Transnationalization and its National Consequences' in J. J. Villamil (ed.), *Transnational Capitalism and National Development. New Perspectives on Dependence*. Hassocks, Sussex: Harvester, 67–94.

SUNKEL, O. (1972), 'Transnationale kapitalistische Integration und nationale Desintegration: Der Fall Lateinamerika' in D. Senghaas (ed.), *Imperialismus und strukturelle Gewalt. Analysen ueber abhaengige Reproduktion*. Frankfurt, Edition Suhrkamp: 258–315.

SUNKEL, O. (1974), *Dependencia y heterogeneidad estructural*. Berlin: Deutsche Stiftung fuer Internationale Entwicklung, mimeo.

SUNKEL, O. (1966), 'The Structural Background of Development Problems in Latin America', *Weltwirtschaftliches Archiv*, 97, 1: 22ff.

SWEEZY, P. M.(1971), *Theorie der kapitalistischen Entwicklung*. Frankfurt, Edition Suhrkamp.

SZLAJFER, H. (1985), 'Sobre el pensamiento y praxis politica de Jose Carlos Mariategui, de manera polemica (en relacion al libro de A.Flores Galindo)', *Estudios Latinoamericanos*. Ossolineum, Wroclaw: Polska Akademia Nauk, 10: 187–204.

SZLAJFER, H. (1977), 'Nachzuholende Entwicklung unter Bedingungen des Weltmarktes: Das Beispiel der polnischen Entwicklung', *Probleme des Klassenkampfes*, 7, 27: 7ff.

SZENTES, T. (1982), 'The TNC Issue. Naive Illusions or Exorcism and Lip Service', *Review*, VI, 2, Fall: 229–52.

SZENTES, T. (1984), 'The Economic Impact of Global Militarization', *Alternatives, A Journal of World Policy*, 10, 1: 45–73.

SZESCI, M. (1977), 'Rueckblick auf die 'Great Transformation', *Wirtschaft und Gesellschaft*, 3, 4: 407–14.

SZYMANSKI, A. (1982), 'The Socialist World-System' in C. K. Chase-Dunn (ed.), *Socialist States in the World-System*. Beverly Hills, London, Delhi: Sage Focus Edition, 57–84.

SWEDBERG, R. (1986a), 'The Critique of the 'Economy and Society' Perspective During the Paradigm Crisis: From the United States to Sweden', *Acta Sociologica*, 29, 2: 91–112.

SWEDBERG, R. (1986b), *Prudence versus Profit: The Role of the Multinational Banks in the Origin of the Debt Crisis, 1974 to 1982*. Paper presented at the XI World Congress of Sociology in New Delhi 18–22 August 1986, Stockholms Universitet, Department of Sociology, mimeo.

TAUSCH, A. (1973), 'Zur Analyse politischer Systeme in Lateinamerika', *Zeitschrift fuer Lateinamerika*, Vienna, 5: 40–56.

TAUSCH, A. (1976), *Die Grenzen der Wachstumstheorie*. Wiener Institut fuer Entwicklungsfragen/Inauguraldissertation, Institut fuer Politikwissenschaft, University of Salzburg.

TAUSCH, A. (1977a), 'Ist der Kapitalismus tot? Zur Verelendung in Oesterreich' in JG in der SPOe Steiermark/Erklaerung von Graz fuer solidarische Entwicklung (eds), *Armut in Oesterreich*. Graz: Leykam, 66–100.

TAUSCH, A. (1977b), 'Neuere Literatur zur Verteilungstheorie', *Oesterreichische Zeitschrift fuer Politikwissenschaft*, 6, 3: 355–8.

TAUSCH, A. (1978a), 'Nicht nur der Artikel 7', *Mladje-Literatura in Kritika* (Klagenfurt-Ljubljana, Slowenisches Wissenschaftliches Institut), 29: 58–90.

TAUSCH, A. (1978b), 'Politische Systeme und Abhaengigkeit. Ein faktorenanalytisches Modell', *Internationale Entwicklung*, I and II: 54–62. Reprinted in A. Tausch (1979b): 53–66.

TAUSCH, A. (1979a), 'Weltweite Armut' in F. Dotter et al. (eds), *Christliche Markierungen*. Vienna: Europa, 137–70.

TAUSCH, A. (1979b), *Armut und Abhaengigkeit. Politik und Oekonomie im Peripheren Kapitalismus*. Vienna: W. Braumueller.

TAUSCH, A. (1980), 'Ruestung und peripherer Kapitalismus' in K. Raffer and M. Kopeinig (eds), *Aktuelle Beitraege zur Entwicklungspolitik*. Vienna, Oesterreichischer Informationsdienst fuer Entwicklungspolitik: 73–120.

TAUSCH, A. (1982a), 'Ruestung und Lebensbedingungen in der Dritten Welt' in P. Sonntag (ed.), *Ruestung und Oekonomie*. Frankfurt: Haag und Herchen, 176–88.

TAUSCH, A. (1982b), 'Gleicher als die Anderen?', *Oesterreichischer Forschungsalmanach*: 200–12.

TAUSCH, A. (1982c), *Aggregate Data Set Eastern Europe*. Cologne: Zentralarchiv fuer empirische Sozialforschung.

TAUSCH, A. (1983), 'Erzwungene Technologie-Abhaengigkeit, Ruestung und Konsum in Osteuropa. Reflexionen ueber Intelligence Research und die amerikanische Aussenpolitik', *Oesterreichische Zeitschrift fuer Politikwissenschaft*, 4: 452–67.

TAUSCH, A. (1984a), 'Zur kubanischen Entwicklungseffizienz', *Zeitschrift fuer Lateinamerika*, Vienna, 25: 33–44.

TAUSCH, A. (1984b), 'Zentrum, Peripherie, strukturelle Gewalt und Superruestung. Unterwegs zu einem politometrischen Modell', *Dialog*, 1, 1: 72–106.

TAUSCH, A. (1984c), 'Umverteilen vor dem Wachstum? Umverteilung, Geburtenpolitik und langfristige Entwicklung in China', *China-Report*, 77–78: 52–66.

TAUSCH, A. (1985), 'Development, Social Justice, and Dependence in Poland', *Occasional Paper*, 9, *Transnational Corporations Research Project*, Faculty of Geography, University of Sydney.

TAUSCH, A. (1986a), 'Costa Rica im System der internationalen Stratifikation' in A. Maislinger (ed.), *Costa Rica*. Innverlag, Studien zur Politischen Wirklichkeit, 3 (ed. A. Pelinka): 197–207.

TAUSCH, A. (1986b), 'Entwicklungsmodell 'realer Sozialismus'-Eine politometrische Untersuchung zu Verteilung, Wachstum und Humanentwicklung in Weltmarkt-abgekoppelten Systemen', *Reader Politikwissenschaft*, Frankfurt: Haag und Herchen, 60–103.

TAUSCH, A. (1986c), 'Was bleibt von der Dependenztheorie?', *Journal fuer Entwicklungspolitik*, 3: 84–90.

TAUSCH, A. (1986d), 'Positions within the Global Order, Patterns of Defence Policies, and National Development: Austria and Pakistan Compared' in S. F. Hasnat and A. Pelinka (eds), *Security for the Weak Nations. A Multiple Perspective. A Joint Project of Pakistani and Austrian Scholars*. Lahore: Izharsons, 245–55.

TAUSCH, A. (1986e), 'Weltentwicklungsbericht 1984', *Kölner Zeitschrift fuer Soziologie*, 1: 164–7.

TAUSCH, A. (1987a), 'Geburtenrate und Weltentwicklung. Die Bedeutung der Bevoelkerungsentwicklung fuer Lebensqualitaet, Wachstum und Verteilung und die krichlichen Nord-Suedbeziehungen', *Dialog*, 8, 1: 239–73.

TAUSCH, A. (1987b), *Jenseits der Weltgesellschaftstheorien*. (*see* 1991a).

TAUSCH, A. (1987c), 'Transnational Corporations and Underdevelopment. Book Review on Bornschier/Chase-Dunn, (1985)', *Acta Sociologica*, 30, 1: 118–21.

TAUSCH, A. (1989a), 'Stable Third World Democracy and the European Model. A Quantitative Essay', *Peace and Development Research Institute*, Gothenburg University papers, ed. Z. Bablewski, and B. Hettne, pp. 131–61.

TAUSCH, A. (1989b), 'Bomshi, Byshi und Brodyagi', *Zukunft*, Dec: 33–46.

TAUSCH, A. (1989c), 'Armas socialistas, subdesarrollo y violencia estructural en el Tercer Mundo', *Revista Internacional de Sociologia*, CSIC, Madrid, 47, 4: 583–716.

TAUSCH, A. (1990a), *International Relations Theory – Beyond Third Debates.* Innsbruck University: Department of Political Science, mimeo.

TAUSCH, A. (1990b), *Some Quantitative Reflections on the Development Theory Significance of the 'Great Transformation'.* Innsbruck University: Department of Political Science, mimeo.

TAUSCH, A. (1991a), *Jenseits der Weltgesellschaftstheorien. Sozialtransformationen und der Paradigmenwechsel in der Entwicklungsforschung.* Munich: Eberhard Verlag, Reihe 'Grenzen und Horizonte'.

TAUSCH, A. (1991b), *Rußlands Tretmühle. Kapitalistisches Weltsystem, lange Zyklen und die neue Instabilität im Osten.* Munich: Eberhard.

TAUSCH, K.J. (1988), 'Stoppt die Unterdrueckung der Frau', *Zyklotron*, Sondernummer, 22a: 78–83.

TEDSTROM, J. (1991), 'Gorbachev the Economist', *Report on the USSR*, 3, 35, 30 Aug: 11–12.

TERHAL, P. (1989), *The Fourth World, Concept, Reality and Prospects.* Paper presented at the RIDC/EADI conference 'The trends towards the globalization of development theory', CSPS, RIDC, Warsaw, 22–23 June 1989.

THERBORN, G. (1986), 'Karl Marx Returning. The Welfare State and Neo-Marxist, Corporatist and Statist Theories', *International Political Science Review*, 7, 2, Apr: 131–64.

THERBORN, G. (1985), *Arbeitslosigkeit. Strategien und Politikansaetze in den OECD-Laendern.* Hamburg: VSA-Verlag.

TAYLOR, C.L. and Jodice, D. (1983), *World Handbook of Political and Social Indicators III.* MRDF, ICPSR, Ann Arbor, Michigan: Yale University Press, New Haven and London.

TAYLOR, C.L. and Hudson, M.C. (1972/75), *World Handbook of Political and Social Indicators*, 2nd edn. New Haven and London: Yale University Press.

THEE, M. (ed.) (1986), 'Arms and Disarmament. SIPRI Findings. 20 years of Studies by the Stockholm International Peace Research Institute', *Bulletin of Peace Proposals*, 17, 3–4.

TIBI, B. (1983), 'Nord-Sued-Konflikt' in W. Mickel (ed.), *Handlexikon zur Politikwissenschaft.* Munich: Ehrenwirt, 313–18.

TILTON, T.A. (1979), ' A Swedish Road to Socialism: Ernst Wigforss and the Ideological Foundations of Swedish Social Democracy', *American Political Science Review*, 73, 2: 505–20.

TIMBERLAKE, M. and Williams, K. (1984), 'Dependence, Political Exclusion and Government Repression: Some Cross-National Evidence', *American Sociological Review*, 49, 1: 141–6.

TREHUB, A. (1989), 'Soviet Economist on US and Soviet Living Standards', *Report on the USSR*, 1, 6, 10 Feb: 4–7.

TREHUB, A. (1988), 'Poverty in the USSR', *Radio Liberty Research, RL 256/88*, Munich.

TREHUB, A. (1987a), 'New Figures on Infant Mortality in the USSR', *Radio Liberty Research, RL 438/87*, Munich.

TREHUB, A. (1987b), 'Social and Economic Rights in the Soviet Union', *Survey*, 29, 4, 127, Aug: 6–42.

TREIMAN, D.J. and Roos, P.A. (1983), 'Sex and Earnings in Industrial Society: A Nine-Nation Comparison', *American Journal of Sociology*, 89, 3: 612–50.

TRUSSELL, J. and Pebley, A. R. (1984), 'The Potential Impact of Changes in Fertility on Infant, Child, and Maternal Mortality', *World Bank Staff Working Papers*, 698.

TUOMI, H. and Vaeyrynen, R. (1982), *Transnational Corporations, Armaments and Development*. Aldershot: Gower.

TYSON, L. D. A. (1986), 'The Debt Crisis and Adjustment Responses in Eastern Europe: A Comparative Perspective', *International Organization*, 40, 2: 239–85.

UN ECOSOC (1978), *Transnational Corporations in World Development: A Reexamination*. New York: United Nations.

UN DEPARTMENT OF INTERNATIONAL ECONOMIC AND SOCIAL AFFAIRS, STATISTICAL OFFICE (1980), *Compendium of Social Statistics: 1977*. New York: United Nations.

UN ECONOMIC COMMISSION FOR EUROPE (current issues), *Economic Survey of Europe*. New York: United Nations.

UNITED STATES CONGRESSIONAL RESEARCH SERVICE (eds) (1981), *Soviet Policy and the United States Response in the Third World*. Washington DC.: US GPO.

UNITED STATES ARMS CONTROL AND DISARMAMENT AGENCY (eds) (Current Issues), *World Military Expenditures and Arms Transfers*. Washington DC: US GPO.

UNITED STATES CENTRAL INTELLIGENCE AGENCY, NATIONAL FOREIGN ASSESSMENT CENTER (1980), *Developed Country Imports of Manufactured Products from LDCs. A Research Paper*. ER 80–10476, Sep (unclassified).

UNITED STATES DEPARTMENT OF DEFENSE (eds) (current issues), '*Soviet Military Power*', Washington DC.: US GPO.

URBAN, G. and Lieven, D. (1991), 'Should There Be a Soviet Union? A Conversation between George Urban and Dominic Lieven', *Report on the USSR*, 3, 29, 19 Jul: 14–19 and 3, 30, 26 Jul: 16–21.

VIENNA INSTITUTE FOR COMPARATIVE ECONOMIC STUDIES (current issues) *Mitgliederinformation*.

VIENNA INSTITUTE FOR COMPARATIVE ECONOMIC STUDIES (1979), *CMEA Data 1978*. Vienna: Nakladal Publishing Company and Austrian Institute for Economic Research.

VALDES, G. and Furtado. C. (1983), 'Dos Reflexiones sobre Crisis Economica y Democracia en America Latina', *Documentos de trabajo, centro de estudios del desarrollo*, 4, Jul, Santiago de Chile.

VALENZUELA, J. S. and Valenzuela, A. (1979), 'Modernization and Dependence: Alternative Perspectives in the Study of Latin American Underdevelopment' in J. J. Villamil (ed.), *Transnational Capitalism and National Development. New Perspectives on Dependence*. Hassocks, Sussex: Harvester, 31–66.

VINTON, L. (ANONYMOUS) (1988), 'POVERTY AND THE SOCIAL MINIMUM', *SITUATION REPORT POLAND*, 2, RADIO FREE EUROPE RESEARCH, MUNICH: 23–9.

VINTON, L. (1991a), 'Balancing Continuity and Change: Walesa Forms a Government', *Report on Eastern Europe*, 2, 3, Jan: 17–20.

VINTON, L. (1991b), 'Walesa's First Challenge: State Workers Reject Anti-Inflationary Wage Controls', *Report on Eastern Europe*, 2, 9, 1 Mar: 23–7.

VINTON, L. (1991c), 'Poland: Disparate Responses to Democracy and the Market', *Report on Eastern Europe*, 2, 13, 29 Mar: 29–37.

VINTON, L. (1991d), 'Walesa, "Special Powers", and the Balcerowicz Plan', *Report on Eastern Europe*, 2, 29, 19 Jul: 15–23.

VINTON, L. (1991e), 'Party X and the "Tyminski Phenomenon"', *Report on Eastern Europe*, 2, 32, 9 Aug: 6–14.

VINTON, L. (1991f), 'The Attempted Coup in the USSR: East European Reactions – Poland', *Report on Eastern Europe*, 2, 35, 30 Aug: 10–14.

VINTON, L. (1992), 'Poland's Governing Coalition: Will the Truce Hold?', *RFE/RL Research Report*, 1, 31, Jul: 34–40.

VISARIA, P. (1979), 'Demographic Factors and the Distribution of Income: Some Issues' in *Economic and Demographic Change: Issues for the 1980s. Proceedings of the Conference*, Liege: IUSSP, vol. 1, 289–320. *World Bank Reprint Series*, 129, Washington D.C.

VOGT, W. (ed.) (1973), *Seminar: Politische Oekonomie. Zur Kritik der herrschenden Nationaloekonomie*. Frankfurt: Suhrkamp Taschenbuch.

VORONINA, O. (1990), 'Die Frau in der sowjetischen Gesellschaft' in K. Segbers (ed.), *Perestrojka: Zwischenbilanz*. Frankfurt und Moscow: Edition Suhrkamp und Progress Verlag, 154–82.

WALDMANN, P. (1985), 'Argentinien: Schwellenland auf Dauer?. *Politische Vierteljahresschrift*, 26, Sonderheft 16: 113–34.

WALLERSTEIN, I. (1974/1986), *Das moderne Weltsystem-Die Anfaenge kapitalistischer Landwirtschaft und die europaeische Weltoekonomie im 16. Jahrhundert. Aus dem Amerikanischen von Angelika Schweikhart*, Frankfurt: Syndikat.

WALLERSTEIN, I. (1976), 'Semi-Peripheral Countries and the Contemporary World Crisis', *Theory and Society*, 4: 461–83.

WALLERSTEIN, I. (1979), 'Aufstieg und kuenftiger Niedergang des kapitalistischen Weltsystems. Zur Grundlegung vergleichender Analyse' in D. Senghaas (ed.), *Kapitalistische Weltoekonomie. Kontroversen ueber ihren Ursprung und ihre Entwicklungsdynamik*. Frankfurt, Edition Suhrkamp, 31–67.

WALLERSTEIN, I. (1982), 'Socialist States: Mercantilist Strategies and Revolutionary Objectives' in E. Friedman (ed.), *Ascent and Decline in the World-System*. Beverly Hills, London, New Delhi: Sage, 289–99.

WALLERSTEIN, I. (1984), *Der historische Kapitalismus. Uebersetzt von Uta Lehmann-Grube mit einem Nachwort herausgegeben von Hans Heinrich Nolte*. Berlin: Argument-Verlag.

WALLERSTEIN, I. (1986), 'Krise als Uebergang' in S. Amin *et al.*, *Dynamik der globalen Krise*. Opladen: Westdeutscher Verlag, 4–35.

WALLERSTEIN, I. (1989), *The National and the Universal: Can There Be Such a Thing as World Culture?*. Fernand Braudel Center for the Study of Economies, Historical Systems and Civilizations, Binghamton, New York: SUNY, Binghamton.

WALLERSTEIN, I. (1990), *America and the World: Today, Yesterday, and Tomorrow*. Fernand Braudel Center for the Study of Economies, Historical Systems and Civilizations, Binghamton, New York: SUNY, Binghamton.

WALLERSTEIN, I. (1991a), *Who Excludes Whom? or The Collapse of Liberalism and the Dilemmas of Antisystemic Strategy*. Fernand Braudel Center for the Study of Economies, Historical Systems and Civilizations, Binghamton, New York: SUNY, Binghamton.

WALLERSTEIN, I. (1991b), *The Concept of National Development, 1917–1989: Elegy and Requiem*. Fernand Braudel Center for the Study of Economies,

Historical Systems and Civilizations, Binghamton, New York: SUNY, Binghamton.

WALTER, F. (1987), 'Verteidigungsausgaben der UdSSR. Dimensionen und Entwick- lungstendenzen' in H. Adomeit *et al.* (eds), *Die Sowjetunion als Militaermacht.* Stuttgart: Kohlhammer: 134–56.

WARD, K. B. (1985), 'The Social Consequences of the World Economic System. The Economic Status of Women and Fertility', *Review*, VIII, 4, Spring: 561–93.

WARD, M. Don (1978), *The Political Economy of Distribution. Equality versus Inequality.* New York and Oxford: Elsevier.

WARD, M. Don (1981), 'Changing Patterns of Inequality in a Changing Global Order', *IIVG preprints*, Berlin: International Institute for Comparative Social Research, 81–101 R.

WEEDE, E. (1970), 'Zur Methodik der kausalen Abhaengigkeitsanalyse (Pfadana-lyse), in der nicht-experimentellen Forschung', *Kölner Zeitschrift fuer Soziologie und Sozialpsychologie*, 22: 532–50.

WEEDE, E. (1975), 'Unzufriedenheit, Protest und Gewalt: Kritik an einem makropolitischen Forschungsprogramm', *Politische Vierteljahresschrift*, 16: 409–28.

WEEDE, E. (1977a), 'Politische Kultur, Institutionalisierung und Praetorianismus: Ueberlegungen zur Theorie und empirischen Forschungspraxis', *Kölner Zeitschrift fuer Soziologie und Sozialpsychologie*, 29, 2: 411–37; 3: 657–76.

WEEDE, E. (1977b), *Hypothesen, Gleichungen und Daten. Spezifikations-und Messprobleme bei Kausalmodellen fuer Daten aus einer und mehreren Beobachtungsperioden.* Monographien Sozialwissenschaftliche Methoden, vol. 1, Kronberg Ts.: Athenaeum Verlag.

WEEDE, E. (1980), 'Beyond Misspecification in Sociological Analyses of Income Inequality', *American Sociological Review*, 45, 2: 497–501.

WEEDE, E. (1981a), 'Militaer, Multis und Wirtschaft', *Schweizerische Zeitschrift fuer Soziologie*, 7, 1: 113–27.

WEEDE, E. (1981b), 'Dependenztheorien und Wirtschaftswachstum', *Kölner Zeitschrift fuer Soziologie*, 33, 4: 690–707.

WEEDE, E. (1982), 'Dependenztheorien und Einkommensverteilung', *Zeitschrift fuer die gesamte Staatswissenschaft*, 138: 241–61.

WEEDE, E. (1983a), 'The Impact of Democracy on Economic Growth', *Kyklos*, 36, 1: 21–39.

WEEDE, E. (1983b), 'Internationaler Konflikt, Militaerdienst, Humankapital und Wirtschaftswachstum', *Politische Vierteljahresschrift*, Sonderheft 14 (Politische Stabilitaet und Konflikt): 66–80.

WEEDE, E. (1985a), *Entwicklungslaender in der Weltgesellschaft'*, Opladen: Westdeutscher Verlag.

WEEDE, E. (1985b), 'Warum bleiben arme Leute arm?', *Politische Vierteljahress-chrift*, 26, 3: 270–86.

WEEDE, E. (1986a), 'Verteilungskoalitionen, Staatstaetigkeit und Stagnation', *Politische Vierteljahresschrift*, 27, 2: 222–36.

WEEDE, E. (1986b), 'Verteilungskonflikte und Arbeitslosigkeit in demokratischen Wohlfahrtsstaaten', *Jahrbuch fuer Neue Politische Oekonomie*, 5, Tuebingen: J. C. B. Mohr, 140–51.

WEEDE, E. (1986c), 'Catch-up, Distributional Coalitions and Government as Determinants of Economic Growth or Decline in Industrialized Democracies', *The British Journal of Sociology*, 37, 2: 194–220.

WEEDE, E. (1986d), *Konfliktforschung. Einfuehrung und Ueberblick*. Opladen: Westdeutscher Verlag.

WEEDE, E. (1986e), 'Income Inequality and Political Violence Reconsidered', *American Sociological Review*, 51, Jun: 438–41.

WEEDE, E. (1987), 'Some New Evidence on Correlates of Political Violence: Income Inequality, Regime Repressiveness, and Economic Development', *European Sociological Review*, 3, 2: 97–108.

WEEDE, E. (1988), 'Price Distorsion, Democracy or Regime Repressiveness and Economic Growth Rates among LDCs, 1973–1983', *Pacific Focus* (Centre for International Studies, Inha University), 3, 2: 23–39.

WEEDE, E. and Jagodzinski, W. (1981), 'National Security, Income Inequality, and Economic Growth', *Social Science and Policy Research* (Seoul), 3, 3: 91–107.

WEIGEL, V. B. (1986), 'The Basic Needs Approach: Overcoming the Poverty of Homo oeconomicus', *World Development*, 14, 12: 1423–34.

WEIL, F. D. (1985), 'The variable effects of education on liberal attitudes: a comparative-historical analysis of anti-semitism using public opinion survey data', *American Sociological Review*, 50, 4: 458–74.

WEINER, M. (1986), 'The Political Economy of Industrial Growth in India', *World Politics*, 38, 4: 596–610.

WEISSKOPF, T. E. (1983), 'Economic Development and the Development of Economics: Some Observations from the Left', *World Development*, 11, 10: 895–9.

WERLHOF, C. von (1975), *Prozesse der Unter-Entwicklung in El Salvador und Costa Rica. Eine vergleichende Studie ueber Prozesse der Unter-Entwicklung und ueber die Reaktionen der Unter-Entwickelten in Zentralamerika*. Saarbruecken: SSIP-Schriften.

WERLHOF, C. von (1983/88), 'Der Proletarier ist tot. Es lebe die Hausfrau?' in C. von Werlhof *et al.* (eds), *Frauen, die letzte Kolonie. Zur Hausfrauisierung der Arbeit*, 2nd edn. Reinbek: 113–36 (engl. transl. in J. Smith *et al.* (eds) (1984), *Households and the World Economy* Beverly Hills, New Delhi and London: Sage, 131–47).

WERLHOF, C. von (1985), *Wenn die Bauern wiederkommen. Frauen, Arbeit und Agrobusiness in Venezuela*. Bremen.

WERLHOF, C. von (1991), *Was haben die Huehner mit dem Dollar zu tun?*. Munich: Frauenoffensive.

WHITE, S. (1990), 'Democratisation' in the USSR', *Soviet Studies*, 42, 1, Jan.: 3–24.

WIGFORSS, E. (1926), *Socialism-Dogm eller Arbetshypotes?* Stockholm: Eskilstuna.

WIGFORSS, E. (1938), *Har Vi Rad Till Sociala Reformer?* Stockholm: Frihets Foerlag.

WIGFORSS, E. (1944), *Broed och Frihet*. Stockholm: Nordisk Rotogravyr.

WIPPERMANN, M. (1983), *Europaeischer Faschismus im Vergleich*. Frankfurt, Edition Suhrkamp.

WOEHLKE, M. (1987), *Umweltzerstoerung in der Dritten Welt*. Munich: C. H. Beck.

WOEHLKE, M. (1985), *Brasilien. Anatomie eines Riesen. Ein Reise-und Studienbegleiter*. Aktuelle Laenderkunden, Munich: C. H. Beck.

WOLF, K. D. (1991), 'Das neue Deutschland-eine Weltmacht?', *Leviathan*, 2: 247–60.

WOOLHANDLER, S. and Himmelstein, D. U. (1985), 'Militarism and Mortality. An International Analysis of Arms Spending and Infant Death Rates', *The Lancet*, 15 Jun: 1375–8.

WORLD BANK (1979), *Brazil: Human Ressources Special Report. A World Bank Country Study*. Latin America and Carribean Regional Office, Washington D.C.: The World Bank.

WORLD BANK (1980), *World Data Tape*. MRDF, Economic Analysis and Projections Department, World Bank.

WORLD BANK (1987), *Poland. Reform, Adjustment and Growth. Volume I. The Main Report. The Economic System*. Washington D.C.: The World Bank.

WORLD BANK (1991), *Staff Appraisal Report Poland*. Country Department IV, Report 9408–POL.

WORLD BANK (current issues), *World Development Report*. New York, Oxford: Oxford University Press.

WULF, H. (1983a), 'Indien' in D. Nohlen and F. Nuscheler (eds), *Handbuch der Dritten Welt*, vol. 7. Hamburg: Hoffmann & Campe, 122–67.

WULF, H. (ed.) (1983b), *Aufruestung und Unterentwicklung. Aus den Berichten der Vereinten Nationen*. Reinbek: Rororo Aktuell.

WYCZANSKI, A. (1979), 'Epoka Odrodzenia' in J. Tazbir (ed.), *Zarys Historii Polski*. Warsaw: Panstwowy Instytut Wydawniczy: 169–230.

ZAMBRANO, L. (1982), *Entstehung und theologisches Verstaendnis der 'Kirche des Volkes (Iglesia popular) in Lateinamerika'*. Frankfurt: Peter Lang.

ZIELONKA', J. (1991), 'East Central Europe: Democracy in Retreat?', *The Washington Quarterly*, 14, 3, Summer: 107–20.

ZIMMERMANN, E. and Saalfeld, T. (1988), 'Economic and Political Reactions to the World Economic Crisis of the 1930s in Six European Countries', *International Studies Quarterly*, 32, 3: 305–34.

ZWICKY, H. (1985a), *Income Inequality and Violent Conflicts*. Paper Presented at the International Sociological Association Conference on Social Stratification in Budapest, September.

ZWICKY, H. (1985b), *Inequality, Repression and Political Violence. Comment on Muller, American Sociological Review, February 1985*. Department of Sociology, University of Zurich.

ZWICKY, H. and Heintz, P. (1982), 'Soziale Ungleichheit, Legitimationsanforderung und Konflikt', *Zeitschrift fuer Soziologie*, 11, 3: 268–78.

ZWIEFELHOFER, H. S. J. (1977), 'Zum Begriff der Dependenz' in K. Rahner *et al.* (eds), *Befreiende Theologie. Der Beitrag Lateinamerikas zur Theologie der Gegenwart*. Stuttgart, Berlin: W. Kohlhammer, 34–45.

Index